Commemorating the Seafarer

Commemorating the Seafarer
Monuments, Memorials and Memory

Barbara Tomlinson

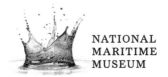

NATIONAL
MARITIME
MUSEUM

THE BOYDELL PRESS

First published 2015
The Boydell Press, Woodbridge

ISBN 978 1 84383 970 5

The Boydell Press is an imprint of Boydell & Brewer Ltd
PO Box 9, Woodbridge, Suffolk IP12 3DF, UK
and of Boydell & Brewer Inc.
668 Mount Hope Ave, Rochester, NY 14620–2731, USA
website: www.boydellandbrewer.com

Published in association with Royal Museums Greenwich, the group name for
the National Maritime Museum, Royal Observatory Greenwich, Queen's House and
Cutty Sark. www.rmg.co.uk

A catalogue record for this book is available
from the British Library

The publisher has no responsibility for the continued existence or accuracy of URLs for
external or third-party internet websites referred to in this book, and does not guarantee that
any content on such websites is, or will remain, accurate or appropriate

This publication is printed on acid-free paper

Dedicated to my splendid aunt,
Mrs Mary Gibson of Christchurch, New Zealand

Contents

Illustrations

Preface

The study of memorials cuts across several academic specialisms, and monuments themselves are generally not found in university or museum collections. They are spread across the country in churches, cemeteries, streets, on hilltops or in other fairly public places. Given their size, their sometimes intimate relationship with buried human remains, and the significance of their location and orientation, this could not be otherwise. Whether tucked behind parish flower arrangements or standing outside in the rain, they act as an expression of grief and a repository of individual and collective memory. Study, recording, publication and publicity can make their messages more accessible, and help to encourage their preservation; but memorials are three-dimensional objects located in a social and geographical context. There is no substitute for seeing them in the flesh and visiting them is always something of an adventure.

This book grew out of a database formally started in 1978 with the encouragement of the deputy director of the National Maritime Museum (NMM), David Waters (1911–2012). Probably inspired by an article by Rupert Gunnis entitled 'History in Marble', published in the August 1955 edition of *Country Life*, the initial objectives were to record important maritime-related sculpture held outside the Museum's collections. However, it soon became apparent that memorials provided much information of historical and cultural importance, potential source material for the maritime historian. The early stages of the project were implemented by Timothy Wilson, later Keeper of Western Art at the Ashmolean Museum, and Bridget Clifford, who went on to become Keeper of Collections at the Royal Armouries. I took it over from them, and that is where the genesis of this book starts. Many entries have since been sent in by NADFAS (National Association of Decorative and Fine Art Societies) volunteers and by members of the public. It was always intended that the records should be digitized at some future date. The later advent of the internet coincided with a burgeoning enthusiasm for family history, in which memorials are key sources. With this market in mind, the database was put online in 2002.

The Museum index includes memorials to British people who made their living through seafaring or related occupations such as shipbuilding, and to those passengers who lost their lives in maritime disasters. Almost all the material included is post-medieval. The memorials recorded are church and cemetery monuments, commemorative stained glass and public sculpture. Database cataloguing tends to suggest avenues for explanation, analysis and further research, and brings up the questions of why memorials were erected and take the form they do. The aim of this book is to explore some of them.

The material culture of commemoration over the centuries has been affected by contemporary politics, religious movements and artistic trends. I have tried to include memorials erected by all sections of society and to look at the cross-cultural influences between them. In addition to the types of memorial included in the NMM database, I also venture into the field covered by the United Kingdom War Memorials Archive.

This publication is an overview of a relatively new discipline, illustrated by representative case studies. It is not, and could never be, an exhaustive catalogue of such numerous items. I have focused on interesting stories and artistically significant monuments that readers may wish to visit. The major figures and best-known narratives are inevitably covered at some length. Cook, Nelson and the loss of *Titanic* are all there, with an attempt to put them in context by including more representative memorials to ordinary seafarers. 'And some there be that have no memorial' (Ecclesiasticus 44: 9) is a biblical line which, of course, covers most seamen but there are also some – probably a large number – whose memorials have been lost through enemy bombing or churchyard clearance, particularly in major industrial ports. Information from the NMM database used here has been checked and supplemented by visits to many churches and cemeteries in Great Britain, largely coastal and mainly in the south. The author expresses her thanks to incumbents and church-wardens who answered her queries and opened remote churches during her visits, notably at Arrow and Great Waltham.

Previous academic work on specifically maritime commemoration is somewhat sparse and begs all sorts of questions about the material culture of the seafarer as a specialist discipline. As part of a long tradition of anti-quarian study of memorials in general, the *Mariner's Mirror* (Journal of the Society for Nautical Research) has regularly published short notes on rele-vant monuments, albeit less frequently today than in its earlier years. David Saunders, an early contributor to the Museum database, was the first to publish on the subject in book form. His *Britain's Maritime Memorials and Mementoes* (Yeovil, 1996) is a gazetteer indicating where in the British Isles maritime memorials, from lych-gates to statues, can be found. He includes some historical background, his particular interest being in twentieth-cen-tury naval history. In recent years, academic study of death rituals and of private and collective memory has also been growing. Archaeologists, most notably Harold Mytum, have been involved in the recording and analysis of nineteenth- and twentieth-century churchyards and cemeteries. As part of this discipline, David J. Stewart of East Carolina University produced a pioneering academic study, mainly of grave markers and funeral rituals among the seafaring community on both sides of the Atlantic — *The Sea Their Graves: An Archaeology of Death and Remembrance in Maritime Culture* (Gainesville, Fl., 2011). Professor Stewart adopts the term 'maritime memorials' (first used by David Saunders) to cover his area of research, which is the precedent followed here.

Acknowledgements

I should like to thank Dr Robert Blyth of the National Maritime Museum for encouraging me to start this project and Dr Margarette Lincoln and Dr Nigel Rigby for supporting it throughout its long gestation period; Rebecca Nuotio for getting it into production; Dr Pieter van der Merwe for editing the manuscript – with enthusiasm; Kara Green, Emma Lefley, Tina Warner and David Westwood for their work on the illustrations; and Sally Badham of the Church Monuments Society who provided invaluable help and advice. I should also like to thank H. Martin Stuchfield and Trevor Parker at the Francis Coales Charitable Foundation for their support; Shaun Tyas for reading the manuscript and providing positive comment; Robin Millerchip for organizing a very useful Church Monuments Society visit to the Isle of Man; my friends and former colleagues Rina Prentice and Christine Parkes for providing illustrations; the churchwardens at Arrow and Great Waltham for going out of their way to assist me, also Christine Reynolds of Westminster Abbey Library, Simon Carter at St Paul's Cathedral and the Reverend Mark Nicholls at St Mary Rotherhithe; and finally all those who have contributed to the Maritime Memorials Database over the past thirty-five years.

This book is published with the assistance of the Francis Coales Charitable Foundation.

Introduction

After a long career at the National Maritime Museum, Greenwich, the present writer has naturally been interested in the way memorials reflect the importance of the sea to the nation at large. Various economic and military imperatives have persuaded the British to risk the hazards of sea travel over the centuries, although in more recent times many have got afloat for the sheer fun of it. A large number of memorials are to those whose voyages ended in disaster: young men who died prematurely, several generations wiped out in the loss of family-owned vessels, entire families drowned in the wreck of passenger ships. For others, the sea offered an occupation which gave status or a reasonably prosperous livelihood, something their family or friends saw as an important part of their identity when seeking to commemorate them.

Memorial types

The most expensive and prestigious memorials were those erected by the monarch or the state. Public memorials to naval commanders came late to Great Britain and the pantheon of national military heroes in St Paul's Cathedral and Westminster Abbey has been extensively researched by Holger Hoock and Matthew Craske. Although commissions went to architects and sculptors of the highest quality, some of the officers they celebrated are now largely forgotten. By the later nineteenth century there was an enthusiasm amongst prosperous citizens (undiminished to this day) for erecting memorials to the long dead, particularly in the form of civic sculpture. This is a good indicator of those historic figures who retained or regained their popularity. Universal education, changing values, national and local identity, not to mention tourism, all played a role in these manifestations of collective memory. War memorials, state or civic, enjoy an increasingly revered status as representing the community rather than the individual. As time has passed, however, they have also come under threat from neglect, vandalism and metal theft: not everyone buys into the idea of individual sacrifice on behalf of the nation.

The Royal Navy dominated maritime art and iconography in Britain from the seventeenth century onwards. Before then, and long after, the division between commerce and warfare at sea was not clear-cut. During the eighteenth century, war was contracted out to privateers; many merchant ships – and certainly major ones such as East Indiamen – carried guns and seamen frequently moved (not always voluntarily) between mercantile and naval service. This is the artistic high point for memorials to wealthy individual officers, eccentric as some of the conventions of late-baroque sculpture seem today. Numerous plainer neo-classical wall tablets were erected during the late eighteenth and early nineteenth century to members of an officer class whose ranks were swollen by war. Very much in the public rather than the private sphere, epitaphs were lengthy, effusive and sometimes very informative.

Commemoration was gradually democratized between the eighteenth and twentieth centuries. Even in the later Middle Ages reasonably prosperous people would have stone churchyard memorials or wooden grave markers (though few of the latter survive). Stone memorials became increasingly common in the eighteenth century with cheaper manufacture and transport. Seafarers are commemorated with other kin, frequently with carvings that combine maritime and religious symbolism. Although these gravestones are an expression of personal grief, it was a grief usually expressed in a very socially constrained, formal way. Philanthropic activity resulting from maritime deaths was another spur to commemoration of the ordinary seafarer, both the event and the contingent charitable support gaining publicity in expanding newspaper coverage. Many memorials to the victims of maritime accidents were erected with the residue of disaster funds for widows and orphans.

The ties between members of a ship's company, particularly in the Navy, stimulated the production of officer and crew memorials throughout the nineteenth century, and shipmates often stood in for family during funeral rites. Such memorials began to appear during the French Revolutionary and Napoleonic Wars, an era in which heady patriotism combined with radical influences. Proposals for state *grands projets*, built or unbuilt, also stimulated all sorts of commemorative activity by individuals or small groups at this time. These memorials, paid for by ordinary seamen and increasingly leaving a record of their names, were another strand in the evolution of the twentieth-century war memorial.

Beginnings

The memorials in this book almost all date from the period after 1500. Surviving church monuments to men of seafaring connection from the late-medieval era, up to 1500, can be broadly divided into military, civilian and clerical. Grave slabs with trade symbols begin to be made in this period, but English examples showing ships are very rare.[1] Some military tombs commemorate men who fought at sea or had other maritime roles. A good example is the effigy in armour at Winchelsea, believed to represent Gervase Alard, Admiral of the Western Fleet during the reign of Edward I (b. 1239; reigned 1272–1307). However there is nothing about the iconography of the tomb itself that would associate the person it represents with the sea.

The late fifteenth and sixteenth centuries saw innovative developments in ship construction including new types of warship, their hulls pierced for guns, and also the beginning of global trade and European colonial expansion. By the end of the sixteenth century, the religious reformation in England had fundamentally changed the nature of commemoration and the country's relationship with the rest of Europe.

In the Scottish highlands and islands, late-medieval military power was based on the galley fleets in the service of the Macdonald Lords of the Isles. Highland galleys or birlinns were square-rigged, double-ended vessels derived from the Viking longship. Used to transport troops to fight on land, they were somewhat modernized by the substitution of a centre-line rudder for a steering oar during the fifteenth century. The Macdonalds forfeited the lordship to the Scottish crown in 1475 but the highland workshops that provided their grave slabs enjoyed a final flowering during the early part of the next century. Their style was as conservative as the ships depicted on them. An excellent example is that of Murchardus MacDuffie (d. 1539) at Oronsay Priory, Argyll. The grave slab is carved with a claymore, a plant scroll, a deer hunt at the top and a galley at the bottom. Alexander MacLeod, chief of the MacLeods of Harris and Dunvegan, has a superb wall tomb at St Clement's church, Rodel, Harris, similar to if less sophisticated than parallel memorials in England and Wales.[2] The tomb was made in 1528, some years before Alexander's death in about 1546 (fig. 1). An effigy of Alexander lies on a tomb chest within an arch carved with religious scenes. The back of the tomb depicts the Virgin and Child in the centre flanked by St Clement and a second bishop. On either side are a galley and castle, emblems of the MacLeods and, in a row below, a deer hunt (Alexander accompanied by two ghillies) and St Michael and Satan weighing souls. This style of highland gothic ended with the Reformation. By 1506, the power of the galley fleets was nearly over. Two years before, in a final struggle with Donald Dubh MacDonald, James IV had sent his heavy guns round the coast by sea and the castles of the island chiefs were bombarded into submission. During this period of decline, galleys achieved a

---

1 Examples have been found at Hartlepool and St George's church, Doncaster (information from Brian and Moira Gittos).
2 See the tomb of Sir Richard Herbert of Ewyas (d. 1510) in St Mary's Priory, Abergavenny.

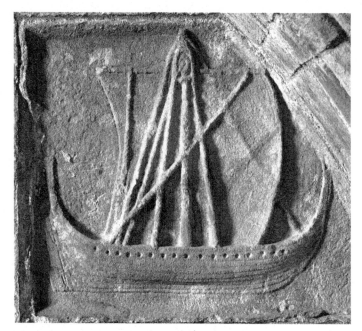

1. *Alexander MacLeod, at Rodel, Harris (detail). © Crown copyright: RCAHMS. Licensor www.rcahms.gov.uk*

late victory in 1533 when a birlinn fleet under Hector Maclean captured the English warship, *Mary Willoughby*, before handing her over to the Scottish king.

The monument of the Hales family in Canterbury Cathedral shows the shape of things to come (fig. 2). The memorial employs classically derived details: the kneeling figure of Alice Hales (d. 1592) is flanked by two obelisks and the inscription tablet by two panels carved with trophies. Behind and above Dame Alice is a relief of a galleon. Its fore- and main masts are square-rigged, while lateen sails on the remaining two masts (the mizzen and bonaventure mizzen) give it added manoeuvrability and the two decks are pierced for artillery. The ship has a beak below the bowsprit and a high, flat stern, defensible against boarders. This type of sailing vessel continued gradually evolving until the early nineteenth century and changes after that were more apparent rather than of essential principle. The ship flies the English flag of St George at the main and the body of Alice's husband, Sir James Hales, is being lowered over the side into the sea. He died of fever in 1589 returning from a disease-ridden military raid on Lisbon led by Drake and Sir John Norris, intended to oust Spain from the Portuguese throne. The objectives of this expedition, on which Hales served as treasurer, were both military and commercial but it failed to provide a return for its investors. The body of

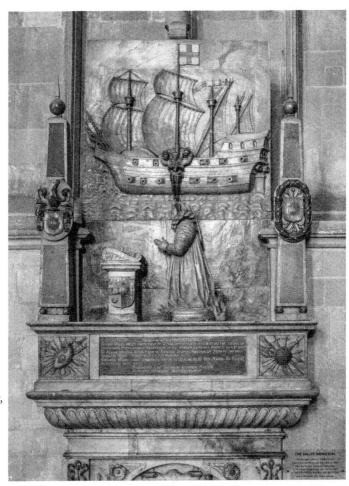

*2. Sir James Hales,
at Canterbury
Cathedral.
© Jay G. Heiser.*

Hales is shown going into the water feet first and is disproportionately large in relation to the ship. The expensive suit of armour which indicates his status may be a touch of artistic licence.

The tombs of Elizabethan and Jacobean merchants could be similarly lavish. At the end of the sixteenth century, England, benefiting from the decline of some of her European rivals, began to undertake longer trading voyages, notably to the Baltic, the Levant and, more gradually, to the East Indies.

If involved in sea trade, the merchant could fall within the scope of maritime-related occupations, putting to sea to manage his import/export businesses. As the financial risk of trade and shipowning was spread between many owners and several voyages, a representative of the investors might be selected to travel with the ship, sell and purchase cargo and generally promote their interests. Later this responsibility was taken over by resident agents and supercargoes (that is, such agents travelling for that purpose on the ships). Investors also financed voyages of exploration or privateering ventures, such backers including Elizabeth I herself. The profits funded commemoration and benefited the general economy. Voyaging is certainly celebrated in merchants' epitaphs: William Bond (d. 1576) at St Helen's, Bishopsgate, in the City of London, 'most famous in his age for his greate adventures bothe by sea and lande …', is compared in his Latin epitaph to Jason bringing home the golden fleece and, indeed, as greater than Jason.

If maritime art was in its infancy, the sea was certainly influencing contemporary English literature, with Shakespeare as usual providing examples, including of the hazards. These are sometimes almost incidental, as in *The Comedy of Errors*:

> With her I lived in joy; our wealth increas'd
> By prosperous voyages I often made
> To Epidamnum, 'til my factor's death,
> And he,—great care of goods at random left,—
> Drew me from kind embracements of my spouse … (I. i)

They can also be more causative as in the shipwrecks which, for example, launch the action of *Twelfth Night* and *The Tempest*, and the rich 'argosies' of Antonio, the 'Merchant of Venice', whose failure to make port until the end of that play obliges him to take out the hazardous loan from Shylock, the money-lender, around which its plot revolves.

The technological advances in navigation that accompanied this age of European expansion are indicated in the cross-staffs, back-staffs, compasses and globes that adorned prestigious funeral monuments during the two centuries that followed. These early maritime memorials commemorate a small number of the elite, but accidents, the health hazards of the tropics and the dietary deficiencies of long voyages led to much premature death among far more ordinary mariners. Commemoration would spread among this community during the centuries that followed and consideration of the forms this took is a large part of what follows here.

1

Shifting loyalties: naval memorials, 1628–1783

To the north side of Henry VII's chapel, in Westminster Abbey, stands the massive tomb of George Villiers, first Duke of Buckingham (1592–1628). In grandeur emulating the royal tombs of the previous century, it is partly the work of the court sculptor Hubert Le Sueur (*c.*1580–1658). The design of the monument does something new in Britain, by using classical symbolism to evoke Villiers's roles as a naval as well as a military commander (fig. 3). The effigies of the Duke and his duchess, Katherine, are surrounded by four obelisks originally decorated with anchors, palm branches and masks. At their feet sit the mourning figures of Mars, shown as a helmeted warrior, and

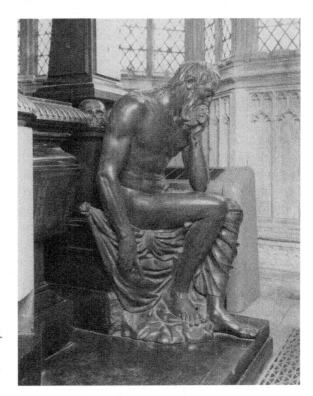

3. George Villiers, first Duke of Buckingham, at Westminster Abbey (detail). © Conway Library, The Courtauld Institute of Art, London.

Neptune as an old man weeping into his beard. Over the next two centuries, Neptune would represent a widely recognized personification of *naval* power. In contrast with conventionally stiff portraits of the Villiers family (the work of Isaac Besnier), the five allegorical figures on the tomb representing the Duke's accomplishments and achievements are in a freer Italianate style.

The courtier

The position of the tomb presents Buckingham as a surrogate member of the royal family. The effigies lie parallel to those of Henry VII and his queen, and the monument balances the tomb of James I's cousin, Ludovic Stuart, second Duke of Lennox and Duke of Richmond, on the south side of the chapel, also by Le Sueur. James I himself, who has no visible tomb, lies in the vault between them.

In common with other contemporary memorials to noblemen, Buckingham is shown as the founder of a dynasty. His four children, three living and one who died before the monument was commissioned, kneel in a niche above their parents. His descendants continued to be buried in a family vault in this hitherto exclusively royal chapel.

A courtier who owed his initial rapid rise to his physical attractions, Villiers was a favourite of James I who appointed him Lord Admiral in 1618. In this role he was actively concerned with the problems of developing the sort of navy demanded by contemporary warfare and foreign threats to trade. A series of reforms had already been proposed and Buckingham supervised their implementation. Financial control was tightened, ships built and repaired, dockyards extended. When James I was succeeded by his younger son, Charles I, Buckingham continued as close personal friend of the monarch. Relations worsened with a Parliament which had no great interest in paying for the king's wars and regarded both Charles and the Duke as harbouring pro-Catholic sympathies. When war broke out, the failure of an expedition against Cadiz further deepened Buckingham's unpopularity and Parliament attempted to impeach him. A combined naval and military expedition against the Ile de Ré, off La Rochelle, was also a failure despite being led by Buckingham in person. By now a popular hate-figure, believed to have enriched himself and his family at the public expense, he was assassinated in Portsmouth on 23 August 1628 during preparations for another expedition. His pregnant wife was upstairs in the Greyhound Inn when her husband was stabbed in a public room below. His posthumous son, Lord Francis Villiers (1629–48), is the youngest of the three living children sculpted on their father's memorial.

As was common before the funerals of seventeenth-century noblemen (which required lengthy organization), the body was disembowelled; and the entrails were buried in Portsmouth. A memorial to this additional burial, probably by Hubert Le Sueur, was placed in the church of St Thomas the Martyr by the Duke's sister, Susan. When it proved politically impossible for Charles to erect a memorial at Westminster, this task was undertaken by the Duchess. As an heiress in her own right, she had the funds to do so and it was completed in 1634 after her husband's affairs had been put in order. Their marriage was much more than one of dynastic convenience and, even if she did not compose the Latin epitaph, the sentiments expressed in it are likely to be her own. Both the Westminster and Portsmouth epitaphs attribute the Duke's downfall to the envy of the mob and, after listing his offices and titles, Katherine upholds the reputation of her husband as beloved spouse and father of their children:

> So memorable a hero was he; highly endowed in both body and mind; the intimate in turn of two most powerful sovereigns, he was famous in peace and war; most famous in the arts; he was a magnificent patron of letters and literary men; of inexhaustible generosity to any worthwhile project, he was unrivalled for his singular humanity and the agreeable nature of his manners; his life was terminated by the most frightful and terrifying murder; to common envy (which is always the partner of virtue and honour) he fell an innocent and undeserved victim. Katherine, most glorious demi-goddess, daughter and sole heiress of the Earl of Rutland, was made by him [Buckingham] a most joyful mother of children of the greatest promise and of either sex … She honoured the most sweet memory of her dearest husband with all possible piety and respect, and saw to it that these titles should be appended, not to satisfy vanity, but to attest the generosity of the greatest Princes: and most sorrowfully enclosed within this monument, which honours him, his sad remains and whatever of him is not yet due to heaven.[1]

The Westminster tomb was also intended to be her own memorial but her circumstances quickly changed when she remarried in 1635, reverting to her original Catholicism and dying in Ireland in 1649.

A second and more literary epitaph, on a gilt-metal tablet on the wall at the foot of the Westminster memorial, seems to have been composed shortly after the murder and shown to the King as an appropriate epitaph for the Duke. This also defends his reputation but is more detached and ironical in describing a man 'who, while he was waging war against the Papists, was accused of papacy: while promoting the Protestant cause, was slain by a Protestant. Behold the dice of human fortunes'. As it emphasizes the Duke's

---

1   All unattributed quotations in the text are from epitaphs or inscriptions. Sources are published in London unless otherwise stated.

Protestantism, this text seems unlikely to have originated with Katherine.[2] The epitaph as a literary form which could be circulated independently of any tomb (of which it is an example) had been popularized by the Italian humanists at least as early as the fourteenth century.

Regime change

After this promising start, the political disruptions of the mid-century held back the development of the naval baroque memorial in England at a time when it flourished in the maritime republics of Venice and the Netherlands. The English sculptor, John Bushnell, worked in Venice in the 1660s, carving reliefs of the siege of Candia (Heraklion) in Crete and the sea battle off Paros in 1651, episodes in a war between Venice and the forces of the Ottoman Empire. These decorate the massive monument in S. Lazzaro dei Mendicanti of Alvise Mocenigo (1583–1654), Captain-General of the Venetian fleet. From the 1650s, the tombs of the naval heroes of the Dutch Republic held them up as examples of patriotic virtue. The States General commissioned, from Rombout Verhulst, a lavish monument for Maarten Harpertszoon Tromp, who fell in battle with the English fleet in 1653. Further splendid memorials adorned with shells, statues, battle reliefs and allegorical figures were erected to naval heroes during the sea wars of the next fifty years, a period in which the deaths of defeated Dutch commanders were symptomatic of the renaissance in English sea power which followed the English Civil War.

The military officers who were effectively in charge of the short-lived parliamentary Commonwealth intended to remain in power and found finance for an expanded and formidable navy, which made the country feared by its European rivals. The political nation was also finally persuaded to support such a navy by means of permanent taxation. However, it was some years before this rise in sea-borne strength was reflected in corresponding naval commemoration.

After his death in 1657, Robert Blake, the most notable of the Commonwealth Generals-at-Sea, was accorded a splendid funeral and buried in Henry VII's chapel. A posthumous victim of regime change, on restoration of the monarchy three years later, his body was removed to the neighbouring churchyard and thrown into a common pit. By the latter part of the nineteenth century he had been rehabilitated as a historic worthy: stained-glass windows to his memory were erected in 1888 at St Margaret's, Westminster, a

---

[2] R.W. Lightbown, 'Isaac Besnier, Sculptor to Charles I, and his work for court patrons, *c.*1624–1634', in David Howarth, ed., *Art and Patronage in the Caroline Courts: Essays in Honour of Sir Oliver Millar* (Cambridge, 1993), p. 148.

monument in the Abbey in 1945 and a statue by Frederick William Pomeroy (1856–1924) at his birthplace of Bridgwater, Somerset in 1900 (fig. 4).

Although his colleague General George Monck, later Duke of Albemarle (1608–70), played a significant role in the restoration of Charles II and retained his naval role afterwards, the King failed to pay his funeral expenses and his memorial in the Abbey was not erected until the 1740s, financed by a bequest from Monck's son. Charles inherited considerable debts from the previous regime and, although he took an informed and active

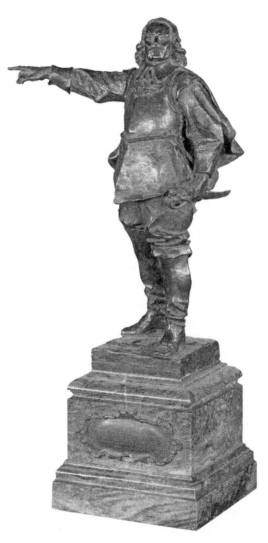

4. *Maquette of the statue of Sir Robert Blake by Frederick William Pomeroy.*
© *National Maritime Museum, Greenwich, London, SCU0007.*

role in promoting the Navy, he had neither the funds nor the enthusiasm for generous artistic patronage, and certainly not in the shape of memorial commissions. Charles's brother James, Duke of York, held the post of Lord High Admiral until he was obliged to resign following the Test Act of 1673, which disqualified Catholics from holding public office. His accession to the throne as James II in 1685, and subsequent fall from power in 1688, also eclipsed his earlier successes as a competent naval commander who was also the last British royal heir-presumptive to command fleets in action.

Careers

Under these two monarchs the officer class was professionalized with an established career path, examinations prior to first commission, and half-pay provided during peacetime – at least for admirals and captains. Charles needed officers of seagoing experience, with humble souls rising by seamanly merit and often from the merchant service, being referred to as 'tarpaulins'. Political debate contrasted them with the 'gentlemen' drawn from the traditional military aristocracy. The community of merchants and mariners in Lowestoft produced a remarkable number of naval commanders during this period. They became very wealthy: rich enough to commission rather undistinguished memorials inside the parish church but not *quite* gentlemen.

'Tarpaulins' were also associated with service in the Commonwealth Navy but this was not necessarily a bar to further employment under a monarchy. One of the Duke of York's senior subordinates at the Battle of Lowestoft in 1665 during the Second Dutch War was a Commonwealth veteran of the First Dutch War, William Penn (1621–70). A career officer with no inheritance, Penn was very willing to change sides where necessary: he prospered accordingly and sometimes controversially. Following his death, his widow erected a wall memorial in St Mary Redcliffe, Bristol, the entablature surmounted by small cannon and powder barrels with Penn's arms placed between them. Funerary armour hangs on the wall above, while the English inscription outlines Penn's personal achievements and rapid career progression under two regimes. His personal banners were also displayed there and have now been replaced with replicas (fig. 5).

It is not dissimilar in design to the splendid memorial of master gunner Valentine Pyne (d. 1677) in the church of St Peter ad Vincula within the walls of the Tower of London. The pilasters of the wall tablet take the form of carved ship's guns with crossed sponges carved on the frieze above. A relief of a galleon in action is placed on the apron below. After his death in 1677, during Charles II's reign, Pyne's memorial could proclaim his impeccable loyalty to the crown. He had been present during the 1625 expedition to Cadiz, and also in that led by Buckingham to the Ile de Ré, and he had served

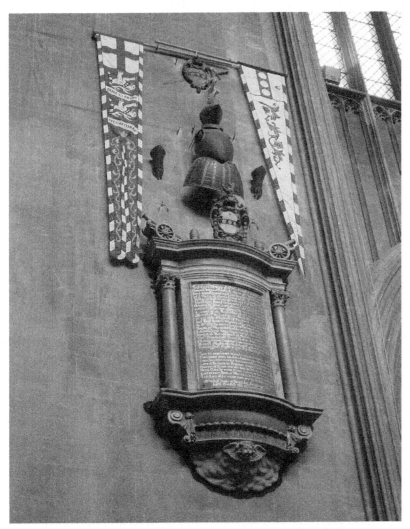

5. Sir William Penn, at St Mary Redcliffe, Bristol. © Author.

in what remained of the royalist navy under Prince Rupert during the Civil War. He returned from exile at the Restoration and picked up his naval career, being appointed master gunner of England.

A field of honour

The nave of Westminster has a wall monument to two junior officers and friends killed in the Battle of Solebay in 1672 – Charles Harbord and Sir Clement Cottrell (fig. 6). Their bodies were lost at sea. The epitaphs are on adjacent panels with a common cornice, the base being decorated with

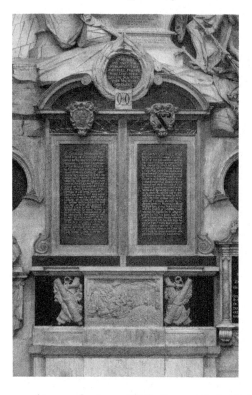

6. *Charles Harbord and Sir Clement Cottrell, at Westminster Abbey.* © *Dean and Chapter of Westminster.*

trophies and a bas-relief of a sea-fight. It has been tentatively suggested that this is a product of the workshop of Willem de Keyser – the Dutch sculptor who produced the battle relief on Verhulst's tomb of Maarten Tromp. It shows the destruction of the English flagship *Royal James* which, having fought off two Dutch fireships, was set on fire and destroyed by a third. This is a more distinctly *naval* memorial than those discussed so far. The English epitaph is a narrative of nautical derring-do, Cottrell 'having returned unwounded into his ship from being the first man that had boarded a Dutch one of LX gun and pulled downe the ensign of it with his own hand'. Harbord was first lieutenant of the *Royal James* and Cottrell a volunteer – the memorial promotes chivalric values not professional ones. The two young men were 'gentlemen' not 'tarpaulins', coming from wealthy, landed families with longstanding associations with the court: Cottrell had gone to sea against his father's wishes. The epitaph stresses their loyalty to their admiral, Edward Montagu, first Earl of Sandwich (who was among the last to abandon ship and was found drowned), their loyalty to each other and the sense of personal honour that led Cottrell to serve at sea. Sir Charles Harbord senior (1595/6–1679) was surveyor-general to Charles II and put up the memorial to his son; the other father, Sir Charles Cottrell (1615–1701), was master of ceremonies at court, a post in which he hoped his son would succeed him, and both were among those who carried bannerolls at the funeral of the Earl of Sandwich.[3] Both had also spent the interregnum in the Low Countries, which may account for the Dutch influences behind this expensive and ground-breaking naval monument.

Royal dockyards

In the expanding domain of the naval dockyards, essential to support the fleet, private and public interests competed. There was a continuing battle to maintain financial control and discourage corruption. The affluence of naval contractors, a business combining public with commercial interest, is reflected in a group of wall tablets whose iconography and manufacture link tomb carving and shipbuilding.

The most famous, Peter Pett (1610–72) was Navy Commissioner at Chatham, and is best known as the builder, at Woolwich in 1637, of the *Sovereign of the Seas*, designed by his father, Phineas. He was one of a family of at least eleven children and was accused of filling the dockyard posts with his numerous relations. Peter Pett (*c*.1592–1652) was his cousin and master shipwright at the Royal Dockyard, Deptford, where he has a war-damaged memorial in St Nicholas's church. This wall monument originally had an architectural surround surmounted with a swan-necked pediment and the Pett arms. The Latin inscription was flanked by two putti, one with a spade and the other with a skull. Below was placed the hull of a warship on the stocks and not yet fitted with her masts and rigging. The inscription claims Pett as the inventor of the frigate. John Evelyn the diarist dined with Sir Anthony Deane on 7 March 1690, and reported a conversation which supported this claim. Deane cited the *Constant Warwick*, built by Pett in 1645. She was a privately owned warship and the first large English frigate, although the term had previously been applied to small Spanish galleys and a type of fast priva-teer. The memorial is attributed to John and Matthias Christmas. Both these men and their father, Gerard Christmas, worked as carvers to the Navy. All three also worked as designers and makers of sets and props for pageants, and as stone and marble carvers, while John also produced monumental brasses. Although repaired in 1822 by a descendant (John David Rolt, Chief Clark of Stores for the Navy), the Pett memorial fell victim to the bombing raids of the Second World War and subsequent vandalism. Now only the inscription tablet survives. The nearby tablet to the Deptford master shipwright, Jonas Shish, and two of his sons, suffered a similar fate.

Joseph Wade (d. 1743), master carver at the Woolwich and Deptford yards

---

3   Though buried in Westminster Abbey, Montagu has no monument there.

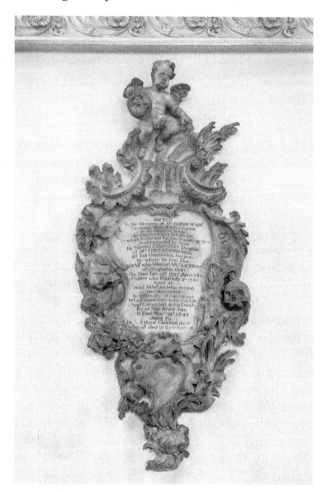

7. Joseph Wade, at St Mary, Rotherhithe. © National Maritime Museum, Greenwich,
London. Courtesy of St Mary's Church, Rotherhithe, London, L7767.

from 1716, has a memorial nearby at St Mary, Rotherhithe (fig. 7). A rococo
cartouche is carved with foliage, a cherub's head and a winged skull; a putto
holds a portrait of Wade, who carved the reredos in this church. In addition
to repairs, replacements and carved work on new ships, he was lucratively
employed on carving for six royal yachts during the reigns of George I and
II. The memorial was erected by his son, Samuel, who inherited the residue
of his estate.[4]

The monument to Philemon Ewer (d. 1750) at St Leonard's, Bursledon,
Hampshire by J. Nutcher of Swathling, is similar to that of Pett, with a

4   The National Archives (hereafter TNA) PROB 11/730/222.

wooden half model of a ship's hull on the base. Ewer, a master shipwright and timber merchant, owned a private shipyard on the Hamble, eventually building vessels on contract for the Navy.

> During the late War with France & Spain
> He built Seven large Ships of War
> For His Majesty's Service.
> In the Execution of that important Trust
> He gained, & deserved, the Reputation
> Of an ingenious Artist
> an excellent workman
> and an honest Man.
> All his Undertakings were crowned with Success,
> And all his Industry justly rewarded
> With a fair Character & a plentiful Fortune
> The first of which he left for ye Imitation
> The second for the Support & Enjoyment
> Of his numerous Family;
> Who in Gratitude erected
> This Monument
> A:D: 1754

Privateering

During the eighteenth century, in addition to the activities of the Navy itself, conflict at sea was also carried on by privately owned ships licensed by government during time of war under what were formally known as 'letters of marque and reprisal'. Privateering was, in effect, subcontracted commerce raiding, difficult to regulate and at times branded as piracy by those on the receiving end. Owners and merchants would invest in ships which were licensed to seize vessels (usually merchantmen) belonging to enemy powers. The profits and risks were divided as shares between the owners and the crew. The Admiralty Courts regulated and administered these ventures which were legitimated by Royal Proclamation or Orders in Council in time of war. Privateering declined during the century as the Navy expanded and took over its role.

In contrast to the popular piratical image of the privateer, a number of high-quality memorials to these men survive from this period, reflecting their connections with established business interests. As in the sixteenth century and later, when it had been the more usual method of naval warfare, commanders, their families and associates had aspirations to social status and to public acknowledgement of their military virtues. Naval officers, by contrast, now looked down on privateer commanders as mercenary, ill-disciplined and in competition with them for prizes and seamen's labour. Admiral Edward Vernon shared this view: 'Privateers doubtless distress the enemy's trade and bring an addition of wealth into the kingdom, but on the other hand they debauch the morals of our seamen ... by which they grow indifferent to the service of their country.'[5]

One such memorial, to the commander of the *Hanover Galley* privateer, was erected in the old British cemetery in Leghorn (Livorno). John Bayley, aged 25, was killed in action with two French galleys on 12 August 1710 during the War of the Spanish Succession. The Latin inscription describing the manner of his death was recorded in 1906.

> Hic jacet
> Iohannes Bayley anglus
> navis Hannover ductor
> qui
> aetatem agens annorum XXV
> in conflictu cum duabus triremibus Gallicis
> strenue pugnans
> die xii Augusti MDCCX
> insigni vulnere percussus
> occubuit[6]

('Here lies the Englishman John Bayley, commander of the ship *Hannover*, aged 25, who died from wounds, received while vigorously fighting in the notable action with two French galleys on the 12 August 1710.')

Bayley was granted letters of marque on 14 June 1706, 24 August 1709 and 27 May 1710.[7] His will indicates that he was resident at Rotherhithe, with a mother in Dover and no living children, and as the monument says, was only 25 when killed. His residual legatee and executrix was his wife, Katherine, assisted by 'my good friend Nicholas Best of Dover', one of the owners of the *Hanover Galley*.[8] The majority of Bayley's backers were London merchants.

Contemporary with the memorial to Bayley is the marble wall tablet

---

5   Vernon to the Secretary of the Admiralty, Portsmouth, 12 August 1745, in Bryan McLean Ranft, ed., *The Vernon Papers* (Navy Record Society, 1958). Vernon was opposed to the privatization of warfare at sea which he considered should be carried out by the Navy.

6   G.G. Milner-Gibson-Cullum and Francis Campbell Macauley, *The inscriptions in the old British cemetery of Leghorn* (Leghorn [Livorno], 1906), p. 28.

7   HCA 26/21, HCA 26/14/178, HCA 26/14/57.

8   TNA PROB11/517/178.

at Paul, near Mousehole in Cornwall, to the captain of another privateer, Andrew Elton, also resident in Rotherhithe and killed in an engagement with a French privateer off Land's End on 4 September 1710. This takes the form of an elaborate cartouche with the inscription on a draped cloth, the family arms above and a winged cherub's head below. He commanded the *Godfrey Galley*, named after Peter Godfrey – a major investor in the vessel, a director of the Bank of England, and of the East India Company, and a Member of Parliament.

The Channel Islands were admirably located as a centre for privateering.

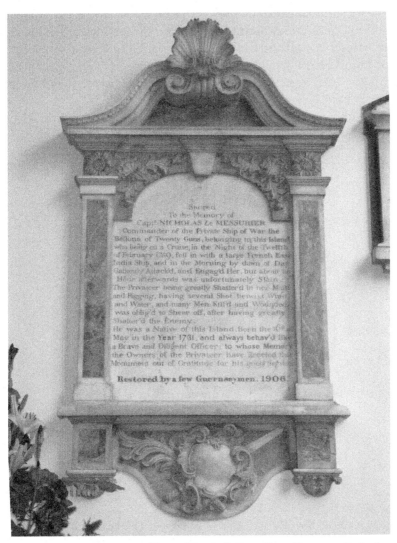

8. *Nicholas Le Messurier, at Town Church, St Peter Port, Guernsey.* © *Author.*

This declined there after 1759 but from that year Guernsey boasts a notable memorial to a 27-year-old privateer captain, Nicholas Le Messurier (fig. 8). He commanded the 250-ton *Bellona*, owned by the local Brock family, and their last major investment in privateering. On 12 February, he fell in with a large merchant vessel, probably a home-bound East Indiaman; his officers were consulted and all agreed to attack her. After an hour's engagement, Messurier sustained an abdominal wound and he died half an hour later, and the *Bellona* was obliged to abandon the action. His wall memorial, erected by the owners of the vessel, has a curved pediment with a shell at the apex, while the arch above the inscription is carved with shells and foliage and the pilasters are surmounted by sunflowers. A cartouche at the base (now plain of heraldry) is placed over a sword and a victor's palm branch. The inscription stresses Messurier's gallantry in taking on a larger opponent. An account in a letter from Guernsey published in the *Edinburgh Evening Courant* on 15 March says: '… it gives us the greatest satisfaction to see how bravely our islanders behave'.[9]

A well-known gravestone at St Nicholas, Great Yarmouth, gives the merchant captain as victim rather than predator:

TO
The Memory of
DAVID BARTLEMAN
Master of the Brig Alexander & Margaret
Of *North Shields*
Who on the 31st of Jan. 1781 on the *Norfolk Coast*
With only three 3 pounders and ten Men and Boys
Nobly defended himself
Against a Cutter carrying eighteen 4 pounders
And upward of a Hundred Men
Commanded by that notorious English Pirate
FALL
And fairly beat him off.
Two hours after the Enemy came down upon him again
When totally disabled his Mate Daniel MacAuley
Expiring with the loss of blood
And himself dangerously wounded
He was obliged to strike and ransom
He brought his shattered Vessel into Yarmouth

9   Quoted in Canon Peter Raban, 'Nicholas le Messurier (1731–1759) a Guernsey privateer captain in The Seven Years War', *Report and Transactions of La Société Guernesiaise*, vol. 22, part 5, 1990, p. 894.

With more
Than the Honours of a Conqueror
And died here in consequence of his wounds.
On the 14th February following
In the 25th Year of his Age.
TO commemorate the Gallantry of his Son
The Bravery of his faithfull Mate
And at the same time Mark the Infamy of a
Savage Pirate
His afflicted father ALEXANDER BARTLEMAN
Has ordered this Stone to be erected over his
Honourable Grave
'Twas Great'
His foe tho' strong was infamous
(The foe of the human kind)
A manly indignation fired his breast
Thank GOD my son has done his Duty.

John Fall was a privateer operating against English east coast shipping under American letters of marque during their War of Independence (1776–83). On 13 December 1781 Nelson chased what he believed to be the same privateer and spent the following Christmas penned up in Yarmouth. Quotations tended to lodge themselves (not always accurately) in Nelson's memory, so conceivably this inscription may be the unconscious source of his last words: 'Thank God I have done my duty'; or perhaps both phrases originate in a third unknown source.

The ancient world revived

The early eighteenth century was the golden age of the naval monument. Trade was booming and, after 1708, naval officers had improved rights to prize money. Prosperous ones were commemorated with maritime iconography appropriated from the Roman world. Since the Renaissance, classical iconography had been used by various governments from absolute monarchs to republics in ways that enhanced their prestige. The political changes that followed the Glorious Revolution of 1688 encouraged identification with the city states of the ancient world. Parliament was in control of military expenditure, the Navy had increasing financial and political support (albeit sometimes subject to ill-informed parliamentary interference) and Britain now held colonies from which, especially in the West Indies, slave-labour was generating growing national wealth. The state's military power to defend as much as expand this rested increasingly on its fleet. Although historical parallels with ancient Athens might have been more apposite, the visual language was Roman. This was partly because art history was in its infancy and Greek and Roman styles of sculpture and architecture were only gradually being distinguished. Roman literature was also more widely read and taught in the original language, although Homer and Thucydides were available in translation. Britain at this time was also an oligarchy (according to Plato's definition) and Greek democracy was regarded with suspicion: the political classes, therefore, identified more with the ideals of Republican Rome. Classical influences were not solely confined to the monuments of Whig aristocrats but can be seen much further down the social scale in the commemoration of people such as privateer John Bayley of Rotherhithe (see p. 18). Bayley would not have completed the Grand Tour or received an academic education but his memorial still proclaims his martial virtue – in Latin.[10]

Initially, production at the top end of the memorial market was dominated by émigré sculptors, notably John Michael Rysbrack (1694–1770) and Peter Scheemakers (1691–1781) who both came from the Low Countries. Talent also follows money. As British classicism had strong antiquarian tendencies at this period, if a sculptor visited Rome and studied surviving antique sculptures (as did sculptor Francis Bird), it gave his work a claim to authenticity: it might also give him contact with potential wealthy patrons who were on the Grand Tour which, although it had seventeenth-century origins, became almost a *de rigueur* conclusion of gentlemanly education in the eighteenth. British classicism consequently took on an increasingly Italian twist as the century progressed.

Westminster Abbey was emerging as a somewhat dilapidated national shrine (repairs were funded by fees and charges to visitors). The nave and transepts were increasingly filled by memorials to those who had gained reputation and wealth through their professions.

The monument to Vice-Admiral Sir Peter Warren (1703–52), by Louis-François Roubiliac, shows Hercules, the hero who memorably chose the hard road of virtue over the easy life of vice, placing the Admiral's bust on a pedestal (classically educated viewers would pick up the references to the terracotta busts carried at Roman funerals). Gazing admiringly at the portrait

---

10 Latin epitaphs remained in use on mariners' memorials throughout the eighteenth century in this particular Italian cemetery. In Britain, they declined in popularity in the latter 1700s, becoming largely confined to memorials to clergymen and academics. See Charlotte Yonge, *The Heir of Redclyffe*, 1853 (repr. Cambridge, 1997), p. 485. The recently widowed heroine asks a male relation to translate her late husband's epitaph: "'Could you, without teasing yourself, put that into Latin for me, by and by? I think it should be in Latin, as it is in a foreign country.' She gave him a paper in her own writing ... 'Will you be so kind as to give it to Arnaud when it is done?' she continued; 'he will send it to the man who is making the cross. I think the kind people here will respect it.'"

is a female figure representing Navigation, in the sense of maritime trade. She has a Union shield, her hair is adorned with the bow of a ship and she holds a cornucopia from which spill the products of agriculture and coins carved with the clearly identifiable head of George II. The message is that Warren's remunerative naval activities (the prizes he took made him very wealthy) also benefited the nation's trade. The carved flag originally placed behind the figures was removed during the 1860s when gothic architecture was more admired than baroque memorials. The erection of the monument had in its turn involved the removal of a smaller one to one Dame Mary James.

Round the corner, outside the chapel of St John the Baptist, stands the memorial to Rear-Admiral Charles Holmes (1711–61) by Joseph Wilton (fig. 9). He is shown in an idealized, youthful manner, dressed as a Roman general but retaining his wig and resting an affectionate hand on the barrel of a meticulously carved and very contemporary gun, draped with a naval ensign. The figure looks backwards to the portraits of seventeenth-century monarchs, sideways to the classical preoccupations of the contemporary landed class, and forwards to the global domination of British firepower. At the time of

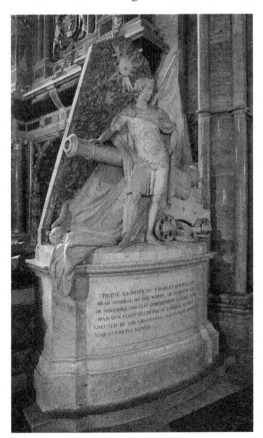

9. *Rear-Admiral Charles Holmes, by Joseph Wilton, at Westminster Abbey.* © *Dean and Chapter of Westminster.*

his death, Holmes was Commander-in-Chief at Jamaica. A codicil to his will dated 9 November 1761 leaves 'to my negroe Boy Charles [his] freedom with an annuity of fifteen pounds sterling for his life' – an act of manumission which re-enacts a Roman custom.[11]

However, people may adopt a fashion for reasons quite removed from the ideas that drive their leaders. The rather old-fashioned iconography of the Holmes memorial is likely to derive from inheritance rivalries within the Holmes family. During the 1760s Charles's oldest brother, Thomas Holmes, was attempting to keep their Isle of Wight estates undivided in a male line and out of the hands of his seven sisters, who retained property in Ireland and Wales. Charles died unmarried and left half the residue of his estates (including land) to his brother-in-law Marmaduke Sowle, a man with no sons and two of whose daughters were the 'Gratefull Neeces' so conspicuously mentioned in the inscription. The memorial at Yarmouth, Isle of Wight, to the most notable member of the family, Charles's grandfather Sir Robert Holmes (*c.*1622–92), also takes the form of a standing figure in armour, right hand resting on a gun, but Charles's memorial is much grander and stands in a more prestigious location. It challenges Uncle Thomas's competing dynastic ambitions.

Trophies

A whole vocabulary of classical symbols came into use in this period, most commonly military trophies, an idea already deployed on the tombs of the Dutch admirals. Sculptors could also offer alternative versions, adapted for military or naval monuments. A tablet at Leatherhead, by the London masons Stanton & Horsnaile, commemorates the Scottish Admiral, Sir James Wishart (1659–1723). It has a Latin inscription relating his Protestant loyalties and military achievements. Surrounding the inscription panel and tucked behind it are weapons, navigational instruments, martial musical instruments, ensigns, military colours and armour. In accordance with contemporary custom, the memorial was placed near Wishart's pew. Later memorials frequently arrange ensigns and guns on either side of a bust or oval portrait, suggesting to the viewer both collective memories of an individual's achievements and personal memories of the man. The idea of the individual life as moral example was beginning to blend into the distinctly un-Christian notion of immortality through worldly fame. A common feature in the art and architecture of seventeenth-century courts, trophies ultimately derive from the practice in the ancient world of erecting displays of captured enemy weapons and arms on battlefields: such arms would also be laid up in temples.

[11] TNA PROB11/874.

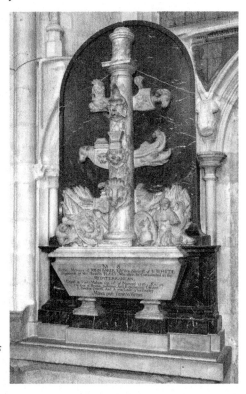

10. *Vice-Admiral John Baker, by Francis Bird, at Westminster Abbey. © Dean and Chapter of Westminster.*

Another Roman custom co-opted by the naval memorial was the column decorated with the beaks, or rostra, of captured galleys, set up on shore sites close to naval victories. One such, in relief, decorates the monument at Westminster to Vice-Admiral John Baker (1660–1716) by Francis Bird (fig. 10). The trophies at the base are, in the main, derived from the ancient world, and Bird distinguishes each prow as originating from a different ship. Bird had a reputation for authenticity to keep up.

The modern world

In spite of this extensive appropriation of 'pagan' iconography, British culture was still Christian and even eighteenth-century naval warfare was of a technical complexity unknown to the Romans. The commissioning and erection of such splendid naval memorials during this period inevitably reflected these facts. Nicholas Read's memorial to the Irish admiral, Richard Tyrrell (*c.*1716–66), revived the medieval subject of the soul of the deceased carried heavenwards (fig. 11). There was much continental Catholic art to draw on here but the work was intended as an illustration of the biblical text, 'The sea shall give up her dead and everyone shall be rewarded according to his

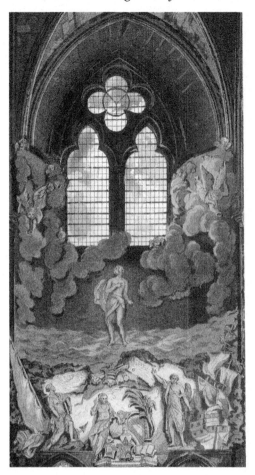

11. *Rear-Admiral Richard Tyrrell,
by Nicholas Read. The complete
monument as illustrated in Rudolf
Ackermann,* The History of the
Abbey Church of St. Peter's
Westminster. © *Dean and Chapter
of Westminster.*

works', being written by the angel on the lower part of the memorial. Tyrrell
died on the *Princess Louisa* and was buried at sea, so the monument is a cenotaph with the figure of Hibernia indicating his final resting place on a globe.
Rising from the dead on the day of judgement, his fate is yet undecided. In
the fulsome words of the *Naval Chronicle*: 'The Admiral's countenance with
his right hand to his breast, is expressive of conscientious hope, while the
position of his left arm appears significant of his seeing something awful
and impressive. He appears rising out of the sea behind a large rock …'[12] J.T.
Smith, biographer of Joseph Nollekens, quotes the latter on his rival, Read's,
production: 'That figure of his, of Admiral Tyrrell going to Heaven out of the
sea, looks for all the world as if he was hanging from a gallows with a rope
around his neck.'[13] Sadly, the modern visitor can no longer pass judgement

[12] *Naval Chronicle*, vol. 10, London, 1803, p. 364.
[13] John Thomas Smith, *Nollekens and his Times* (1829), vol. 2, p. 96.

on the completed work, as the upper part was removed during the nineteenth century to make room for another memorial.[14] The lower figures and the stern of the ship, *Buckingham*, in which Tyrrell gained fame, remain and are still impressive.

New British sculptors like Read began to take over the monument trade from immigrant masters as the century progressed. In parallel, a native school of marine painters was inspired by its Dutch predecessors. Naval officers were the main market for their battle scenes, accurately depicted but with a view-point chosen showing the client's ship in a prominent position. The painting would be an heirloom transmitting his deeds to his family, and the artists could also exploit the interest of a patriotic public through versions produced by the print trade. Paintings might also be reproduced in relief on memorials. The lower part of Sir Charles Wager's monument at Westminster is carved with a view of his action off Cartagena in 1708, based on a painting by Samuel Scott owned by the sculptor who executed the piece, Peter Scheemakers.[15]

Patriotic martyrs

After the Jacobite threat had been suppressed in 1745, the Protestant succession was secured and the related religious passions began to subside. However, there was a lingering fear that a Hanoverian monarchy was putting continental interests before those of Great Britain. This encouraged a stance of patriotic opposition to government among influential networks of the elite, expressed at more popular level though a lively print culture.

The loyalties of the vastly expanded Royal Navy were increasingly focused on the profession and the state. Competing loyalties to family among well-born officers were never quite eclipsed; although the sort of dynastic claims put forward by the epitaph to Rear-Admiral Sir Thomas Hardy (1666–1732),[16] in which his ancestry is traced back to 1381, were increasingly seen as pretentious and old-fashioned.

Although, the House of Commons controlled defence expenditure, foreign policy remained in the hands of the King's ministers. The memorial to Captain James Cornwall by Robert Taylor was the first to be erected by parliamentary subscription (fig. 12). The circumstances of its commission were a result of tensions between opposition and government. A Latin inscription and a battle relief after Samuel Scott are set into a grotto-like

---

14 The figure was placed in the treforium and the clouds are now lost. The complete memorial is illustrated in publisher Rudolph Ackermann's *Westminster Abbey: The History of the Abbey Church of St Peter's, Westminster, its Antiquities and Monuments* (1812).

15 This memorial is now inaccessible behind the ticket office in the North Transept entrance.

16 The memorial is inside the West Door of Westminster Abbey: Hardy's effigy in Roman armour reclines on a sarcophagus.

rocky base. Britannia and Fame stand above, supporting the hero's portrait. Before it was cut down and moved to the cloisters of Westminster Abbey from its former position in the nave, the top of the rock sprouted a palm and a laurel tree supporting the Cornwall arms. The action off Toulon in which Cornwall died on 27 February 1744 was indecisive, a fairly common occurrence at this period before the British established a marked advantage in tactics and firepower. It was followed by another battle in the press, fought between Admirals Mathews and Lestock over the body of Cornwall, whose ship his comrades in arms – Lestock in particular – had failed to support, and who had died after losing both legs to a single shot. The ghost of popular hero John Benbow hovered over these proceedings: in 1702 Benbow had also died of similar wounds, but not before court-martialling the captains who had similarly failed to support him in action. Two of them, Kirby and Wade, were shot.

A patriotic versifier in the *Gentleman's Magazine* enquired:

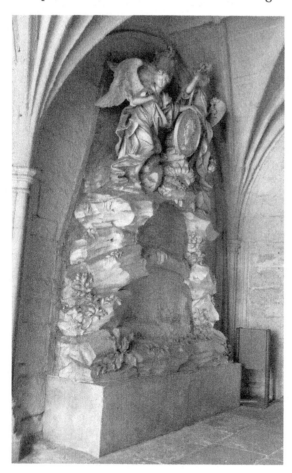

12. *Captain James Cornwall,*
by Sir Robert Taylor, at
Westminster Abbey.
© *Author/Dean and Chapter*
of Westminster.

If Greece and Rome for fame of old renown'd
With deathless palms the happy victor crown'd
Or when the hero for his country bled,
With lasting statues grac'd his honour'd shade!
What mark shall speak Britannia's fond regret,
Lamented Cornewall! For thy mournfull fate!
What honours shall she pay, what statues raise?
Or must the poet only give thee praise![17]

The writer (who supported Mathews) goes on to draw parallels between the conduct of Kirby and Wade and that of the commanders involved in the Toulon débâcle.

A parliamentary committee of inquiry was held. It had been requested by disgruntled Tory backbenchers who wished to embarrass those former leaders of their faction who had accepted posts in the current administration. Tories generally supported Lestock and had the support of government allies in the Admiralty who wanted naval reform.[18] The inquiry duly decided in favour of Lestock and in the courts-martial that followed, Lestock was acquitted and Mathews was cashiered (rather implausibly) for failing to mount a close attack and pursue the enemy. Lestock could claim that he had stuck punctiliously to the rules and Mathews should have waited for him to catch up, but the Navy and public opinion were outraged at this outcome.

In May 1747 it was proposed in the Commons that a monument be erected to James Cornwall in Westminster Abbey and that: 'this house will make good the expense'. The proposer, Thomas Carew, with his seconder, George Lyttelton, and a thirder, General James Oglethorpe, were acknowledged with many personal compliments by James's brother, Velters Cornwall. Lyttelton was the nephew of Richard Temple, Viscount Cobham (1675–1749), Cobham and his circle being staunch Whig patriots. The other proposers were Tories. The erection of the memorial indicated the House of Commons' sometimes ill-informed interest in the conduct of its naval officers.

Cobham's cubs acquired their own patriotic martyr in the same year. Thomas Grenville was killed in the first Battle of Finisterre on 3 May 1747 (Old Style). His siblings planned a monument in the Abbey with a full-length effigy of Grenville in modern dress, and an English epitaph comparing him to the sixteenth-century poet and soldier, Philip Sidney, was written by

---

17 *Gentleman's Magazine*, September 1744, p. 502.
18 P.A. Luff, 'Mathews *v.* Lestock: Parliament, Politics and the Navy in Mid-Eighteenth-Century England', *Parliamentary History*, vol. 10, 1991, pp. 45–62.

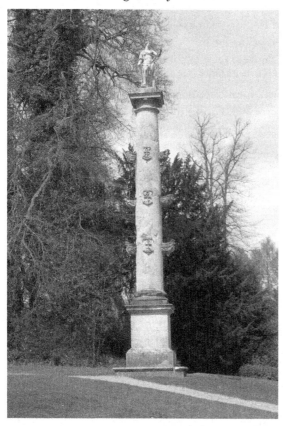

13. *Captain Thomas Grenville,*
at Stowe. © *Author.*

the same George Lyttelton MP and published in the *London Magazine*.[19]
Designed by John Pitt and Prince Hoare of Bath, this conscientious expression of indigenous culture was never completed. It was left to Grenville's uncle, Viscount Cobham, to add a rostral column to the numerous classical structures he erected in the grounds of Stowe, a scheme which represents patriotic Cobham politics set in stone (fig. 13).[20] The Latin inscription (by Lyttelton again) quotes the famous last words: 'he … declar'd it, in his last Moments, infinitely better to perish, than to be brought to Judgement for Cowardice'. The Toulon débâcle was still on everyone's mind in 1747.

The Admiralty – led by the Duke of Bedford, the Earl of Sandwich and above all Vice-Admiral George Anson – was now determined to initiate

[19] George Lyttelton (1709–73), MP for Okehampton, poet and classicist. *London Magazine* (December, 1747), p. 576.
[20] Viscount Cobham's heir – Richard Grenville (1711–79, later Grenville Temple), second Earl Temple – moved the column to the Elysian Fields area of the garden. The figure of Neptune holding a splinter of ship's timber was replaced with the muse of heroic poetry in 1756. The column could now be seen framed in the door of the nearby Temple of Ancient Virtue.

reforms that would tighten up naval discipline and encourage an aggressive pursuit of military objectives. A Navy Bill was passed in 1749 which revised the Articles of War and to a degree achieved these aims.[21]

During this era of controversies and quarrels, epitaphs and memorials were one way the family could have the final word. Following the loss of Minorca after an inconclusive action and an unnecessary withdrawal from the Mediterranean, the British commander John Byng was court-martialled and shot on 14 March 1757 for 'failure to do his utmost' in the face of the enemy. He had fallen victim to the Admiralty's new and tougher requirements for zeal and activity in its officers. Although he had political friends in office, this was not enough to save him from 'the anger of the king, the fury of the public and the disgust of his naval colleagues'.[22] The stone sealing the coffin into its shelf in the family vault at Southill reads:

To the perpetual Disgrace
Of PUBLICK JUSTICE
The Honble. JOHN BYNG Esqr:
Admiral of the Blue
Fell a MARTYR to
POLITICAL PERSECUTION
March 14th in the year 1757
when BRAVERY and LOYALTY
were Insufficient Securities
For the
Life and Honour
of a
NAVAL OFFICER

The son of an eminent naval officer (Admiral George Byng, Viscount Torrington), Byng's tragedy was that family connections had raised him to a command for which he lacked the personality, the experience and adequate resources to carry out the task given him.

---

[21] Anno 22 ° Georgii II c.33 CAP XXXIII II, 10: 'Every Flag Officer, Captain or Commander in the Fleet, who, upon Signal or Order of Fight, or Sight of any Ship or Ships which it may be his duty to engage, or who, upon Likelihood of Engagement, shall not make the necessary Preparations for Fight, and shall not in his own Person and according to his Place, encourage the inferior Officers and men to fight courageously, shall suffer death.'

[22] N.A.M. Rodger, *The Command of the Ocean* (2004), p. 267.

Naval supremacy

The reforms initiated by Anson had their effect. After the triumphs of the Seven Years War, Great Britain commanded the seas and had made unprecedented gains in colonial territory. Admiral Sir Edward Hawke (later Lord Hawke, 1705–81) was one of the few officers to emerge with any credit from the Mathews-Lestock débâcle, owing to his decision to leave the battle line and launch a pugnacious attack on the Spanish 60-gun *Poder*. Hawke pursued aggressive tactics and was prepared to take risks. This won him a crushing victory at Quiberon Bay in 1759. He has a monument by John Francis Moore, of somewhat conventional design, at North Stoneham in Hampshire. An obelisk flanked with flags bears the Hawke arms and below it is a sarcophagus carved with a relief of Hawke's most famous victory, based on a painting by Dominic Serres. Hawke's flagship *Royal George* is at the centre of the composition. The inscription claims: 'The Annals of his Life compass a Period of Naval Glory unparallel'd in later time For wherever he sailed Victory attended him.' Hawke's doctrine of engaging the enemy at close quarters was taken to heart by Nelson, whose victories would surpass his: this is unsurprising given that his own mentor, William Locker, was himself a follower of Hawke.

Edward Boscawen, Viscount Falmouth (1711–61), prefigures the other side of the Nelsonic persona. The monument erected by his wife and made by Robert Adam and John Michael Rysbrack stands in the church at St Michael, Penkevil, in Cornwall.[23] The design has a bust in Roman armour flanked by trophies, with a pyramid behind. The inscription on the plinth is flanked by a naval and a mural crown, indicating his civic service as MP for Truro. The epitaph, composed by his wife (whose affectionate letters also survive), dwells on Boscawen's professional merit and virtues:

> ... His Birth, tho' noble
> His Titles, tho' Illustrious
> Were but incidental Addition to His Greatness:
> HISTORY
> In more expressive & more indelible characters
> Will inform latest Posterity
> With what ardent Zeal,
> With what successful Valour,
> He serv'd His Country!
> And taught Her Enemies
> To dread Her Naval Power.
> In Command

---

[23] The preliminary drawings, including the executed version, are in the collections of Sir John Soane's Museum, SM Adam volume 19/1.

He was equal to ev'ry Emergency,
Superior to ev'ry Difficulty;
In his High departments, Masterly & upright
His Example form'd while
His Patronage rewarded
MERIT
With the highest Exertions of Military Greatness,
He united the gentlest offices of Humanity.
& concern for the Interests & unweary'd Attentions to the Health
of All under his Command
Soften'd the necessary Exactions of Duty,
And the Rigours of Discipline
with the Care of a Guardian & the Tenderness of a Father

Boscawen's care for the health of his men helped his squadron remain at sea for extended periods. His command of the fleet at the capture of Louisbourg in 1758 opened the way for Wolfe's conquest of Quebec in the following year.

Imperial conquests

British colonial acquisitions in North America and India introduced an element of exoticism into the iconography of military memorials. Two Pequot Indian allies support the carved sarcophagus on the Westminster Abbey memorial to Lieutenant-Colonel the Hon. Roger Townsend, killed on the second expedition to Ticonderoga in 1759. The victories of the ancient world had been celebrated by sculptures of conquered barbarians or personifications of captured cities, and to the eighteenth-century artist they suggested suitably classical ways in which they could represent individuals from other cultures. One of the most brutally triumphalist of these ancient memorials, that made for Attalus of Pergamon (269–197 BC) to celebrate his victory over the Galatians, was unknown at this time: dying enemies had covered it like a huntsman's kill. However, Roman copies of these statues survived, if wrongly identified, of which the most famous was believed to represent a dying gladiator.

The memorial to Admiral Charles Watson (1714–57) was erected in Westminster Abbey by a grateful East India Company for the enormous sum of £1000 (fig. 14). Watson, who died in India where he is buried, had acted as the naval arm of Robert Clive in the capture of the pirate stronghold of Gheriah, the recapture of Calcutta from Siraj ud-Daula and more indirectly in Clive's final victory at Plassey. Designed by James Stuart and executed by Peter Scheemakers, the monument utilized the gothic arcade at the end of the west aisle of the north transept. Until 1957 the pillars were disguised by palm trees,

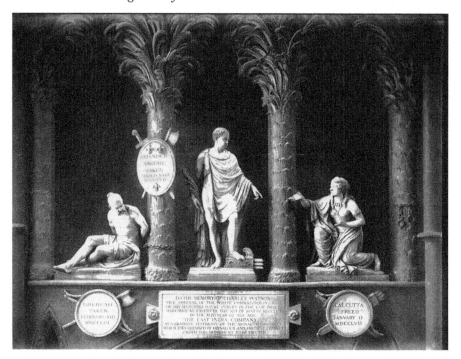

14. *Vice-Admiral Charles Watson, by Peter Scheemakers, after a design by James Stuart, at Westminster Abbey. The photograph shows the palm trees on the monument before their removal.* © Dean and Chapter of Westminster.

when these were removed. The central space was occupied by the Admiral who, clad in a toga and holding a palm branch, extends a hand to a female figure in a sari representing the liberated Calcutta (her manacles are hung on the palm tree behind).[24] Gheriah is shown as a chained Indian captive, and the third of Watson's victories, in which Chandernagore was taken from the French on 23 March 1757, is represented by an inscription only.

Other ranks

A few modest memorials to the men and junior officers of this period survive. The style and inscriptions are vernacular and the tone forlorn. A lively school of masons, probably based in Chichester, seem to have specialized

[24] Matthew Craske, *The Silent Rhetoric of the Body* (New Haven and London, 2007), attributes the source of the figures to plates of ancient coins in Joseph Spence, *Polymetis*, London, 1747. The bound captive is similar to one depicted on a *Judea capta* coin, one of the series issued by Vespasian. Spence in pl. XXXII also shows a coin with a kneeling figure, hand extended, titled 'JUDEA REST'.

in unfortunate accidents. A much eroded stone at Warblington, Hampshire, shows an exploding warship with the inscription:

> To the memory of
> William son of John & Sarah Bean
> [Who] lost his life by some powder
> taking fire in his Majesty's ship the
> Torbay in Portsmouth harbour
> September the 27th 1758 Aged 20 Years.
> Unhappy late impressed and forced was I
> From every Friend to Fight the Enemy
> Yet harder fate by Strange Explosion sent
> From fire to Water mark the dire event:
> Two Elements conspire to set me free
> Lord from life's Tempest rest my Soul with thee …

William Bean appears in the ship's pay book on 28 June 1758 and was discharged dead on 28 September as 'drowned'. The damage to *Torbay* does not seem to have been structurally serious.[25]

A nearby stone to William Coopper (d. 1755, aged 17) is carved with sea shells, the stern of a warship and a mariner holding a backstaff. The verse below takes a decidedly negative view of his naval career.

> Unhappy Youth imprest, thou needs must go
> To serve thy King and scourge th'insulting Foe
> From Parents Friends and every Joy to Part
> This more than Wars dread thunder pierced thy heart
> Heaven heard thy grief and brought thee a release
> From hostile War to Realms of endless peace

In conclusion, the naval monument was slow to develop in England during the seventeenth century, owing to the political and religious upheavals of the time and their impact on the state. Rapidly expanding in the following century as an agent of national and commercial power, the Navy provided its officers with a distinctly maritime as opposed to military identity, expressed in iconography drawn from ancient and modern republics. The epitaph held its subject up as an exemplar of public-spirited and increasingly meritocratic virtue. Nevertheless, the majority of memorials were still dynastic, often commissioned by women or the heirs of the deceased.

---

[25] National Maritime Museum (hereafter NMM) ADM354/160/119; TNA ADM33/593.

2

The age of heroes: naval memorials, 1783–1815

The Great War with France was the apogee of British naval success but it began with a failure: in 1783 the Treaty of Paris sealed the foundation of the United States and the loss to Great Britain of many of her North American colonies. However, George Rodney's victory at the Battle of the Saints, fought to the north of Dominica on 12 April 1782, following a preliminary action closer in on the 9th, ensured she retained her valuable sugar-producing islands in the West Indies. The wider European involvement in the American war left France with crippling government debt, which would sow the seeds of future revolution.

On 22 May, Charles James Fox, in his brief tenure as Foreign Secretary, proposed that the House of Commons present their thanks to Rodney; after various members had proposed thanks to other officers: 'Mr B. Gascoigne said that all the Living had been attended to, but he wished that some Regard should be paid to the Dead.'[1] His motion that Captains Bayne and Blair, killed in Rodney's actions, and also Captain Robert Manners, who died later of his wounds, should be commemorated by publicly funded monuments erected in Westminster Abbey was suitably rephrased to state their dates of death correctly and passed the following day. His seconder, Sir Grey Cooper, mentioned the precedent of the monument to Captain Cornwall, of 'inferior rank' like Bayne, Blair and Manners, but unlike them killed in the course of a British defeat. The three men were the highest-ranking British casualties of the actions concerned

Through the Royal Academy, founded fourteen years earlier, Joseph Nollekens (1737–1825) was appointed to undertake the commission at a cost of £4500, later reduced to £3500. The three casualties were to be commemorated by a single monument on which each individual was represented by a portrait in relief. In one of Nollekens's earlier designs, Fame with her attribute of the trumpet is placed in the centre, flanked by a seated Britannia on the right and on the left by Neptune about to plunge his trident into a prostrate woman

---

1   *Public Advertiser*, 23 May 1782.

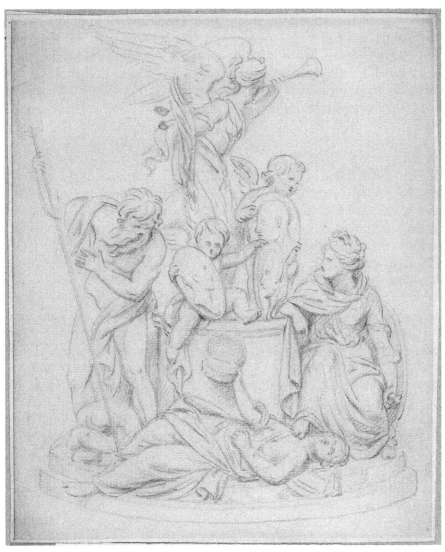

15. *A design for the memorial to Captains Bayne, Blair and Manners by Joseph Nollekens. © Victoria and Albert Museum, London.*

representing France.[2] The enemy figure holds an empty box representing the state of the French treasury (fig. 15). In the final version, which has a flat grey pyramid behind it, a standing Britannia and recumbent Neptune admire the heroes' portraits, now hung on a Doric rostral column by a cherub, with a small figure representing Fame placed at the top. After the delayed

---

2 The original design is in the Victoria and Albert Museum; chalk on paper, E.448–2010.

completion of the typically brief inscription, Nollekens put in a request for his final payment in 1793, the year war was declared with Revolutionary France. His creation, which survives intact, was the only public commission he executed: transitional in style between baroque and neo-classical, none of the public naval memorials subsequently erected in Westminster Abbey and St Paul's surpassed it in magnificence.

Glorious First

The first major action of the French Revolutionary War was hailed as a victory for Great Britain, although a vital grain convoy got through to feed the citizens of France while their fleet engaged the enemy. Although overshadowed by later and more decisive naval battles, the Glorious First of June 1794 was lavishly commemorated. The senior British casualties were Captains James Montagu, who was killed during the action, and John Hutt and John Harvey, who died from their wounds after returning to Portsmouth. Harvey's ship, *Brunswick*, had been involved in a lengthy and vicious duel with the French *Vengeur du Peuple*. He remained on deck until wounded for the third time. Parliament voted two separate memorials in Westminster Abbey to the three men. Montagu's was designed by an up-and-coming John Flaxman (1755–1826). It shows the captain as a standing figure in contemporary uniform, leaning on his sword, crowned by Victory and backed by naval ensigns. The statue is placed on a drum-shaped plinth which is carved with a relief of the action and flanked by lion figures. This design exerted a long-term influence on later naval monuments. The Harvey and Hutt monument was designed by John Bacon senior but signed by John Bacon junior. An urn with profile portraits of the two officers is garlanded by Britannia (now without her attributes) while Fame indicates the names of the deceased. The lower part of the memorial, with its relief of the action, is now at St Mary's church, Eastry, Kent, with an inscription commemorating Harvey alone. William Vincent, Dean of the Abbey from 1802 to 1815, separated these two monuments, which originally stood side by side in the nave. Harvey and Hutt now partially obscure a window, and Montagu stands in a cluttered corner just inside the entrance.

National pantheon

It was at this point that Westminster Abbey became overcrowded. In response, George III decided to excavate a new royal vault at St George's chapel, Windsor, and future memorials to military heroes were put up in the vast and then largely empty interior of St Paul's. This plan to form a national pantheon was conceived as a response to that established by the

French government in the former church of Sainte Geneviève (today's Panthéon). The remodelling of culture in Revolutionary France was simultaneously an inspiration and a threat to the British, national monuments playing a role in a propaganda war, and a series of expensive memorials were voted by Parliament during the course of what came to be seen as a fight for national survival. While the army came to prominence in the war's Napoleonic phase (1803–15), especially during the Peninsular Campaign, the early victories were predominantly naval. Early royal influence on the choice of design gave way in 1802 to a treasury-appointed 'Committee of Taste' – a group of experts including connoisseurs and collectors set up to supervise sculptural competitions, approve the designs, award commissions and supervise progress. Press coverage was usually favourable, but Joseph Farington's diary recorded occasional private criticisms of sculptors' work voiced by his fellow Royal Academicians. The patriotic memorials certainly included some interesting failures. They exerted a wide influence on national culture, being reproduced in prints, copied and satirized.

The forgotten captain

Memorials were erected to commanding officers and to the highest-ranking junior officers who died in the course of an important battle (in these wars we can say in an important victory). The occasional act of exceptional bravery was also rewarded, notably in the memorial to Captain Robert Faulknor, one of the first three installed in St Paul's Cathedral (fig. 16). This monument was singled-out for especial mockery by Robert Southey, in the guise of visiting foreigner 'Don Manuel Alvarez Espriella'. Regarding the new installations at St Paul's, he notes: 'they now seem to have discovered the nakedness of this huge edifice, and to vote parliamentary monuments to every sea captain that falls in battle'.[3] Faulknor died in a five-hour, single-ship action on 5 January 1795 between the *Blanche*, 32 guns, and the French *Pique*, 36 guns. He was shot dead about three hours after the combatants had opened fire. He did not, as *Lloyd's Evening Post* said, expire 'contented after having seen the Enemy's colours struck'[4] but he did die after the bowsprit of the *Pique* had been lashed to the capstan of the British ship.[5] A contemporary print, after Thomas Stothard, shows Faulknor falling dead in the midst of crew members carrying out this action, while the inscription on the print, like that of the monument, insists that it was performed 'with his own hands'. At the time of his adoption as a national hero, Faulknor had already shown promise and the war was going badly for the British. *The Sun* noted a proposal to erect a pillar:

---

3   Robert Southey, *Letters from England by Don Manuel Alvarez Espriella* (1807), vol. 1, p. 312.
4   *Lloyd's Evening Post*, 11 February 1795.
5   A lieutenant's log, NMM ADM/L/B/97, says: '… we lash'd her Bowsprit to our capstan'.

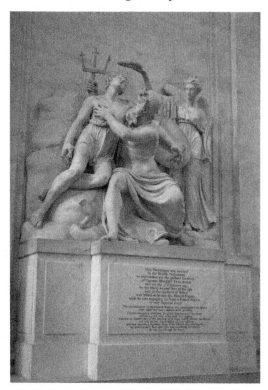

16. *The monument to Captain Robert Faulknor RN, by Charles Felix Rossi, at St Paul's Cathedral. © National Maritime Museum, Greenwich, London & the Chapter of St Paul's Cathedral, London, L7778.*

'There is a novelty and grandeur too in the idea of erecting it upon some eminence on the sea coast.'[6] The City, with financial interests in the West Indies where the action took place, voted money for a monument and there were lengthy debates in Parliament over the erection of a national one. *The London Packet or New Lloyd's Evening Post* accused objectors of being miserly. The *St James's Chronicle*, by contrast, compared the manner in which the Opposition supported the proposal, to 'the farce and *fourberie* of the French Convention; where actions, less meritorious than those daily performed by our common soldiers and sailors are made the theme of ridiculous Applause, and idle Gasconade'.[7]

The commission went to John Charles Felix Rossi (1762–1839). Based on a design by Richard Smirke, the monument is allegorical in conception and shows Faulknor as a Homeric hero supported by Neptune and crowned by Victory. The work excludes the backing pyramid, Britannia and the British lion, which were part of the original conception: as completed in 1803, it presents a more up-to-date neo-classical group. Although of Italian origin, Rossi was British-born: determined lobbying secured him commissions for

6   *The Sun,* 28 February 1795.
7   *St James's Chronicle or the British Evening Post,* 14 April 1795.

six naval and military memorials within St Paul's, although the response to these works from his fellow sculptors was mixed.

Stylistic problems

These commissions presented new opportunities to native sculptors and, thanks to the nation's trade, the British state had deep pockets. There was a growing attempt to develop a national school but British sculptors had difficulty in attaining the technical polish of continental rivals like Antonio Canova. The war made it harder to view continental sculpture, both ancient and modern, and even made the supply of marble problematic. Contemporary sculptors such as Flaxman now had a much more sophisticated grasp of what the canon of classical sculpture actually was – mainly restored Roman marble copies of Greek bronze originals. Going back to earlier, purer sources and adapting them to serve modern purposes was far from easy. The hero dying in the service of his *polis*, who they were attempting to commemorate, was not a youthful Greek warrior with muscles toned in the gymnasium. He was more probably a flabby, middle-aged British officer. As in the aftermath of the First World War, there were lengthy discussions on whether to adopt a timeless ancient style or include modern uniforms and technology.

In Thomas Banks (1735–1805), the cognoscenti thought they had a rising star. The radical politics he adopted at the beginning of the French Revolutionary War appealed to progressives like Southey, if not to all Banks's fellow Royal Academicians. Talented and innovative, particularly in the production of reliefs and free-standing sculpture, he was chosen to make a monument to Captain Richard Rundell Burges (fig. 17), among others. This officer was killed during the Battle of Camperdown in 1797, a victory in the North Sea over the Dutch fleet of the short-lived 'Batavian Republic', gained in a year in which the British had been obliged to withdraw their own fleet from the Mediterranean. The monument was completed in 1806, the year after Banks's death. Flaxman, normally an admirer of Banks, disliked both the memorial to Faulknor and that to Burges but said: 'there are beams of light in that by Banks, though mixed with much imbecility'.[8] Both monuments represented the deceased as an active participant in his own allegory, rather than being represented by a portrait or bust. This discomfited the viewer: 'Falling into Neptune's arms;—a dreadful situation for a dying captain it would be.'[9] Burges, naked except for minimal drapery, receives a sword from a hovering, personified Victory. Between them is placed the breech of a naval gun, as if about to fire through the wall of the cathedral. The original design showed

---

8   *The Diary of Joseph Farington*, 14 May 1806.
9   Southey, *Letters from England*, vol. 1, p. 311.

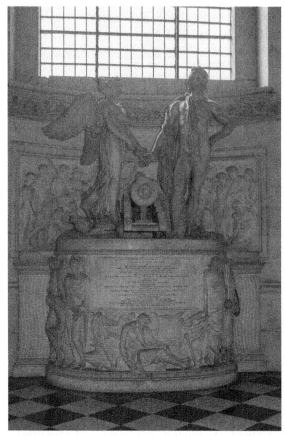

17. *Captain Richard Rundell
Burges RN, by Thomas Banks,
at St Paul's Cathedral.* ©
*National Maritime Museum,
Greenwich, London & the
Chapter of St Paul's Cathedral,
London, L7774.*

the sort of idealized male nude typical of ancient Greek military art,[10] but this subsequently acquired a portrait head and the drapery was extended to spare passing ladies embarrassment. It all combined to ruin Banks's original conception. The fine carving on the base combined the hull of a contemporary warship with depictions of Dacian prisoners borrowed from Trajan's Column. This is now less visible, following removal of the high plinth on which the monument originally stood.

The older generation

The war began with the Navy under the leadership of an elderly generation of commanders. Of the two major veterans of the War of American Independence, Lord Rodney died before the outbreak of war with France in 1792. Richard, Earl Howe, having achieved a victory over the French fleet at the Glorious First of June 1794 and acted as negotiator in the closing stages of

[10] TNA MPD/1/78.

the Nore Mutiny, died at the age of 73 in 1799. Both were awarded state monuments for their considerable lifetime achievements: Rodney's memorial is by Rossi, Howe's by Flaxman. They are both based on a fairly safe formula whereby a full-length statue of the veteran admiral, in contemporary uniform, is accompanied by female personifications representing their legacies – young, beautiful and scantily clad women representing History and Victory. On Howe's monument, completed in 1811, Britannia is seated between them with a British lion to the right of Howe (fig. 18). The monument, partly completed by assistants, had to be cut down to the correct size.

Adam Duncan, after achieving his victory over the Dutch at Camperdown in 1797, died in 1804 and did not receive his state memorial until 1823, well into the post-Napoleonic peace. In the same year, his contemporary John Jervis, Earl St Vincent, also died at the age of 89, after a long active career.

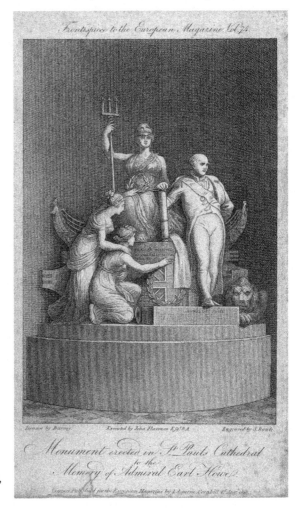

18. *Monument erected in St Paul's Cathedral to the Memory of Admiral Earl Howe. Frontispiece to the European Magazine', 1818.* © *National Maritime Museum, Greenwich, London, PAD0107.*

Their monuments in St Paul's are both full-length statues by Westmacott and Baily respectively.

In the early stages of the French wars, commemoration of senior officers celebrated the living rather than the dead, with the much younger Nelson treated as the last in a set. The form might be portable. In about 1800 Henry Webber (brother of John, the last of Captain Cook's voyage artists) produced 'Britannia Triumphant' for Wedgwood – a group piece in jasperware showing Britannia treading underfoot a dishevelled female figure representing France. Britannia holds a medallion showing George III and by her side are a cornucopia and a lion, which eyes France warily. The drum-shaped base is decorated with the medallion portraits of Howe, Duncan, St Vincent and Nelson, modelled by De Vaere in 1798.

On top of a steep hill called the Kymin, near Monmouth in South Wales, local gentry had built a small banqueting pavilion with good views. To this, in 1800, was added a small building known as the Naval Temple. It was surmounted by a figure of Britannia and round the walls were the names of sixteen British admirals with the dates of their victories, their flags, and a representation of the Battle of the Nile. Most had taken part in the current war and were then still living. Though dead, Rodney and Boscawen were also included (Boscawen's daughter, the Duchess of Beaufort, having been involved in the project). The Kymin was one of the attractions on a route down the Wye valley, fashionable with middle-class travellers attracted by its picturesque scenery. Admiral Nelson, taking a rare holiday during the Peace of Amiens, visited Monmouth in July and August 1802. He travelled with members of his family and the more culturally sophisticated Sir William and Lady Hamilton. On the return trip he visited the Kymin and observed that

> the Temple was the only Monument of the kind erected to the English Navy in the whole range of the kingdom; … The nation has been engaged, for some time in collecting money, in order to erect, by public subscriptions, a magnificent structure of this kind, without accomplishing its purpose. – This at the Kymin is enough; and for which the admirals, whose services are here recorded, *are very much obliged to you.*[11]

Nelson was here contemplating something resembling a bus shelter while addressing Mr Hardwick of Monmouth, treasurer of the building projects on the Kymin. The more 'magnificent' scheme to raise a national naval monument, alluded to, was one launched in 1799. The Duke of Clarence, the future William IV, was presiding over the competition and submissions

---

[11] Charles Heath, *Descriptive account of the Kymin Pavillion* (Monmouth, 1808).

included a design for a colossal standing Britannia by John Flaxman, to be erected in Greenwich Park, overlooking the Royal Hospital for Seamen. The project failed when subscriptions raised insufficient funds but the publicity for it inspired two small summer-house-like structures, similar to the temple on the Kymin, which were completed at Thorsby Hall and Storr's Hotel, Windermere.

James Gillray produced his own satirical design, in which Britannia stands on a column dashed by waves and struck by lightning bolts. This edifice is constructed of a messy pile of naval trophies and French republican artefacts such as caps of liberty, clogs and a banner inscribed 'EGALITÉ'. The most conspicuous feature is a trousered French backside peppered with shot.

Nelson: an exemplary death?

Two of Nelson's iconic quartet of battles, namely St Vincent and Copenhagen, were fought under the overall command of a senior and more cautious admiral. The Nile in 1798 was probably his greatest triumph and firmly established him as the pre-eminent naval hero. He successfully exploited British superiority in discipline and firepower to achieve crushing victories and his premature death in action at Trafalgar in 1805 completed his deification. His final battle sealed British hegemony at sea for over a century, its heavy casualties being overwhelmingly French and Spanish combatants. Nelson's death was unusual because fleet commanders were rarely killed during victorious actions (although, in battle, the quarterdeck was one of the most dangerous places in the ship). Defeat was another matter: the Spanish commander Federico Carlos Gravina was also mortally wounded in the carnage of Trafalgar and, as we have seen, there was a regular attrition of more junior officers throughout the war.

As we have seen, by 1800 a narrative of exemplary naval death in action had become established. Of Aristide-Aubert-Dupetit Thouars, captain of the French *Tonnant* during the Battle of the Nile, it is said that 'Round shots deprived him successively of his right arm, his left arm, and one of his legs; whereupon the heroic officer, instead of letting himself be taken below, caused himself to be placed in a tub of bran, whence he continued to give his orders until from loss of blood he became insensible.'[12] This is an extreme example (inspired perhaps by revolutionary zeal) but, even on the British side of the Channel, the public liked to read that mortally wounded heroes had stayed on deck, remained in charge and retained their faculties and sangfroid until they expired in the knowledge of victory gained.

---

12 William Laird Clowes, *The Royal Navy: A History*, vol. 4 (1899), p. 367.

Nelson, on being fatally wounded by a French sniper, was immediately carried below to the orlop deck below the waterline. Paralysed and with blood flooding his lungs, he died among the other wounded there three hours later, and the British reading public naturally wanted an account of the circumstances of his death. A certain amount appeared shortly afterwards in the newspapers, followed in 1806 by the publication of surgeon William Beatty's *Authentic Narrative of the Death of Lord Nelson*. This drew on Beatty's own eyewitness recollection of the event and that of Nelson's chaplain, Alexander Scott, Walter Burke (*Victory*'s purser) and Captain Hardy. Other sources indicate slight variations in the witnesses' memories. The patient spoke with considerable difficulty and Beatty's account renders the occasion much more dignified and sanitized, repairing Nelson's broken sentences: readers would have expected no less from a competent author. The bloodstains on Nelson's uniform confirm the accuracy of the early part of the narrative and his reported words, though rewritten, are in character. He too read the newspapers and knew what was expected. He survived until victory was complete and produced some suitably patriotic last words, but he was out of the action for much of the battle (and did not entirely retain his sang-froid). Depictions of his death persist in showing him wounded but before being carried below, implying he remained on deck; his body cradled by supporters lent itself to 'deposition-from-the-cross' artistic compositions. Benjamin West's early picture (1806) follows this formula and disappointed Joseph Farington, after he had the truth from a seaman who was present: 'West has made a picture of what might have been not the circumstances as they happened.'[13] The painting by Arthur William Devis (1807) which shows the hero's last moments in *Victory*'s cockpit, though also firmly in the 'deposition' mode, had more claim to authenticity but did not exert much influence on contemporary iconography.

State commemoration

Nelson's public funeral was organized by the College of Arms to include the traditional heraldic accoutrements befitting the (recently) ennobled. Other more specifically naval elements were added, such as the ship-shaped funeral carriage. The grave in the crypt of St Paul's remained open, provoking complaints in the press until the tomb above it was completed. It was eventually surmounted by a black marble sarcophagus which had originally borne a bronze effigy of Cardinal Wolsey by Benedetto da Rovezzano. This had been appropriated to form part of the monument of Henry VIII at Windsor and

---

13 Farington, *Diary*, 8 July 1806.

was later stripped of its bronze fixtures during the Commonwealth period: the four bronze angels have recently been rediscovered, two of them after many years at Great Harrowden Hall, now the clubhouse of a golf club.

By 1805 the King's vandalized tomb was in the way of excavations for the new royal vaults at Windsor. Henry Westmacott was put in charge of recycling the sarcophagus, presented for the purpose by George III, as part of a suitably impressive memorial to the national hero (fig. 19). He decided to place a viscount's coronet on the top, a task completed in 1817. The additional state monument in the nave of the cathedral was based on a design by Henry's brother, Richard Westmacott (1775–1856), and carried out by Flaxman (fig. 20). A full-length statue of Nelson, in contemporary uniform and with the stump of his amputated arm covered by the pelisse given him by Selim III, Sultan of Turkey, leans on an anchor. The whole adopts the conceit of a sculpture within a sculpture, as on a lower part of the plinth a motherly

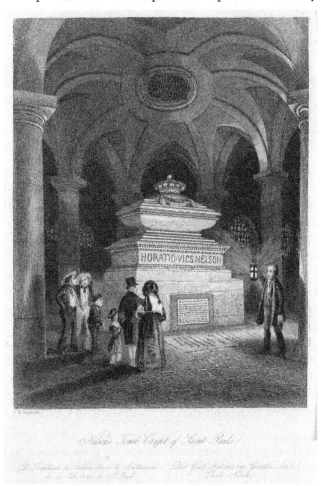

19. *'Nelson's Tomb, Crypt of Saint Pauls',* c.*1830, after a sketch by Thomas Hosmer Shepherd.* © *National Maritime Museum, Greenwich, London, PAD3922.*

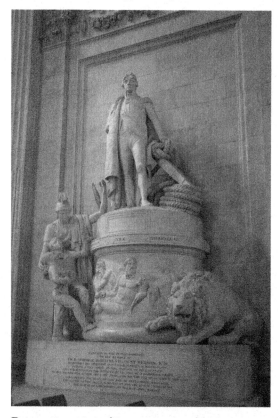

20. *Monument to Vice-Admiral Nelson, by John Flaxman, at St Paul's Cathedral.* © *National Maritime Museum, Greenwich, London & the Chapter of St Paul's Cathedral, London, L7773.*

Britannia points him out as a glowing example to two small boys in sailor dress. The British lion stands guard to balance the composition. The monument is scarcely bigger than that commemorating Captain Faulknor but cost as much as those to Howe and Rodney.

George III also approached the Royal Academy to provide ideas for a memorial to Nelson. The President, Benjamin West – the King's favourite artist – produced, as a painting, a design for a monument flanked by columns similar to a side-altar. Although never built in this form, the 'altarpiece' it framed was subject of an accompanying commemorative painting by West entitled *The Immortality of Nelson*, in which the body of the hero is handed to Britannia by Neptune and Victory in a complex and rather surreal allegory. West also produced a triangular tympanum design based on this composition, which was installed during 1812 in the colonnade pediment of the King William Courtyard at the Royal Hospital for Seamen, Greenwich. It was modelled by Joseph Panzetta, and made in Coade stone.[14]

---

[14] West's paintings were both shown at the Royal Academy in 1807: the former is in the Yale Center for British Art, the 'altarpiece' detail and the tympanum design drawing in the NMM (both Greenwich Hospital Collection).

Civic commemoration

No sooner had the news of victory at Trafalgar and Nelson's death arrived in England, than memorial schemes on every scale were organized. The earliest to survive, and one of the most spontaneous, was a monolith at Taynuilt, Loch Etive, erected by local ironworkers perhaps as early as November 1805.

The common council of the City of London voted to erect a monument which was eventually placed in the Guildhall. Political divisions among their numbers denied the commission to Rossi (favoured by the artistically entrepreneurial Alderman Boydell) and the work went to Flaxman's former assistant, James Smith. This was the only major monument that Smith completed before his early death in 1815 (fig. 21). A rather cluttered design shows a personification of the City of London inscribing Nelson's three major victories on an obelisk, flanked by the usual Britannia, Neptune, the British

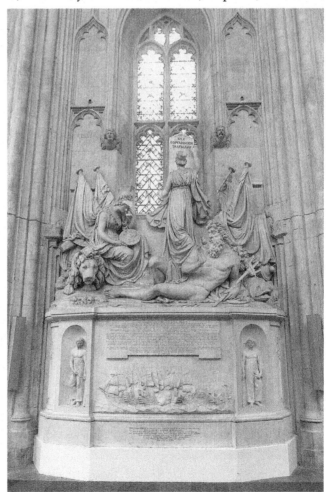

21. *Nelson monument by James Smith, at the Guildhall, City of London. © National Maritime Museum, Greenwich, London, E9054.*

lion and numerous banners. A relief of the action is carved on the base, with two figures of seamen in niches holding inverted torches. Nelson's personal merits are described at some length.

At Liverpool, Richard Westmacott was chosen to carry out a design by Matthew Cotes Wyatt (fig. 22). Not deterred by the mixed reception given to Banks's designs, Wyatt presents a classical allegory with Nelson as a heroic nude figure, one foot placed on a cannon, the other on a fallen enemy. Victory drapes him in a captured flag and adds the crowns of four victories to his sword. Death, represented as a skeleton, lurks in the folds of drapery and a British seaman stands ready to avenge him. A mourning Britannia forms the

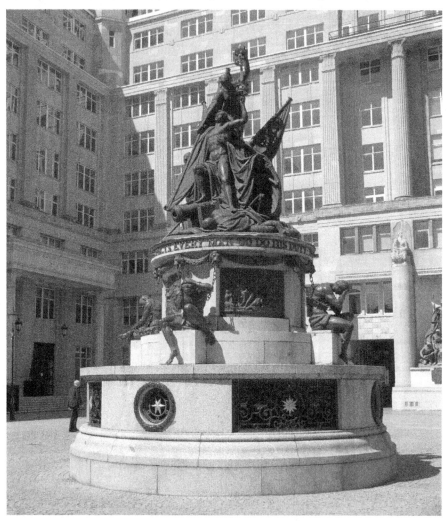

22. *Nelson monument by Sir Richard Westmacott, after a design by Matthew Cotes Wyatt, at Liverpool. © Author.*

fifth figure. The memorial stands in a square behind the town hall, the figure group on a drum-shaped plinth bearing slightly classicized reliefs of Nelson's victories, with four chained prisoners seated around the base. The casting of the main elements in bronze contributes to the success of this somewhat eccentric memorial, restored for the Trafalgar bicentenary in 2005.

Other towns and cities put up memorials – a tower at Calton Hill, Edinburgh, statues at Birmingham and in Barbados, pillars at Great Yarmouth, Dublin and Montreal, among many others. There are no memorials erected by Nelson's family but among the private monuments erected on estates is one put up by Nelson's prize agent and banker, Alexander Davison. A modest obelisk of 1807, in the grounds of the now demolished Swarland Hall, Northumbria, it is dedicated 'To the memory of private friendship'.

Private and commercial commemoration

This unprecedented explosion of public commemoration inspired the production of related memorabilia both commercially and privately. William Holland published a caricature protesting at the 2d entrance charge at St Paul's: 'Sailors should have free admission' (fig. 23). The British tar has erected his own memorial in his back garden consisting of his sea chest chalked with a biblical text, two barrels of grog, crossed officer's swords, Nelson's uniform

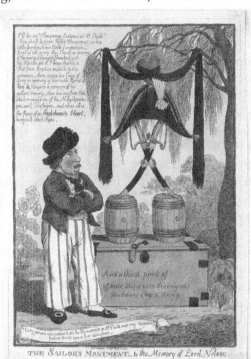

23. *'The Sailor's Monument to the Memory of Lord Nelson', by William Holland. © National Maritime Museum, Greenwich, London, PAG8562.*

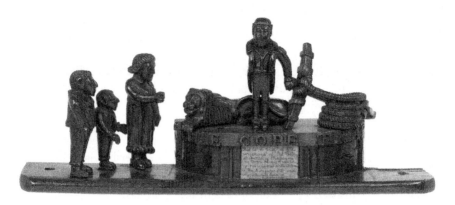

24. *Veteran's wood carving of Flaxman's monument to Nelson in St Paul's Cathedral.* ©
National Maritime Museum, Greenwich, London, REL0580.

hat and 'the figure of an Englishman's heart hung with black crape [*sic*]'.

Popular prints, and the coloured transfers on glass which derived from them, were produced in some numbers in the months following Trafalgar. They typically show Nelson falling wounded on deck, or rather modest, old-fashioned memorials. These scenes include marines, naval officers and seamen shown as mourners and supporters. They are accompanied by personifications such as Britannia, Victory, Neptune and Hope. Patch boxes were a more expensive collectable but one which offered more restricted scope for decoration. Their painters favoured a small plinth base surmounted by a bust or urn, one mourner and an appropriate caption.

William Holland's fictional sailor was not alone in making his own memorial. A rather primitive British carving in the National Maritime Museum collection has a label which says: 'This is a piece of the wreckage of "The Victory" at the Battle of Trafalgar[,] was taken care of and carved by one who was with Nelson in 3 engagements and who afterwards lived in Twickenham' (fig. 24). It is clearly based on Flaxman's Nelson monument at St Paul's, including Nelson, Britannia, the two boys and the lion, much rearranged and simplified.

Concrete and lasting commemoration in all its forms took place amidst what one might call performance or installation art. As had become traditional, victory and death were accompanied by patriotic illuminations and theatrical interludes. The Theatre Royal, Covent Garden, responded more quickly than its rival at Drury Lane, slotting into its programme a short 'Loyal Musical Impromptu', which relied on patriotic songs and backdrops including a representation of a naval battle. Additionally, a few nights later and doubtless after it had been specially painted, 'a picture of Lord NELSON is let down, where he appears expiring—VICTORY crowning him with a laurel wreath, and FAME proclaiming his actions with her eternal trumpet'.[15]

Illuminations were a more contentious issue. They were supposed to be a spontaneous expression of rejoicing by the populace, so it was difficult to get the tone right. As after previous victories, public and private buildings were decorated with back-lit transparencies and designs formed of lamps and candles. Those who did not light up their premises were liable to have their windows broken by the mob. With some approval, however, the press noted the occasional subdued response: 'several had the laurel bound round with crepe, and a light barely sufficient to let the public see what was the feeling of the proprietor of the house upon this occasion ... others exhibited the words "Sacred to the Memory of the Immortal Nelson" and other expressions similar to that, which had more the appearance of readings in Westminster Abbey than transparencies on a rejoicing night'.[16] Funereal imagery had invaded the display.

Trafalgar Square

Plans for a memorial to Nelson, to be set up in a public place in London, saw a subscription opened in November 1805 by a donation from the Prince of Wales. The fund failed to raise sufficient money to erect an adequately imposing monument and contributions up to that point were invested. In the depression which followed the end of the war in 1815, enthusiasm for patriotic memorial projects waned but, with the redevelopment of the Charing Cross area by John Nash, a site became available in the new square Nash created on the south side of the old King's Mews there. During 1832 to 1838 the mews were replaced by the new National Gallery and Trafalgar Square was adopted as the name for the piazza in front in 1830, shortly after work began to lay it out. In 1838 the Nelson Memorial Committee was revived, holding its first meeting on 22 February under the chairmanship of Admiral Sir George Cockburn. Its work was primed with the money from the previous project, which had been building up interest, and what we now know as Nelson's Column in the new square was the end result.

The winning design was by architect William Railton (1800–77). He submitted an artist's impression rather than a model and the project ran into a long series of modifications and problems before final completion by the addition of the flanking lions in 1867. John Lough, the original sculptor commissioned to produce these beasts, dropped out; Thomas Milnes's lions

---

15 *Mirror of Fashion*, 8 November 1805.
16 *Morning Chronicle*, 9 November 1805.

were rejected and are now at Saltaire.[17] In 1858, Sir Edwin Landseer was given the job. Although a well-known animal painter, he had little experience of sculpture, but he successfully fulfilled what proved a ten-year task, modelling the quartet in clay before they were eventually cast in bronze (by Baron Marochetti), rather than being carved in granite. By 1844 the committee had run out of money and had to approach the Treasury to make good the shortfall. As a cost-saving measure, the steps on the column plinth were scrapped, which rather spoiled the architectural relationship between the lions and the pillar. Instead of spectators walking up the steps to admire the bronze reliefs of Nelson's four battles (descent-from-the-cross compositions much in evidence),[18] the base below them became a vantage or performance point for active young men who climbed onto it during festivities or demonstrations. As in so many civic schemes of the period, the provision of public access to new, prestigious spaces was accompanied by worries about how the masses would behave. The wide basins of the fountains were designed to obstruct the space in which mobs could assemble. However, the new square was initially much used as a public lavatory and the homeless slept in it.

The project faced heroic engineering challenges. The column had to be reduced by thirty-three feet and had concrete foundations sixteen feet deep on a bed of gravel. Steam was used to lift the components. The battle reliefs and the lions posed considerable casting problems and, as usual, a combination of classical and more recent design elements did not appeal to all. Hippolyte Taine in 1852 compared the general effect to: 'a rat on top of a pole'.[19]

When hoisted into place in 1843, the giant statue of Nelson by William Hodges Baily (1788–1867) was, by then, wearing historic costume: the Victorians would have regarded it as such and were careful to get it right. The colossus had also assumed a personality in its own right: it was impossible to ignore and the vicissitudes of the project, and its position, kept and keep Nelson's reputation in the public eye.

By the end of the century, British domination of the seas was beginning to face challenges from a newly united Germany. In 1894 the Navy League was founded, a pressure group whose objectives were to promote increased expenditure on the Navy. The following year they laid a wreath in Trafalgar

---

[17] Milnes did, however, receive a commission in 1847 for the statue of Nelson in the Cathedral close, Norwich.

[18] St Vincent by Musgrave Lewthwaite Watson (1804–47), the Nile by William Frederic Woodington (1806–93), Copenhagen by John Ternouth (*c*.1796–1848), Trafalgar by John Edward Carew (*c*.1785–1868).

[19] Hippolyte Taine, 'Notes on England', in Charles Morris and H.G. Leigh, eds, *With the World's Great Travellers* (Chicago, 1901), p. 49. Taine found London's combination of classical architecture, rain and air pollution depressing.

Square on Trafalgar Day (21 October) and in 1896 the column was decorated with wreaths and garlands of evergreens (a mode of decoration copied from the French).[20] Trafalgar Day subsequently became popular nationwide but the League regarded this involvement with heritage as a distraction from its contemporary political objectives.

The twentieth century and beyond

During the twentieth century some Nelson memorials were destroyed in the break-up of the empire his victories had helped create. The Coade-stone statue and pillar erected in 1808 in Montreal still survives, as does the version of Richard Westmacott's Birmingham statue erected in Barbados. The Irish memorials did not fare so well. In 1966 nationalists demolished the memorial arch erected by the men of the Sea Fencibles at Castletownsend, near Cork. This had been the first one to go up, in a record five hours. The Nelson pillar in Dublin was blown up in the same year by (apparently maverick) members of the IRA.[21] It had always been a traffic obstruction, although journalist Desmond Ryan wrote in 1955: 'We believe that Horatio Nelson's Pillar is his castle; and he is a true Dublin citizen by squatter's rights, by a century and a half's public repentance for widely publicized human frailty [and] by his unique contribution to the symmetry of the main street of our capital city.'[22]

This sums up the public relationship to Nelson after the Second World War. He had become a local hero, more a 'character' than a glowing example. Portsmouth erected a new statue by Frederick Brook Hitch (1897–1957) in 1951. The city and its naval base had suffered severe enemy bombing in the Second World War and the inscription mentions destruction of the George Hotel in the High Street, where Nelson spent his last night in England, and war damage to HMS *Victory*. The statue itself was presented by a local Nelson enthusiast, Dr Herbert James Aldous, and was based on his own design. Originally overlooking the beach where Nelson left England for the last time, it was re-sited in 2005, the bicentenary of Trafalgar. The continuing appeal of Nelson and the Napoleonic period in the late twentieth century was also expressed in the restoration of existing memorials, a task in which the 1805 Club played an important role. Founded in 1990 as a splinter group of the Nelson Society, its first objective was to preserve 'the historic environment

20 *The Builder*, 24 October 1896, p. 326: 'In Paris the decoration of statues and monuments at anniversaries has long been a habit, in London we have hitherto paid little attention to this decorative manner of celebrating an anniversary. It is pleasant to see some life and colour given to our streets by such decoration as has been carried out at the Nelson Monument.'
21 The statue on the pillar was by Thomas Kirk (1781–1845).
22 *Irish Press*, 9 November 1955. Quoted in Micheál O' Riain, 'Nelson's Pillar, a controversy that ran and ran', *Trafalgar Chronicle*, 2001, pp. 98–108.

of the Georgian sailing navy; as represented by its monuments, graves and memorials'.[23]

New statues of popular local celebrities, frequently prominent in film or sport, play a role today in promoting the tourist industry. During the Trafalgar bicentenary a new bronze Nelson statue of this type, by local artist Lesley Pover, was put up outside the historic Trafalgar Tavern in Greenwich, within yards of the Old Royal Naval College and National Maritime Museum. The cartoonish tone of this work was hardly reverential but undoubtedly added to the appeal of the venue until 2012, when the statue apparently became victim of attempted metal theft, which caused damage, and it was then removed completely. This provoked much comment online and in the local press, and while opinion on the work's merits was sharply divided, its presence was certainly missed. In April 2014, despite the company which ran the Tavern going into administration in the meanwhile, it reappeared to much acclaim and in repaired order, in its old position but now overlooking the Thames. The controversy revealed some of the ambiguities inherent in placing privately-owned commemorative sculpture in public places.

The diversity and wealth of London in Olympic year (2012) was reflected in the installation of Yinka Shonibare MBE's *Nelson's Ship in a Bottle* outside a new south entrance to the National Maritime Museum. Originally placed on the fourth plinth in Trafalgar Square, this very popular contemporary work explores the long and not always happy relationship between Britain and West Africa. A giant acrylic bottle contains a model of HMS *Victory* – which itself owes its survival to being a Nelson memorial – the sails made of the Dutch-wax printed cotton manufactured in Europe for the Nigerian market.[24] Shonibare is taking a well-worn symbol of British heritage and putting a new, personal slant on it to say something about the changing nature of present-day national identity. The Georgian caricaturists did something very similar in producing their own take on the state memorial projects of their time, and present-day visitors to Greenwich enjoy making their own appropriation of Shonibare's work by attaching themselves to the bottle in mobile-phone snaps.

23 Peter Warwick and John Curtis, 'Such Graves to Share; Twenty Years Conserving Memorials to Georgian Naval Heroes', *Kedge Anchor* (Newsletter of the 1805 Club), November 2010.
24 Note also Claes Oldenburg's 1993 'Bottle of Notes' sculpture at Middlesbrough, which obliquely references Captain Cook.

Successor

Cuthbert Collingwood (1748–1810) was Nelson's second-in-command at Trafalgar and was in charge for much of the battle. Throughout much of his career, he had been a personal friend of Nelson and, though older, was always slightly behind him on the promotion ladder. He also outlived Nelson by only five years, dying of natural causes (possibly stomach cancer) in 1810 before he could return home from the Mediterranean. His plain tomb in the crypt of St Paul's is overshadowed by that of his illustrious colleague but his memorial by Richard Westmacott, in the main body of the church, shows some originality in its design by returning to the old idea of including a recumbent effigy of the deceased. In an era fascinated by personality, this type of memorial tended to obscure the face (fig. 25). Collingwood lies on a stylized antique galley, his head cradled by a kneeling Victory. Beside the vessel is a reclining river-god figure, representing the Thames, with his tributaries shown as putti. This was based on the famous Roman statues of the Nile and Tiber, which were spoils of Napoleon's conquests in Italy and were ceded to France by treaty in 1797: Nile was returned to the Vatican in 1816 while Tiber remains in the Louvre. More putti in little boats representing 'the progress of navigation' are carved

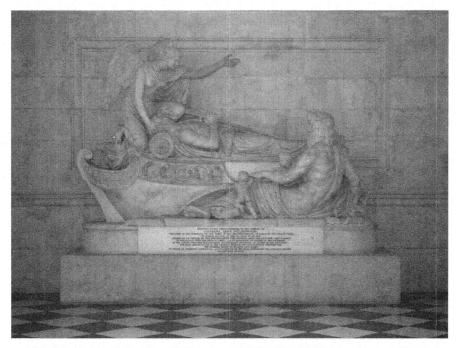

25. *Vice-Admiral Cuthbert Collingwood, by Sir Richard Westmacott, at St Paul's Cathedral.* © *National Maritime Museum, Greenwich, London & the Chapter of St Paul's Cathedral, London, L7766.*

along the side of Collingwood's funeral barge. This state monument gives a short account of Collingwood's public services.

The family memorial in St Nicholas's Cathedral, Newcastle upon Tyne, was commissioned by Lady Collingwood and inscribed after her death in 1819 by her two daughters. Collingwood's marriage (unlike Nelson's) had survived the stresses of separation and he left legitimate children. The long inscription stresses not only his professional skills but his lineage, ties to Newcastle, private virtues and personal sacrifices: 'He became anxious to revisit his native land; but being informed that his service could ill be spared in those critical times, he replied that his life was his country's, and persevered in the discharge of his arduous duties, till exhausted with fatigue, he expired.' The designer was architect Charles Robert Cockerell (1788–1863) and the monument takes the form of a bust of Collingwood by Charles Felix Rossi standing on a plinth in front of a draped cenotaph which bears his sword and coat of arms. The plinth is carved with a rostral column, and the names of Collingwood's three victories – the Glorious First of June, St Vincent and Trafalgar – are carved within wreaths.

In 1845, during the revival of interest in Trafalgar sparked by the Nelson memorial in London, Newcastle subscribers set up a large statue of Colling-wood as their local hero on a short column serving as a sea-mark, at the entrance to the River Tyne. The plinth is reached by steps and is guarded not by lions but by four guns from his ship, *Royal Sovereign*. John Graham Lough (1798–1876), the locally born sculptor who had given up the Trafalgar Square lions, produced the statue. The architect was John Dobson (1787–1865), another local man, who was to rebuild central Newcastle during the same period in a neo-classical style, funded by coal and heavy industry.

From the officers and crew …

The commissioning of memorials to officers, paid for by their peers or by fellow officers and crew, was well established during the Napoleonic Wars. Nelson and his officers commissioned a memorial to Captain Ralph Willett Miller (1762–99). Miller had been present at the Nile but died afterwards in an accidental shipboard fire and explosion during the siege of Acre, so would not have qualified for state commemoration. Nelson led this enterprise and was prepared to pick up the bill for any financial shortfall. The result was a particularly successful tablet by Flaxman carved in high relief, still to be seen high in the south transept of St Paul's: it shows Britannia and Victory hanging Miller's portrait on a palm tree, with the British lion to the left and Miller's ship, *Theseus*, to the right. Letters survive from Nelson and his Nile flag captain, Sir Edward Berry, concerning this commission. Neither man is concerned about its appearance: 'Flaxman is the artist, and in him we may all trust.'[25] They are both preoccupied with the finances of the project and who should be allowed to subscribe. This honour, thought Berry, should be reserved for comrades in arms and not even extended to Nelson's prize agent, Alexander Davison, who was handling the money. Nelson has decided views on the style of the inscription: 'The language must be plain, as if flowing from the heart of one of us Sailors who have fought with him.'[26] Their views suggest that there was an aspirational aspect to memorial subscription.

Deal in Kent was the site of two early (and exceptionally rare) shipmates' memorials to naval seamen. Naval vessels operated from the Downs – the important anchorage between Deal and the Goodwin Sands – against smugglers and French privateers, both capturing such prizes and taking part in operations against the enemy-held European mainland. Remaining relatively near this base they were able to bury some of the casualties on British soil and carry sick and wounded to the nearby military hospital. A gravestone (now lost) at St George's church, Deal, erected 'by his shipmates', commemorated Andrew Woodburn of HMS *Clyde*, who died on 20 August 1808 in the hospital after being wounded by musket fire in a boat action on the 8th of that month.[27] A mural tablet in the shape of an obelisk on ball feet, still *in situ* on the south wall, commemorates two seamen killed during an engagement between the *Naiad*, *Rinaldo*, *Redpole*, *Castilian* and a division of seven French 12-gun *prames*. This took place off Boulogne, where the Emperor Napoleon had been reviewing his invasion flotilla on 20–21 September 1811 and, finding the presence of the British frigate *Naiad* just outside the port more than he could stomach, sent these vessels out to engage her and her smaller consorts. The British considered the outcome a success and a personal humiliation for Bonaparte. The Royal Navy's losses were one officer and two seamen of *Naiad*, James Draper and John Ross, 'truly good men, who so nobly fell in the just cause of their Country'. The body of Draper was interred at St George's on 27 September.[28]

In 1812 war broke out between Britain and the United States, a sideshow at the end of the long French wars as far as the British were concerned, but crucial to the emerging national identity of the USA and what, later, would be Canada. Memorials to the British casualties include a rather unusual

---

25 Berry to Thomas Troubridge, 28 March 1801, in Nicholas Harris Nicholas, ed., *The Dispatches and Letters of Vice Admiral Lord Viscount Nelson* (repr. 1998), vol. 4, pp. 276–77.

26 Nelson to Sir Edward Berry, 26 January 1801, in ibid.

27 TNA ADM51/1894; inscription recorded in 1950s.

28 For other early crew memorials see NMM PAF8557, a sketch made in 1818 by Midshipman C.W. Browne of a memorial in the form of a notice board to the crew of HM ship *Julia*, lost at Tristan da Cunha in 1817. Matthew Flinders erected a plaque at Memory Cove, South Australia, in 1802: engraved on a sheet of copper, it commemorated eight seamen drowned in a boat accident.

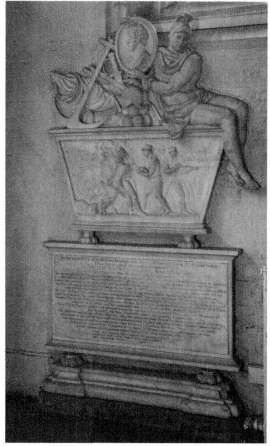

26. Sir Peter Parker by Christopher Prosperi, at St Margaret's, Westminster. © Dean and Chapter of Westminster.

officer-and-crew example in St Margaret's, Westminster (fig. 26), to a promising and popular naval captain killed in a land skirmish in North America. During the combined military and naval campaign in the Chesapeake that culminated in the burning of the public buildings of Washington, including the White House, Sir Peter Parker and men from the *Menelaus* landed at Belle Air near Baltimore on 30 August 1814, to create a diversion. They encountered spirited resistance from a party of local militia in an action now known as the Battle of Caulk's Field. Parker is said to have been wounded 'in the moment of VICTORY' but 'continued to cheer his men'. The acting commander of *Menelaus* also reported a victory but with heavy losses.[29] US sources, unsurprisingly, claimed it as a British defeat.[30] Whatever the truth, Parker bled to death and, were one to believe its representation in the

---

[29] Letter from Acting Commander Henry Crease in the *London Gazette*, 27 September 1814.
[30] Theodore Roosevelt, 'War with the United States', in Clowes, *The Royal Navy: A History*, vol. 4, p. 144.

Westminster monument, in an exemplary manner. His memorial inscription there also devotes a line to his extensive naval family connections and ends in a quotation from the *Aeneid* (X: 467): 'Every man has his appointed day; life is brief and irrevocable; but it is the work of virtue to extend our fame by our deeds.' Quotations from Virgil were used on monuments to officers killed on both sides of this conflict.[31] Parker's memorial, by Christopher Prosperi, shows him in relief, dying while supported by two seamen, with marines opening fire on the enemy to the right: the stern of Parker's ship, *Menelaus*, is on the left. Naval trophies are carved above, with a full-length figure of the Greek hero, Menelaus, supporting a profile portrait of Parker. The memorial makes a number of allusions to the Trojan War and with a suitably Homeric twist to the narrative: Parker's men, determined that the body should not fall into enemy hands, carried it five miles to the shore. It was embalmed on board ship and buried with full military honours in Bermuda.

When Parker's wish to be interred in the family vault at St Margaret's was known, his remains were repatriated and reburied within a year in a second military funeral, attended by many senior officers. Thirty seamen from *Menelaus* carried the bier which supported the (doubtless lead-lined) coffin. After the ship returned to Britain, Lieutenant Henry Crease wrote to Parker's widow via her father, presenting her with £300 that the ship's company had subscribed for a memorial. She promised to acknowledge their contribution in the inscription. According to Crease, it had come out of the crew's prize money: 'I was under the necessity of most positively limiting the sum – finding, poor fellows, on the very mention of the subject, instinctively, at a moment, they crowded around me with every farthing they possessed.'[32]

Family grief

The toll that the long French wars of 1793–1815 might take on one family is illustrated by a plain but lengthy memorial at Bridlington Priory. John Pitts and Frances, his wife, daughter of James Hebletwayte, lost three sons in the course of the conflict. Two were midshipmen in the Navy: William drowned in 1806 and Frederick died at sea, of disease, in 1814. Thomas, who served in the Royal Engineers, was present during most of the major battles of the Peninsular War, falling in 1814 during the capture of the city of Hastingues, just over the border in France as French forces retreated.

---

31 The memorial to Lieutenant Augustus Ludlow USN (d. 1813) at Trinity church, New York, also employs a quote from Virgil, *Aeneid*, IX, 182: 'One love united them, and side by side they entered combat'.

32 Henry Crease, 19 May 1815. Sir George Dallas, *A biographical memoir of the Late Sir Peter Parker: Baronet … (1815)*, p. 108.

IF THE FATHER WAS TOO PROUD, THE MOTHER TOO FOND

OF SONS LIKE THESE,

THEY HAVE BORNE THE LOSS OF THEM WITH SUBMISSION TO THE WILL

OF GOD

WHOSE MERCY THEY HUMBLY ACKNOWLEDGE

THAT IN THIS SAD BUT SOOTHING OFFICE

OF INSCRIBING A MONUMENT OF THEIR CHILDREN

NOTHING WOULD BE RECORDED

THAT DID NOT REFLECT HONOR ON THE AUTHORS OF THEIR BEING

This memorial is unusual for its period in mentioning the role played by its erection in consoling the bereaved.

Ordinary seamen

In the years during and after the war, the neo-classical wall tablet (in a simplified form affordable to the middle-class purse) spread across the walls of the nation's churches. If the middling sort were gaining a new individual identity, the naval seaman failed to escape his role as a generic patriotic symbol. However, the totally inclusive monument was beginning to appear in Prussia and in schemes mooted in Revolutionary and Napoleonic France. In 1807 the liberal writer, Southey, put forward the idea that, if the commander-in-chief survived a victorious action, and if 'it be thought expedient ... that every victory should have its monument, let it be, like the stone at Thermopylae, inscribed to the memory of all who fell'.[33] At the end of the war Parliament voted to erect memorials to all who were killed at Trafalgar and Waterloo. Robert Smirke's design for the naval monument was recommended by the Committee of Taste in 1817 and a budget of £100,000 was allotted to it; but, in the event, neither monument was erected.

The British tar generally featured on the memorials of officers as a mourner or supporter – supporters, in the heraldic sense, in the case of the seamen who flanked Nelson's newly granted shield of arms; a supporter in the literal sense in the case of the sailor whose muscular back dominates the memorial to Captain Edward Cooke (d. 1799) in Westminster Abbey: he is holding up his fatally wounded captain. Seamen and marines as mourners appear in the popular glass pictures and prints mentioned above and, in a similar composition, a three-dimensional tar weeps beside the sarcophagus of Captain George Duff (killed in the *Mars* at Trafalgar in 1805), by John Bacon junior, in St Paul's Cathedral.

---

[33] Southey, *Letters from England*, vol. 1, p. 312.

Individual warrant officers were quite commonly commemorated on family memorials. This was a rather mixed group which included not only the surgeon and the chaplain, who had prospects of second careers in civilian life, but also the master, bo'sun, carpenter, gunner and sail maker. Standing warrant officers (the carpenter, gunner and bo'sun) had some prospect of continuous employment as they remained with the ship between commissions. A well-preserved sandstone headstone at Arbroath Abbey commemorates James Kiell, 'late gunner in the Royal Navy who died 30th March 1816 aged 83': a naval cannon is carved in relief on the reverse (fig. 27). The ordinary seamen of the Napoleonic period are mostly without memorials, although their names were recorded in the bureaucratic records kept to track pay owed and deserters. Internet genealogical records are now immortalizing these formerly anonymous individuals. Later in the nineteenth century the physical commemoration of war dead would take a more inclusive direction as revolutionary continental practices were quietly adopted in Britain for conservative motives.

The French Revolutionary and Napoleonic Wars represented the high point of the nation's naval success. Nelson's achievements were never overshadowed by those of successive heroes and the appeal of his personality to succeeding

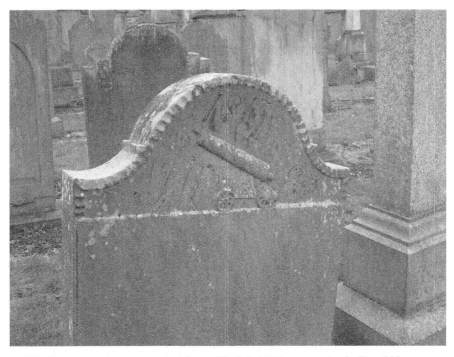

27. *Gravestone commemorating James Kiell, d. 1816, gunner in the Royal Navy, at Arbroath Abbey. © Author.*

generations is reflected in continuing re-evaluation and commemoration. It continues to survive, although the cult of the dying warrior as practised in his era now seems strange, mediated as it was through contemporary art to a public generally far removed from the conflict.

The pantheon of military heroes of this period in St Paul's is now obscured by later re-ordering of the memorials, some of them (notably Rodney) long relegated to obscure corners of the crypt. As the late Georgians became early Victorian there was a growing ecclesiastical resistance to the cathedral's purpose as a house of prayer for the living being obstructed by a marble congregation of the heroic dead. Nevertheless, the project which put them there had challenged the abilities of a generation of British sculptors and these monuments were the subject of unprecedented public interest in an era when popular patriotism had no other outlet but war.

3

Pax Britannica: naval memorials, 1815–1914

During the years following the defeat of Napoleon, the Royal Navy was a victim of its own success. In peacetime, there were fewer ships in commission and less opportunity for gaining prize money. The military careers of many younger officers were virtually over. Unable to live on the reduced pay provided when they were not actively employed by the Navy, they sought other opportunities in civilian life. More senior officers, if better-off on half-pay, could similarly only look forward to long periods of unemployment. While some men gained distinction in expanding areas such as surveying and Arctic exploration, the Navy had largely ceased to be a route to social advancement through fighting prowess.

On the beach

Naval seamen could, in theory, return to the merchant service, although many seem to have worked as farm labourers or in more urban trades. If significantly disabled, chronically infirm, elderly and also – or thereby – destitute, some veterans became Greenwich Hospital in-pensioners (resident at the Hospital) or out-pensioners drawing a charitable income from it but living elsewhere. Memorials to any of these individuals are rare.

The original Hospital burial ground was on Maze Hill, in the north-east corner of Greenwich Park, but a new site was opened adjacent to the present Romney Road in 1749 including a new vault for officers. Pensioners were buried in sixteen-foot pit graves, two abreast, in hexagonal, single-break wooden coffins, with iron breastplates and grips. The cheapness of the coffin plates would make future identification of individual graves impossible.[1]

The last surviving Greenwich Pensioners gained a sort of celebrity and were given individual identity in contemporary paintings and photographs. In 1857 their second cemetery closed and, although a third was opened about

---

[1] Ceridwen Boston, Annsofie Witkin, Angela Boyle and David R.P. Wilkinson, *Safe Moor'd in Greenwich Tier* (Oxford, 2008), p. 73.

a mile to the east (now a park called Greenwich Pleasaunce), the Hospital, facing a declining number of applicants for admission, was itself closed in 1865, except for 'helpless' cases finally rehoused in 1869. When a cut-and-cover railway tunnel was constructed across the second burial ground, opening in 1878, about 1400 bodies were moved to a mass grave in the third.[2] They were followed by about another 4000 prior to the building of the Devonport Nurses Home (now Devonport House) on the site from 1925. An 1875 wall tablet at the Pleasaunce commemorates them all: 'They served their country in the wars which established the naval supremacy of England and died the honoured recipients of her gratitude.'

Surgeons and chaplains, both warrant officers in inconstant employ, were men with transferable skills. A wall tablet at Paul parish church, near Mousehole in Cornwall, was erected 'In memory of EDWD. LEAH M.R.C.S. of this parish Esqre. Having served in foreign climes for many years as a surgeon R.N., he settled at Penzance where it pleased God to afflict him with a lingering mortal disease of intense suffering which he was mercifully enabled to bear with Christian fortitude and resignation, he died Decr. 27th MDCCCLIII [1853] in the 51st year of his age.' Though he would have been part of the post-war intake, the 1851 census notes his occupation as surgeon RN and general practitioner, and that he was (not unusually) living near his birthplace. The status of the surgeon, frequently Scottish, was rising during this period, reflecting his marketable skills and involvement in scientific enquiry. He might also seek employment in the East India Company or at a shore-based naval hospital.

The chaplain could also find employment on shore. Nelson's foreign-language secretary, the Reverend Alexander John Scott (1768–1840), famously present at both his death and thereafter in constant attendance on his body until the funeral, is commemorated by a chest tomb at St Mary's church, Ecclesfield, South Yorkshire. This records his later joint role as Vicar of Catterick, Yorkshire, and Southminster, Essex.

Unlike the cadet classes (below the rank of lieutenant), unemployed commissioned officers were retained on half-pay. Those of post rank (captains upwards) enjoyed continuing promotions by seniority – irrespective of whether further actively employed – filling dead men's shoes until, by the mid-century, the Admiralty had difficulty finding senior officers young and fit enough to provide effective wartime leadership. Death and something resembling a modern retirement scheme, introduced in 1847, finally thinned the ranks at senior level and allowed the emergence of talented younger men.

The mid-century memorials to senior officers should be viewed with this

---

2   Three thousand according to the plaque at Greenwich Pleasaunce.

long period 'on the beach' in mind. A pedestal tomb at Kensal Green Cemetery in London commemorates Rear-Admiral Thomas Tudor Tucker, who died aged 78 in 1852. Captain Tucker saw plenty of action during the French Revolutionary and Napoleonic Wars, being wounded during the hard-fought capture of the USS *Essex* on 28 March 1814, and rising to rear-admiral on the retired list in 1846.[3] The 1851 census indicates his modest London establishment: the Tuckers had no live-in servants; and the Admiralty, seeking to reduce the superfluous number of flag officers, did not fill his place on the list when he died. His memorial is crowned with naval trophies and has a sword and wreath at the base: the inscription is now only partially legible. This type of monument was not only unfashionable during the 1850s but condemned by contemporary writers as unchristian: 'Surrounding a boastful list of their exploits, which might have applied with as much truth to a heathen centurion, as to a Christian soldier ... flags hung on dumpy halberds, muskets, bayonets, swords.'[4] The wall tablet to Benjamin William Page (1765–1845) in his home town of Ipswich is unabashedly Georgian in tone:

> during a long public life, he honorably & successfully accomplished every appointed service, twice received the thanks of British merchants in the East Indies and by God's blessing in the zealous discharge of his duties, reached the summit of his profession & acquired the character of a good sailor a kind friend, a bounteous master & a munificent relation.

A captain at the close of the war, Page did not go to sea again but rose steadily in seniority, becoming an Admiral of the Blue in 1841. Rebuilding of the church of St Mary-le-Tower began in 1850, shortly after Page's memorial was erected there. The architect of the new church was Richard Makilwaine Phipson (1827–84). Phipson's cathedral-like gothic church was utterly in accord with the stylistic preferences of the Oxford Movement but not with classical wall tablets. Page's memorial was reinstalled in a low and dark position on the south side of the nave and it was lucky to survive at all.

In foreign service

One way out of the unemployment problem was to seek service with foreign navies. By the end of the war, the career prospects for Thomas, Lord Cochrane (1775–1860), were particularly bleak. After a promising naval career, he had reached the rank of captain but was stripped of his knighthood and dismissed

---

3 The Admiralty, at this time, was reducing the number of older captains on the active list by offering retirement with a nominal promotion to flag rank.
4 The Reverend Edward Trollope, *Manual of Sepulchral Memorials* (1858), introduction, p. 3.

from the service following his association with a stock-market swindle engineered by a shady uncle, Andrew Cochrane-Johnstone, in 1814. His radical connections led to his recruitment in 1817 as commander-in-chief of the newly created Chilean navy, although he had previously commanded nothing bigger than a frigate. During the French occupation of Spain, an independence movement had sprung up in South America. An independent Chile was led by General José San Martin and Bernardo O'Higgins, under whose strategic direction Cochrane prosecuted the naval arm of the campaign against Spanish rule in Peru. The Chilean navy was established on the British model and initially manned by British and American seamen. Its personnel were mainly Chilean by the time Cochrane left for Brazil, where he was similarly successful in commanding its navy against the Portuguese.

After his return to Britain in 1825, a threat was made to prosecute him under the 1819 Foreign Enlistment Act, which prohibited service in foreign wars in which Britain was neutral. Two unsuccessful years in command of the Greek navy followed, fighting for Greek independence from Turkey. A change of government and the accession of the 'sailor king' William IV in 1830 made conditions favourable for Cochrane's rehabilitation and he was given a final command in the British Navy. He was buried in the centre of the nave at Westminster Abbey with an inscription which states that 'who … by his exertions in the cause of freedom and his splendid services alike to his own country, Greece, Brazil, Chili and Peru, achieved a name illustrious throughout the world for courage, patriotism and chivalry'. The epitaph was written by Lyon Playfair, first Baron Playfair (1818–98), a fellow liberal and Scot who shared Cochrane's scientific interests. The ledger is carved with Cochrane's arms as tenth Earl of Dundonald (he succeeded his father in 1831) and the shields of Chile, Peru, Brazil and Greece. Once a year, representatives of the Chilean navy still lay a wreath on his grave.

A statue of Cochrane was erected by public subscription at Soto Mayor, Valparaiso, in 1873 (fig. 28). The Chileans chose a fellow countryman of Cochrane's to execute the commission – the Scottish sculptor George Anderson Lawson (1832–1904). The likeness was based on a bust by Canova and a portrait by Sir George Hayter, and the attitude was said to be 'suggestive of his daring and energetic character'.[5] It was unveiled by the President and veterans of Cochrane's daring capture of the Spanish *Esmeralda*, 44 guns, at Callao in 1820; members of the Cochrane family were also present. Moved to its present location in 1920, the statue became part of a larger naval monument surmounted by an obelisk and adorned with the bronze prows of ships.

[5]   *The Graphic*, 22 February 1873, p. 170.

Gothic

The term 'chivalry' in Playfair's epitaph for Cochrane is perhaps significant, not so much with regard to Cochrane's conduct but as a reflection of the ethos of mid-century Britain. When Augustus Welby Northmore Pugin published *An Apology for the Revival of Christian Architecture in England* in 1843, various revivalist styles were already in fashion. Pugin championed gothic as particularly Christian and English. His ideas for reviving the gothic memorial brass utilize contemporary women's fashions and men's robes of office to achieve a medieval effect. However, he did not offer any solutions to the problem of depicting modern military uniform. Although Pugin's circle was Catholic, the Oxford Movement and associated reform within the Anglican Church also rehabilitated the Middle Ages and encouraged a new type of clergyman: active, resident rather than absentee, and much more concerned about the

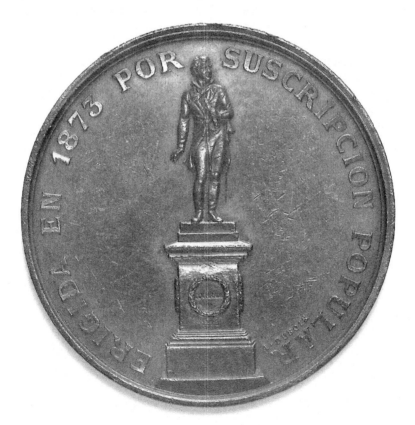

28. *Medal depicting the statue of Admiral Thomas Cochrane, by George Anderson Lawson, Valparaiso, Chile.* © *Robert Cutts (*http://www.flickr.com/photos/21678559@N06) *from Bristol, England, UK (CC BY 2.0).* © *National Maritime Museum, Greenwich, London, MEC 2515.*

appearance of his building. This extended to sepulchral monuments: 'nothing can be more offensive and unsightly than monumental tablets like blisters stuck up against the wall and pillars of a church'.[6] Monumental brasses were less intrusive additions to the fabric of the interior. They had a good medieval pedigree and, in a crude form, they had never quite gone away.

The memorial to Commander Armine Wodehouse, captain of HMS *Cormorant*, sunk in action against the Peiho forts in 1859 during the Second China War, consists of an inscription painted in gothic letters between the arcades on the south side of the nave of Norwich Cathedral, seeking to integrate this addition with the architecture of the building. The brass at Rochester Cathedral to Joseph Oates Travers (d. 1869), a colonel in the Royal Marines, combines a gothic architectural frame and personal heraldry with the Marines' globe-and-laurel symbol. The dedication of church fittings, stained-glass windows, church extensions, repairs or even new churches were suggested to the bereaved as appropriate memorials. Naval officers, however, frequently had close relatives in the clergy and strings could be pulled to ensure the insertion of the memorial their family wanted. The church monument did not entirely disappear, though social and religious pressures weighed more heavily upon its content. Biographical details were curtailed in the inscription and biblical texts included.

Among the relatively small number of exuberant naval gothic monuments, that to Commander Charles Spencer Ricketts (1788–1867) at Kensal Green Cemetery stands out (fig. 29). Reminiscent of a shrine, it consists of a sarcophagus decorated with shields supported on green Cornish serpentine colonnettes, under a canopy on red Peterhead granite colonnettes with cusped arches, crockets and gargoyles. Ricketts served as a midshipman under Cochrane in the *Speedy*, 14 guns, including in his celebrated capture of the 32-gun Spanish xebec-frigate *El Gamo* off Barcelona in 1801. He ended the war with the rank of lieutenant, after which he remained on half-pay, though his finances were augmented by his marriage to Elizabeth Sophia Aubrey, who in 1826 inherited a large part of her uncle's estates. This allowed Ricketts to become a keen collector of china and *objets d'art* and later to commission a large painting of the 1801 action by Clarkson Stanfield (exhibited at the Royal Academy in 1845), including himself hauling down the Spanish colours.[7] The designer of his monument was Pugin's disciple and builder of Cardiff Castle, William Burges (1827–81), the most flamboyant exponent of Victorian gothic.

Another gothic memorial at Kensal Green commemorates Commander

---

6 Pugin, quoted in David Meara, *A.W.N. Pugin and the Revival of Memorial Brasses* (1991), p. 31.
7 His daughter bequeathed this to the South Kensington Museum in 1901: it is now V&A ref. 364–1901.

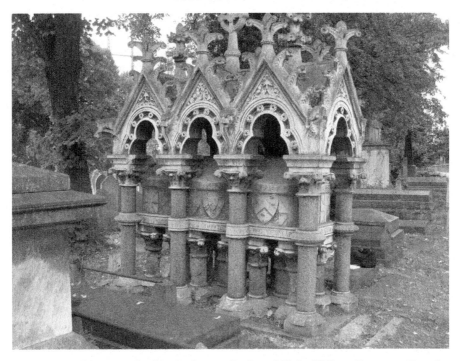

29. *Tomb of Commander Charles Spencer Ricketts RN, by William Burges, at Kensal Green Cemetery. © Lucy Saint and Eleanor Baugh.*

James de Bertodano Lopez (1846–89), whose grave is marked by a tall column topped with statues of four religious figures: St James the Great, the Virgin Mary, Christ and St John. Lopez was London-born and he made a promising start: 'Knows Spanish and Italian and sings Tenor, of great tact in dealing with others ... shows great zeal and judgement'.[8] However, his career and life were cut short by a mental affliction, probably syphilitic in origin. Like Ricketts, the iconography of his memorial is religious, rather than naval.

The Seymour family maintained a vault at Arrow church in Warwickshire and the church contains many memorials to Seymours and Seymour-Conways. The head of the family, the Marquis of Hertford, was patron of the living, and the church, with its family vault, also functioned as a mausoleum. It houses a reclining effigy commemorating Admiral of the Fleet, Sir George Francis Seymour (1787–1870). Although this type of memorial was popular among aristocratic patrons of the period, this particular example is unusual in depicting a uniformed naval officer (fig. 30). It was erected by Seymour's son, Francis, 5th Marquis of Hertford, and executed by his son-in-law, Prince

8   TNA ADM196/39/45.

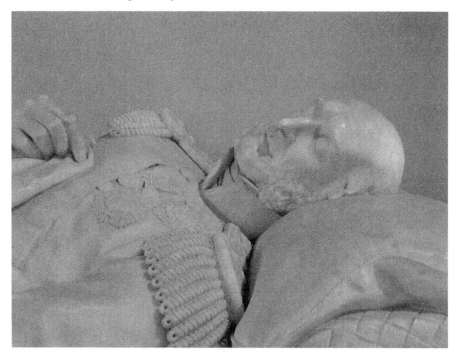

30. Sir George Francis Seymour, by Count Gleichen, at Arrow, Warwickshire (detail).
© *Author.*

Victor of Hohenlohe-Langenburg (1833–91), more generally known after his marriage (for reasons of German protocol) by his secondary title of Count Gleichen. A naval officer and nephew of Queen Victoria, Gleichen had served in Seymour's flagship, HMS *Cumberland*, during the Baltic campaign of 1854. In retirement from the Navy, he forged a second career as a good professional sculptor, with a socially elevated clientele. The monument to his father-in-law was exhibited at the Royal Academy in 1873 and was described by a reviewer as: 'simple, grave, and manly in feeling and execution, and the introduction of the Admiral's dress is as appropriate as the harness of the old knightly effigies'.[9]

---

[9]   *Illustrated London News*, 7 June 1873, p. 546. In 1870 Gleichen exhibited a posthumous plaster bust of Seymour at the Royal Academy. The finished marble version (done as a family memorial later that year) is now in the NMM collection (SCU0050). Seymour's recumbent figure and the chest tomb on which it lay, as shown by Gleichen at the RA in 1873, may have been the plaster version later placed in the chapel vestibule of the Royal Naval College, Greenwich, and currently (2014) in store there.

Burial reform

The ideas of Edwin Chadwick, crusader for public health reform, were a long way from the romantic notions of Pugin's circle. Committed to achieving the greatest good of the greatest number, he was a man lacking in empathy or artistic sensibility. His *Report on Intra-Mural Interment* of 1843 was crammed with stomach-turning examples of unsanitary corpse-disposal practices, such as burial in overcrowded urban churchyards and delayed funerals. A cholera epidemic was raging at the time, but the link with contaminated water supplies was not established until the 1850s and the disease was still being attributed to bad air. The National Society for the Abolition of Burial in Towns was pressing for legislation by 1845. The Burial Act of 1853 established that places of burial including graveyards, churches and chapels within cities could be closed by Orders in Council. It was one plank in a whole raft of such legislation and a further discouragement to the erection of memorials in or near churches. W.H. Hale, Archdeacon of London, published a response in 1855, entitled *Intramural Burial in England, not injurious to the public heath, its abolition injurious to religion and morals.* The archdeacon's scientific arguments now look unconvincing, to say the least. However, his cultural arguments are not without basis: 'To bury the dead in places apart from human habitation is to overwhelm their memories in darkness.'

Garden cemeteries had already opened in the London suburbs, the earliest being established at Kensal Green in 1833. The architecture initially evoked the Classical period, when tombs were located outside the city walls. The additional space in these new cemeteries, besides allowing more hygienic, less crowded burials, also permitted landscaping and the allotment of space to other dominations and religions. Pugin mocked their essentially commercial nature, noting that their blank walls provided space for advertising and that there was usually a public house: 'The Green Man and Dog' across the road.[10] Initially, the prime sites encouraged the erection of large and prestigious monuments like those described previously to Thomas Tudor Tucker and Charles Spencer Ricketts.[11] Clergymen or monumental masons associated with the larger cemeteries sought to encourage general visitors: 'In strolling through them, who does not stop to read the records? – and how profoundly natural it is! Every man has one chance of being "read"; he may hope to have a reader for his gravestone.'[12] Ultimately, however, with the decline of these formerly prestigious burial places, they bore out Archdeacon Hale's warning. Gravestone inscriptions (now unread except by close family) changed from

10 A.W.N. Pugin, *An Apology for the Revival of Christian Architecture in England* (1843), p. 12.

11 A trend for erecting elite memorials in churchyards was already well established.

12 Joseph Barlow Robinson, *Epitaphs collected from the Cemeteries of London, Edinburgh, Glasgow, Hull, Leicester, Sheffield …* (1859), introduction, pp. 8–9.

being public declarations to private messages – effusive or reticent according to the class and taste of the author. The focus of public commemoration shifted to the erection of civic sculpture.

Ratings remembered

By the 1830s changes were taking in the commemoration of the lower ranks of the Navy. Steam could be applied to the cutting and transport of stone, and the cheaper headstone eventually became a universal badge of respectability. As late as 1831, the levelling, by the unpopular rector, of the mounds over the graves round the dockyard church of Stoke Damerel, near Plymouth, provoked a dispute: 'They then pointed out that the levelling of the graves was especially offensive to the poor of the parish who, unlike the richer parishioners could not afford head and footstones … the only mark they had of their dead relatives' and friends' resting places were the mounds above the graves.'[13]

Something resembling the modern military war memorial had evolved by the 1860s. In the Navy, shipmates' memorials to seamen killed in action or accidents began tentatively in the early years of the century, as noted in the previous chapter. The practice had become more common by the 1830s and by the 1850s numerous group memorials to crew members were being erected in Britain and overseas. They tended to commemorate men who died during a particular commission, of any cause; disease and accident as well as warfare. The British collective naval memorial, honouring each deceased crew member by name, was developing at a time when changes were taking place in the Navy's relationship with its personnel, and was perhaps symptomatic of this. Social mobility had declined within the Navy: after 1815 promotion from the lower decks practically ceased and the basis of officer selection became narrower. However, in 1853, the principle of long-term service was introduced whereby the Navy was to maintain a standing force of full-time seamen as opposed to engaging them for each commission. This in turn necessitated the creation of a reserve in the merchant marine that could be drawn upon in time of war. These changes had an impact on discipline: 'We had the cat and no discipline; now we have discipline and no cat.'[14] Attempts to improve the morale and behaviour of seamen increasingly favoured the carrot rather than the stick and sought to encourage identification with the service as a whole. They were, after all, now in it for the long term.

---

[13] Patricia Grey, *The Home of Grave Robbers and Murderers* (1979), p. 60.
[14] Lord Charles Beresford, quoted in E.R. Freemantle, *The Navy as I have Known it* (1869), vol. 2, p. 144.

Memorialization, with other changes in service culture such as the provision of uniform and the award of campaign medals to all ranks, helped to achieve this end.

Mainly medals

The first government-issued campaign medal awarded to all naval personnel was the First China War Medal issued to all British forces who had taken part in the first of the Opium Wars, 1839–42. Shortly afterwards the Naval General Service Medal was instituted for those who had participated in successful actions from 1793 to 1840. Awards to all ranks by other nations spurred the changes and British war medals were issued regularly after every subsequent conflict.

A marble wall tablet in Rochester Cathedral commemorates Commander Henry Lushington Comyn Robinson who died in 1872, aged 40, after an active career which included service in the Baltic, Crimea and New Zealand Wars (fig. 31). His marble wall tablet by J. Bedford of London is carved with his sword and medals: the Baltic Medal, Crimea Medal, Turkish Crimea Medal and New Zealand Medal. The epitaph, on a carved scroll, gives a complete career résumé. Although Robinson had some clerical connections,

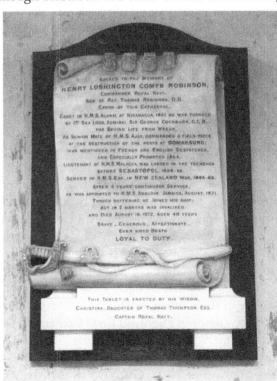

31. *Commander Henry Lushington Comyn Robinson RN, at Rochester Cathedral.* © *Author.*

as his father, the Reverend Thomas Robinson, was a canon of Rochester, the memorial has remarkably little Christian content. A more forceful and aggressive ethos was permeating national culture during this period of increasing European rivalry and imperial expansion. Military memorials in general have a strong presence in this building as in so many other cathedrals.

Another marble wall tablet at Christchurch, Chorleywood, Hertfordshire, states:

TO THE MEMORY OF
CHARLES AUGUSTUS HAYWARD,
MIDSHIPMAN OF H.M.S.VIRAGO,
WHO DIED AT MONTE VIDEO OF YELLOW FEVER,
AGED 19;
SECOND SON OF JAMES AND RACHEL HAYWARD
OF LOUDWATER.
HE RECEIVED FOR HIS SERVICES
WITH THE NAVAL BRIGADE IN THE CRIMEA,
THE CRIMEAN MEDAL WITH TWO CLASPS,
THE CROSS OF THE LEGION OF HONOR,
THE SARDINIAN MEDAL,
AND THE TURKISH ORDER OF THE MEDJIDIE.
OBIIT 27TH FEBRUARY 1858

The memorial is carved with a fouled anchor, hung with a wreath and carved with the group of medals mentioned in the text which clearly had a certain novelty value at this date. The mixture of British and foreign awards is not untypical.

The most prestigious gallantry award was the Victoria Cross, instituted by Queen Victoria in 1856 and open to all ranks. The first winner from either service to be invested in 1857 was Mate Charles Davis Lucas, who died aged 81 in 1914 at Great Culverden and was buried at Mereworth near Maidstone, where his grave is marked by a Celtic cross. He had reached the rank of rear-admiral on the retired list by the time of his death. A wall tablet in the church vestry briefly outlines his career, with the text from Matthew 5:8: 'Blessed are the pure in heart for they shall see God'. His Victoria Cross is depicted in relief, in the top left-hand corner.

William Nathan Wright Hewett, also awarded his Victoria Cross for service in the Crimea, reached vice-admiral rank and was buried with some naval ceremony in Highland Road Cemetery, Portsmouth, in 1888. His family grave is marked with a very ordinary memorial consisting of a cross, carved anchor and chain on rocks and an inscription which includes a somewhat low-brow verse: 'NOT GONE FROM MEMORY, NOT GONE FROM

LOVE BUT GONE TO HIS FATHER'S HOME ABOVE.' It makes no special mention of his award other than the abbreviation which follows his name. An officer of equivalent rank in the eighteenth century would have had something grander, or at any rate something grander than those below his station. Naval memorials were now typically marked by some piece of ship's equipment, mainly anchors and rope. There has been a move in recent years to refurbish grave memorials or mark the unmarked graves of Victoria Cross winners. This work by individuals and voluntary bodies is moving these modest, private cemetery memorials back into the public sphere.[15]

Steam

Steam in the Navy first made its appearance in the royal dockyards for dock pumping and as part of the production process of building wooden sailing ships. Nelson, visiting Portsmouth Dockyard on 14 September 1805 before leaving England for the last time, would have caught a whiff of coal smoke from the first two steam engines to be installed there. They powered pumps by night and woodworking machinery by day. Machine-tools for making ship's blocks, designed by Marc Isambard Brunel and constructed by Henry Maudslay, had been installed earlier in 1805, powered by these same engines. This was, in effect, the world's first industrial production line. The Brunels, father Marc and son Isambard, are buried in Kensal Green. The epitaph to the father, who died in 1849, echoes that of Sir Christopher Wren: 'He has raised his own monument by his public works at Portsmouth, Chatham and the Thames Tunnel'.

As steam moved afloat, initially in the form of paddle tugs, Woolwich became the most important dockyard in the development of the steam navy, being near to the steam-engine manufacturing works on the Thames. Maudslay was buried in the churchyard of St Mary's church, Woolwich, in 1831. He is said to have designed the tomb within railings which marked the spot. Cast iron plates, commemorating Maudslay and other members of his family, covered the sides, the last dating from sometime after 1864. They were likely to have been cast in the Maudslays' Lambeth foundry. Maudslay's inscription was as follows:

TO THE MEMORY OF
HENRY MAUDSLAY
BORN IN THIS PARISH 1771

---

15 This charitable work is currently being carried on by the Nottingham and Nottinghamshire Victoria Cross Committee and the Victoria Cross Trust which care for and mark Victoria Cross graves.

DIED AT LAMBETH FEB. 15TH 1831
A ZEALOUS PROMOTER
OF THE ARTS & SCIENCES
EMINENTLY
DISTINGUISHED AS AN
ENGINEER
FOR MATHEMATICAL ACCURACY AND
BEAUTY OF CONSTRUCTION
AS A MAN FOR
INDUSTRY & PERSEVERANCE
AND AS A FRIEND FOR A KIND &
BENEVOLENT HEART[16]

Maudslay's tomb fell victim to churchyard clearance and was dismantled in about 1965. Before the plates could be re-erected along the boundary wall, the one that commemorated Maudslay himself was stolen. The remaining three plates were temporarily housed at the National Maritime Museum for safekeeping, before being transferred to the Greenwich Borough Museum (now Greenwich Heritage Centre) in 1993.

The dockyards also had a role in training ship's engineers. The Royal Naval Engineering branch was formed in 1836 with a set of warrant officers rated below the ship's carpenter but paid rather more. Their responsibilities were significant but their status was poor. After 1847 engineers were appointed by commission and a highly educated engineer-officer class gradually emerged. Prejudices were slower to disappear: a *Punch* cartoon at the time of the Royal Naval Exhibition, held at Chelsea in 1891, depicted the show as advertising 'Engineer snubbing at intervals throughout the day'. However, by the First World War, this branch of the service enjoyed reasonable status.

A memorial to one of this new breed of officer was recorded by Frederick Teague Cansick at Highgate Cemetery.[17] Captain John Dinnen (1807–66), at the time of his death working at the Admiralty in Whitehall, was Chief Inspector of Steam Machinery afloat of Her Majesty's Fleets and Dockyards, Member of the Institution of Civil Engineers and Member of the Institution of Naval Architects. He 'met his death by accident in the midst of his hard labours, having devoted a life of 39 years in bringing Her Majesty's Steam Navy to its present important position amongst nations'. The unfortunate Captain Dinnen was not killed by an exploding boiler but walked into the path of a cab horse, having partaken of a glass of Burton ale in a nearby public house after work. He died later in the night of a cerebral haemorrhage. The

---

[16] Maudslay Society, *Henry Maudslay 1771–1831: and Maudslay, Sons & Field* (1949).
[17] Frederick Teague Cansick, *Epitaphs of Middlesex* (1872), vol. 2, p. 144.

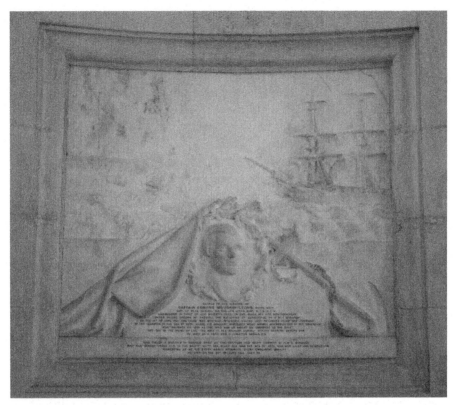

32. *Captain Edmund Moubray Lyons RN, by Matthew Noble, at St Paul's Cathedral.* ©
National Maritime Museum, Greenwich, London & the Chapter of St Paul's Cathedral,
London, L7776.

coroner exonerated the beer and stated 'that several eminent men who were
wrapped up in thought had met with similar deaths'.[18]

Steam really took off during the Crimean War, when the inefficient paddle
steamer, easily vulnerable to enemy fire, began to give way to screw propulsion. A rare depiction of one of these pioneer steam warships appears on
the memorial to Captain Edmund Moubray Lyons (1819–55) by Matthew
Noble, which was placed in the nave of St Paul's Cathedral (fig. 32). The son
of the commander-in-chief in the Black Sea – Rear-Admiral Sir Edmund
Lyons (also commemorated in St Paul's) – Lyons was having a successful war,
leading an expedition to attack Russian bases in the Sea of Azov. He was badly
wounded in the leg on 18 June while engaging the batteries at Sevastopol and
'Amputation was, unfortunately, not resorted to in the first instance …'[19] By

18   *The Times*, 9 January 1866.
19   *The Times*, 4 July 1855.

the time he arrived at the naval hospital at Therapia (present-day Tarabaya), it was too late for such an operation and he died on 23 June from the resulting infection. The memorial is carved with a portrait of Lyons in relief and a depiction of his vessel, the steam corvette HMS *Miranda*, and was erected by the officers and ship's company. Powered by screw rather than paddle wheel, a tell-tale funnel can be seen amid the vessel's masts. Such depictions of the now rapidly evolving warship became rare: as a naval writer later observed, 'Ships get out of fashion nearly as quickly as ladies' hats'.[20] By contrast, the old wooden ship of the line, little changed for over two hundred years, had been an instantly recognizable motif, easily put to all sorts of decorative uses.

Some senior officers, whose early career was spent in the sailing navy of the Nelsonic era, regarded steam power with surprising enthusiasm. Peacetime defence cuts were more of a block to progress than attitudes of the commanders. Sir Charles Napier (1786–1860) was a committed advocate of steam, losing a considerable commercial investment in a scheme to introduce steam boats on the Seine. Finally reaching flag rank in 1846 after forty years as a captain, Napier conducted steam trials which persuaded the Admiralty to adopt screw propulsion for all future warships. At the start of the Crimean War he was given command of the Baltic Fleet but was unable to achieve the desired results against the main, and strong, Russian bases of Sveaborg (in Finland) and Kronstadt. Renewal of serious hostilities during the second half of the century revealed serious weaknesses in the Navy. Napier had enjoyed a parallel parliamentary career, campaigning for improved conditions of naval service, particularly for petty and warrant officers, and the abolition of corporal punishment and impressment. He is commemorated at his burial place at Catherington, Hampshire, by a discreet family memorial uncharacteristic of the braggart nature of the man – though a great fighter, he had a difficult personality. As befits his importance as a naval and politically radical figure during this challenging period for the service, Napier also has a wall memorial at St Paul's Cathedral by George Gamon Adams (1821–98), which includes a portrait and battle scenes in relief. Another memorial was erected at Portsmouth with donations from warrant and petty officers, seamen and marines: 'to commemorate the untiring efforts of a gallant officer and true-hearted man in advancing the welfare of the British sailor' (fig. 33). This monument, reminiscent of a well-known one in the Piazzetta in Venice, was a column of red sandstone surmounted by a lion, with its paw on a bomb-shell in allusion to the Napier crest rather than the lion of St Mark. It was designed by the architects Wilson & Nicholl, while a relief portrait of the mature Napier, set into the column, is by the Belgian sculptor, Theodore

---

[20] E.H. Seymour, *My Naval Career and Travels* (1911), p. 171.

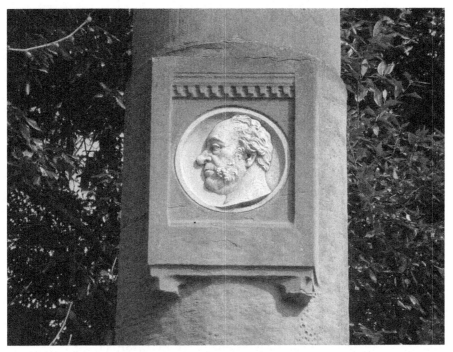

33. *Sir Charles Napier, by Theodore Phyffers, at Victoria Park, Portsmouth (detail).*
© *Author.*

Phyffers. The memorial originally stood, surrounded by railings, between the Lion-gate and Commercial roads, Landport, but was moved to Victoria Park to ease the flow of traffic in 1878.

A change of role

For almost two hundred years the Navy played a key role in protecting the British colonies and the trade of the West Indies, whose lucrative sugar was produced by slave labour. During times of war it guarded convoys and fought European rivals in the region, both at sea and on land. Islands were invaded and captured to be exchanged for other concessions at the end of the war.

After 1815, the West Indies was less a focus of rivalry between European powers and more a scene of internal dissent, which continued even after the abolition of slavery in 1833, when local assemblies were abolished in many islands and replaced by Crown Colony government. The Navy, still maintaining a squadron in the area, continued to suffer heavy losses through the repeated yellow-fever epidemics that swept the islands. A small obelisk on the seafront at Southsea commemorates forty-eight officers and men from HMS *Aboukir* who died of the disease at Jamaica during 1873–74.

After British abolition of the slave trade in 1807, the Navy found itself no longer protecting but suppressing this traffic, which other nations continued. This was a long process involving both military and diplomatic pressure, and gave naval officers, in particular, direct experience of the dreadful conditions in which slaves were transported across the Atlantic. It was an early use of military forces in relief work. The mosquito-borne diseases of the tropics were also a hazard to naval personnel engaged in anti-slavery operations off the African Coast, as they had always been to European seamen (often unwillingly) involved in the trade itself.

The memorial to James Still, at St Mary the Virgin, High Pavement, Nottingham, commemorates one casualty and suggests that he died in the course of a moral crusade.

Sacred to the Memory
of
LIEUTENANT JAMES STILL; R.N.
Who
in the 22:nd year of his age,
fell a victim to the ravages of the Yellow Fever,
on board His Majesty's Ship, THE PHEASANT,
while stationed off SIERRA LEONE,
on the 12th October 1821.
For four successive years
he had been employed in the fatal service
of enforcing obedience
to that sacred Law, which to the honour of his Country
and in the spirit of Christian Love,
forbade
the Traffick in Human Blood.
That he possessed the best feelings of the heart
was manifested in his unwearied watchfulness over those
whose aid he was in sickness,
and who,
withering like the blighted shoots of Spring,
left their blessings upon him.

In the early years of the African Preventative Squadron, financial incentives to the officers and crews in the form of bounties paid for each slave liberated were relatively generous. Until the abolition of slavery itself in 1833 the fate of the freed slaves was not necessarily freedom. Black American loyalists, with British support, had established a colony at Sierra Leone and this served as a base for the Navy's operations. Abolition involved the promotion of legitimate trade in crops, such as palm oil, and led to increased British military involvement in West Africa. A marble wall tablet at St Ann's church, Portsmouth, surmounted by trophies and flanked by palm trees, records the naval casualties of a boat attack on Lagos, Nigeria, in December 1851. It was then still a centre of the slave trade and the British were supplanting an 'intractable' local ruler.

The fatalities sustained by the Navy in suppressing the slave trade in West Africa are believed to be around 2000 – mostly from malaria and other tropical diseases.[21] Invalids from the West Africa squadron were sent north to Ascension Island where a hospital was set up in 1849. A memorial at St Mary's church there lists a total of thirty-two crew members of HMS *Scout* who died between 1836 and 1839. Some were buried elsewhere on Ascension, some at Sierra Leone and others at sea. The ship's commanding officer, Lieutenant Charles Baldwin Dyke Acland (d. 1837), also has a memorial at All Saints church, Selworthy, Somerset, which he shares with a younger brother. A draped sarcophagus with two relief portraits, this wall monument was commissioned from Sir Francis Legatt Chantrey (1781–1841) at the cost of 200 guineas. An earlier memorial of similar design had been commissioned from Chantrey to their uncle Charles Richard Dyke Acland, who had died of blackwater fever at the Cape of Good Hope, while on anti-slavery duties in 1828. The introduction of quinine, in the 1840s, as a regular prophylactic against malaria made European incursions into tropical Africa a much less lethal proposition.

From the mid-century, after a successful campaign in West Africa and the abolition of both slavery and the slave trade by other European nations and the United States, the focus shifted to East Africa and the interception of the Arab trade from Zanzibar to the French colonies in the Indian Ocean. E.R. Freemantle, writing in 1904, suggested that the East African cruises of the second half of the century were regarded by junior officers as a chance for promotion and prize money, as well as welcome danger and adventure for midshipmen, who were away for weeks in boats: compared to the moral self-congratulation seen in the early years of abolition, the outlook of the latter part of the century was more self-interested.

Sir Edward Pellew's attack on Algiers in 1816 was also seen as an attack on slavery, but this time white slavery. One of a number of operations against the corsairs (or 'Barbary pirates') who operated from the Islamic city states of North Africa, it released over 1000 European captives and the imprisoned British consul. Pellew's memorial at Cristow in Devon mentions that he risked his life 'to break the chains of Christian brethren mourning in helpless

---

21 Bernard Edwards, *The Royal Navy versus the Slave Traders: Enforcing Abolition at Sea 1808–1898* (Barnsley, 2007), p. 183.

captivity, in a heathen land'. The officers under his command commemorated this by presenting him with a massive silver-gilt table centrepiece by Paul Storr. The lighthouse fort at Algiers is surrounded by four modelled figure groups, two representing a British seaman unchaining a Christian slave, and the other two showing a seaman on the point of slaying an Algerine corsair (fig. 34).

Raids

The second half of the nineteenth century saw naval brigades – seamen acting as soldiers – deployed on shore in conflicts outside Europe. Initially, they were better armed than Asian opponents, whose population centres near the coast or major rivers were vulnerable to European attack, particularly after the introduction of steam. The 1850s saw British intervention in India, China, Japan and Burma. These campaigns were by no means a walkover. The attack on the Taku Forts on 25 June 1859, during the Second China War, was the heaviest defeat the Navy suffered during the nineteenth century.

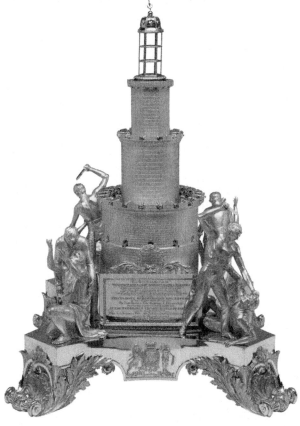

34. Centrepiece presented to Admiral Edward Pellew, 1st Baron Exmouth, by the officers who served under him at the Bombardment of Algiers, 27 August 1816, by Paul Storr. © National Maritime Museum, Greenwich, London, PLT0047.

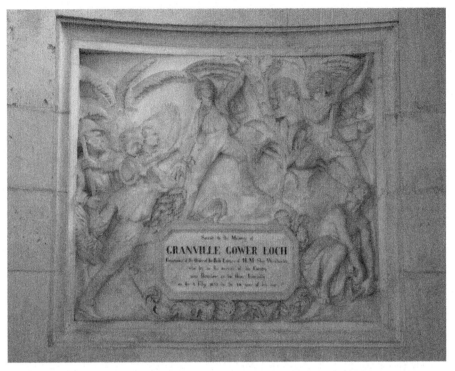

35. *Captain Granville Gower Loch RN, by Carlo Marochetti, at St Paul's Cathedral.*
© *National Maritime Museum, Greenwich, London & the Chapter of St Paul's Cathedral, London, L7775.*

The memorial by Carlo Marochetti in the nave St Paul's Cathedral to Granville Gower Loch provides an image that sums up these imperial wars (fig. 35). Surrounded by tropical forest, Loch leads an attack against the half-naked Burmese. While he was commanding a punitive raid against a local dacoit (bandit) called Myat Tun, in the aftermath of the Second Burmese War, Loch's party was ambushed. Mortally wounded, he died two days later on 6 February 1853. It was specifically a naval defeat, since only the steadiness of the Bengal Infantry prevented the Burmese from cutting off the whole column. Loch was buried in Rangoon, where his grave was marked at the expense of the officers and men of his ship, HMS *Winchester.*

Victorian hero

The most notable naval hero of the mid-century was Sir William Peel, a younger son of the Prime Minister, Sir Robert Peel (d. 1850). He led naval brigades in the Crimea (where the term was coined) and afterwards during the Indian Mutiny. The primary role of these brigades involved the deployment of naval guns on shore in siege operations, sometimes dragged about with a boat's ensign attached and a fiddler sitting on top. The men acquired a reputation for competence and cheerfulness. Staff officer to grumbling member of naval brigade: 'I thought you fellows were always cheery and contented?' 'Oh, that's where you are wrong. I ain't a Bluejacket now – nothing but a broken down *blessed* commissariat mule.'[22]

With a brigade formed from the men of his ship, the frigate *Diamond*, Peel took part in the siege of Sevastopol. In 1854 he was awarded the Victoria Cross for throwing a live Russian shell over the wall of his battery. During the Mutiny, another brigade (this time from his *Shannon*) aimed their big guns at the walls of resisting Indian cities – manpower in dragging ships' guns here being enhanced by bullock and elephant power. Peel was badly wounded in the thigh and was offered the option of travelling to Cawnpore (present day Kanpur) in a carriage looted from the King of Oude with 'HMS Shannon' painted over the royal arms. Peel decided instead to be carried in a doolie like one of his blue-jackets, and he died from smallpox contracted in Cawnpore, though the story went about that he had caught it from a previous patient who had travelled in the doolie. Peel is buried at Mirpur Cemetery, Kanpur, with the inscription:

> To the memory of William Peel. His name will ever be dear to the British inhabitants of India, to whose succour he came in the hour of need and for whom he risked and gave his life. He was one of England's most devoted sons, and with all the talent of a brave and skilful sailor, he combined the virtues of a humble and sincere Christian. This stone is erected over his remains by his military friends in India and several of the inhabitants of Calcutta. Captain Sir William Peel, R.N., K.C.B., was born in Stanhope-Street, Mayfair on the 2nd November 1824 and died at Cawnpore on the 27th April 1858.[23]

A statue by William Theed the younger, raised by public subscription in 1863, originally stood to the south side of Auckland (later Eden) Gardens, Calcutta. It was removed in the 1980s (as were many such colonial monuments) and is now under the portico of the Temple of Fame at Barrackpore, looking out on the Hooghli River. Two more versions were made by Theed, one (dated 1861) now at St Swithun's church, Sandy, Bedfordshire near Peel's former home at The Lodge. The third currently stands in the Neptune Court

---

22 Quoted in Richard Brooks, *The Long Arm of Empire: Naval Brigades from the Crimea to the Boxer Rebellion* (1999), p. 20.

23 E.A.H. Blunt, *List of Inscriptions on Christian Tombs and Tablets of Historical Interest in the United Provinces of Agra and Oudh* (Allahabad, 1911), p. 127.

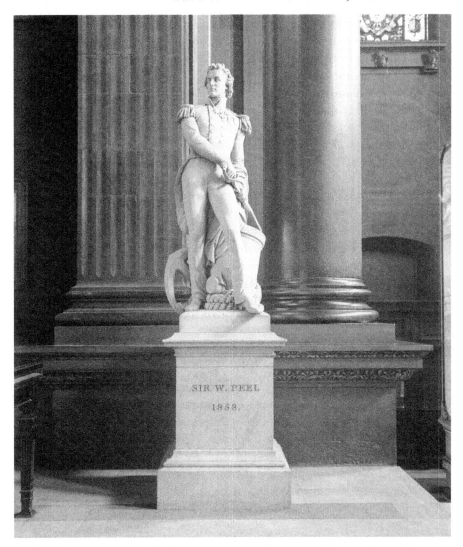

36. *Sir William Peel, by William Theed junior, shown in its original position in the Painted Hall, Greenwich. © National Maritime Museum, Greenwich, London, neg. 1526.*

of the National Maritime Museum, signed and dated 1860, and wearing the Victoria Cross that Peel did not live to receive. It was presented to Greenwich Hospital by his elder brother, Sir Frederick Peel MP, and installed in the Naval Gallery, where it completed a quartet in the four corners of the lower Painted Hall with three earlier marbles of distinguished naval officers of an older generation (fig. 36). These were all executed as national monuments to them pursuant to vote of Parliament, moved, in 1842, by Peel's father, Sir

Robert, when he was Prime Minister. The Greenwich version of Peel shows him advancing and drawing his sword 'as if about to lead a charge of his blue-jackets'.[24] The Calcutta figure is shown in repose, the right hand of the figure resting on an anchor and coil of cables, the left holding a telescope.

The memorial to the seamen and marines of Peel's *Shannon* who died during the Mutiny stands on the seafront at Southsea, Portsmouth, erected in 1860 by the surviving officers and crew of the ship. It has a tapering plinth set with granite panels and terminates in bronze trophies made from a gun captured at Lucknow and presented by the commander-in-chief of the Army, Colin Campbell, Lord Clyde. Four cannon are embedded in the plinth. A memorial plaque to Peel in the Royal Garrison church, Southsea, was destroyed by enemy bombing in 1941.

Although Peel retains a reputation for high-Victorian chivalry, his forces were involved in looting and harsh retribution meted out in revenge for sepoy atrocities. Edmund Verney records in January 1858 that a party led by Lieutenant Thomas Young of the *Shannon* hanged 127 rebels from one tree at Mhow: 'These dreadful, though absolutely necessary severities are most painful to recollect and to commemorate.'[25]

China Wars

The series of wars that weakened central authority in China and opened the country up to Western trade were even more contentious. Naval brigades continued to be deployed and more collective memorials were erected at Portsmouth and Happy Valley Cemetery, Hong Kong, to commemorate British casualties. The same team of architect and artist who erected the memorial to Napier completed a memorial commemorating those men of HMS *Chesapeake* who died in battle or from disease and accident, during an eventful four years commission between 1857 and 1861.

> The memorial consists of a column, of a free Romanesque treatment, with plinth and sub plinth resting on a pedestal, the summit being ornamented with a naval crown of gilt bronze, elevated on a tripod also of bronze … The sculptured capital, the base and band of the column, the sub-plinth and the die of the pedestal and the step, are of Portland stone. The base of the tripod and the cornice and plinth to the pedestal are of the grey Forest of Dean stone.

---

[24] *Illustrated London News*, 12 December 1863, p. 591. The earlier statues are of Sir William Sidney Smith (by Thomas Kirk, 1845), Edward Pellew, Viscount Exmouth (Patrick Macdowell, 1846), and James Saumarez, Viscount Saumarez (Sir John Steell, 1853).

[25] Edmund Hope Verney, *The Shannon's Brigade in India: being some account of Sir William Peel's Naval Brigade in the Indian Campaign of 1857–1858* (1862), p. 70.

The shaft of the column is in red Aberdeen granite, polished, and the plinth is of grey granite, also polished. The plinth has on it a representation in bronze of the attack on the Taku Forts. The sculptor who executed this portion of the work was Mr T. Phyffers.[26]

The Taku forts guarding the mouth of the Peiho River were taken by the French and British on 20 May 1858. During a brief peace the forts were reoccupied and strengthened by the Chinese and a second British attack on 25 June 1859 was driven off. They were re-taken by an Anglo-French force, from the land side, on 21 August 1860. Both the second and third attacks involved the men of HMS *Chesapeake*. The relief depicts a boat action with a junk in the background. The forts were eventually stormed again and largely demolished during the Boxer Rebellion of 1900.

A bell, said to have been captured from the north-west fort, was placed in a bell tower of Chinese design erected in Victoria Park, Portsmouth (fig. 37). It was erected to commemorate the men who died during the commission of HMS *Orlando* from 1899 to 1902. They had been deployed in the final attack on the Taku forts on 17 June 1900, the defence of Tientsin and the relief of Peking. The bell was removed for safety during the Second World War, not being reinstated until 1960. Then, following defacement by vandals, it was removed again for safekeeping. In 1993, Bob Holmes, in a letter to the local Portsmouth paper, *The News*, suggested that the bell had been taken from a temple and should be returned to its owners. It was doubtless removed in the extensive looting which took place in Chinese cities, particularly Beijing and Tientsin, following allied victory, and was returned to the Deputy Mayor of Tanggu in 2005: a replica, made by a foundry in that city, replaced it at Portsmouth in 2007.

New identities

The memorial erected at Portsmouth to members of the naval brigade of HMS *Centurion*, who died during the same conflict, is decorated with the head of a centurion bearing the vessel's name on a ribbon (fig. 38). This iconography relates to the development of unofficial ship's badges, as figureheads – primarily a feature of sailing ships – became increasingly obsolescent. They began as an initiative by the officers who used them on ship's stationery, after heraldic printed notepaper became available: less fanciful designs were fixed to the ship's boats. The crested-notepaper type of design is shown on the top of a memorial plate at St Ann's church, Portsmouth, commemorating crew

---

[26] *The Builder*, 6 December 1863, p. 862.

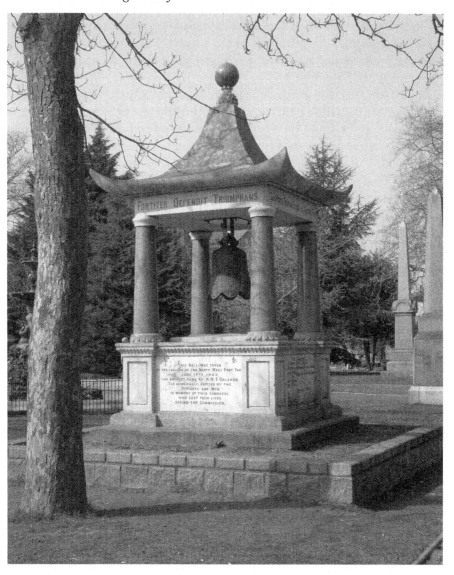

37. *Memorial to the crew of HMS* Orlando, *at Victoria Park, Portsmouth.* © *Author.*

members of HMS *Narcissus*, lost in a boat accident in 1896. A late example of a gothic memorial brass, it shows Narcissus falling in love with his own reflection, with the flower of the same name into which he was transformed. Any homoerotic overtones seem to have passed the Navy by. After the First World War these designs became formalized as an official symbol of each vessel and, in a growing world of trademarks and corporate branding, they were used in a very similar way to the house flags and cap badges of the merchant lines.

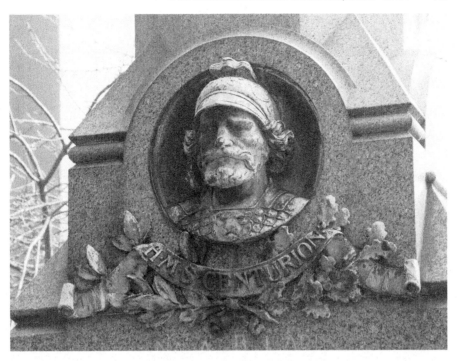

38. *Memorial to the crew of HMS* Centurion, *at Victoria Park, Portsmouth (detail).*
© *Author.*

South Africa

By the end of the century, Great Britain had new naval rivals in the USA, Germany and Japan. Between 1899 and 1902 it also faced a difficult war in South Africa against the two still-independent Boer (Dutch settler) republics there, the Orange Free State and the Transvaal, and this became another stage for the exploits of the naval brigades. A pom-pom gun captured by the men of HMS *Doris* from Boers at Paardeberg was utilized as a memorial at Devonport Park, Plymouth, to fourteen of her crew members who died in this conflict – a modern twist on the ancient display of military trophies (fig. 39). The men of HMS *Powerful* are commemorated nearby and by a granite obelisk in Victoria Park, Portsmouth. Her men became celebrities as a result of their role in the defence of Ladysmith. Men from *Powerful* transported overland the powerful guns needed to keep the besiegers at bay – first by train, then pulled by oxen, finally hauling the guns themselves. They were invited to a reception by the Corporation of Lloyd's on 7 May 1900 and a banquet in Portsmouth Town Hall on 24 May.

Although the naval brigades kept the Navy in the public eye during the latter part of the century, its fighting role was relatively minor compared

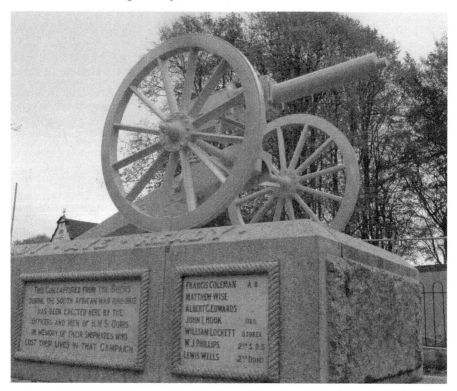

39. *Captured pom-pom gun, commemorating the naval brigade of HMS* Doris, *at Devonport Park, Plymouth.* © *Author.*

to the army it supported. Nevertheless, by Queen Victoria's death in 1901 after a reign of sixty-four years, her Navy had helped consolidate a British maritime empire spread across much of the globe, and in expanding its trade networks. Coaling stations, naval bases and associated naval cemeteries were established worldwide to support it, and Royal Naval identity became more corporate, with the state exerting tighter control over recruitment, training and retirement. Commemoration was to a degree more democratic, though maintaining nice bureaucratic distinctions of rank, even in death: lists of names on naval memorials were always tabulated strictly in order of rank and hierarchy.

4

Stormy weather: conflict and sacrifice in the twentieth century

The technical advances in place by the beginning of the twentieth century were to involve both the Navy and the merchant marine in conflict of unprecedented ferocity. After the carnage of the First World War, European war dead were commemorated with unprecedented reverence. In an increasingly democratic society, there was a groundswell of feeling that all life sacrificed in conflict should be commemorated. All casualties, not just officers, had been named on Boer War memorials. After the 'Great War', the nineteenth-century custom of listing them in order of rank gave way to tablets listing names in alphabetical order.

The majority of First World War conscripts had been drafted into the army, which was supplemented by two naval brigades officered by naval reservists. In spite of its smaller size, the historic importance of the Navy and its prominence in the previous 'Great War' of 1793–1815 were reflected in those civic war memorials whose design included figures representing different branches of the services. A figure from an earlier South African War memorial of this broad type stands on the south wall of the Old Library at Lichfield. It represents a sailor in field service order holding a Mark 1 Lee-Enfield rifle, with 'HMS POWERFUL' on his cap ribbon. Designed by George Frederick Bodley, the Ketton-stone figure was intended for a gothic war memorial at Duncombe Place, York, with eight figures representing all services. The sailor was rejected as overly aggressive and was replaced with an unarmed one who is nevertheless holding a length of rope with a chain and hook attached, probably to haul a heavy gun.[1] A particularly splendid First World War memorial with just two sculpted servicemen was erected at Keighley in 1924 and has been recently refurbished (fig. 40). The general scheme is classically inspired: Victory, holding a laurel wreath and a palm branch, surmounts an obelisk

---

1 Pieter van der Merwe, 'Another Lichfield Sailor', *Mariner's Mirror*, vol. 95, no. 4 (November 2009), p. 483.

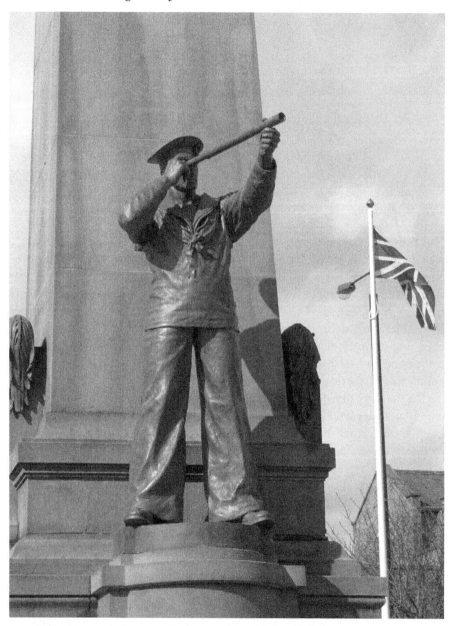

40. *Sailor, by Henry Charles Fehr RA, on the war memorial at Keighley, West Yorkshire.*
© *Author.*

flanked by realistic modern figures of a soldier and sailor. The rating raises a telescope to his eye rather than holding a weapon. The figures were praised by the *Keighley News* as 'giving an impression of alertness and vigour, but without any hint of aggressive force'.[2] The sculptor was Henry Charles Fehr RA (1867–1940), a Londoner of Swiss origin and the artist of the nearby city memorial at Leeds. There are no officer-heroes on the monument, just two ordinary servicemen drawn from the working population of this Yorkshire mill town. Although most of them would have joined the army, Keighley men did serve in the wartime Navy in spite of the town's inland situation far to the north of the traditional naval ports. Their industrial skills were in tune with the new warfare.

The citizen takes up arms

The major architectural schemes erected near First World War battlefields sought to commemorate casualties with no known graves. For the Navy, this was nothing new, but in parallel to the military monuments, a series of major sea-mark memorials were planned near the shore at Chatham, Plymouth and Portsmouth. They were all unveiled in 1924. The Imperial War Graves Commission asked the Scottish architect, Sir Robert Lorimer (1864–1929), to submit a design. He had established a practice in England and had designed war cemeteries in Italy and also the Scottish National War Memorial. Lorimer took the Navy's favoured (and now somewhat hackneyed) obelisk and modernized it. The top of the granite pylon was stepped, terminating in four ships' prows with female figures representing the four winds supporting a large copper sphere symbolizing the world. The base was surrounded by couchant, rather Assyrian-looking, lions. Although basically conservative in design, the influence of a new taste for clean lines and archaeological influences can be seen. The panels of names were set in enclosures around the base, varying in layout according to the setting of the three memorials. Although individual actions were not commemorated by bars on First World War campaign medal ribbons, they found a place on the base of the obelisk which was decorated with battle reliefs and names of general actions, single-ship actions and amphibious actions. The sculpture was by Henry Poole (1873–1928).

In Portsmouth and Chatham the monuments are outside the centre of town on shore or hilltop sites. By contrast in Plymouth, thanks to the blitz of the Second World War and Sir Patrick Abercrombie and Paton Watson's post-war 'Plan for Plymouth', the monument is now the focus of the main

---

2   *Keighley News*, 6 December 1924. Quoted in Alex King, *Memorials of the Great War in Britain: The Symbolism and Politics of Remembrance* (Oxford, 1998), p. 176.

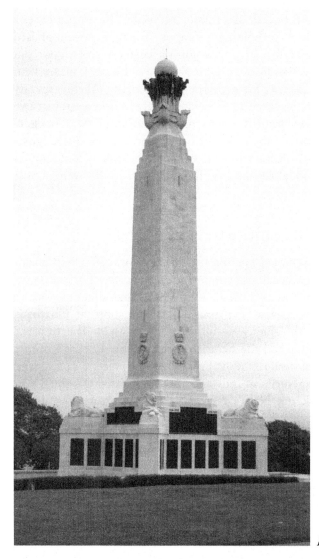

41. *The Naval Memorial at Plymouth, designer Sir Robert Lorimer. © Author.*

vista through the shopping centre (fig. 41). On general civic and state memorials, individual names are recorded but no individual narratives, no outstanding heroes.

The Church

The rehabilitation of medieval religious practice that had taken place in the Church of England continued to inspire novel forms of commemoration. Military chapels were dedicated in cathedrals in an echo of the old chantry chapels, where in the late Middle Ages priests were paid to say prayers and masses for the dead. Maritime chapels are less common and were mainly established after the Second World War. The Scottish National War Memorial, dedicated in 1927, was erected on the site of recently vacated barracks in Edinburgh Castle. The architect, Sir Robert Lorimer again, suggested a shrine and cloister with stained-glass windows by Douglas Strachan and a roll of honour (the names of the dead being enshrined at the centre of the complex). Because of the Calvinist tradition of the Scottish lowlands any suggestion that the building was a church provoked strong opposition and was played down. The scheme commemorates all services, with a section devoted to the Royal Navy which features windows with a theme of 'water'.

In spite of Scotland's strongly Protestant history, a figure of St Michael still overlooks the roll of names. The dragon-killing military Saints Michael and George were frequently invoked in the iconography of the Great War. Both are shown in a window commemorating Edward Henry Swinburne Bligh in the north transept of Winchester Cathedral. Bligh was a lieutenant in the Royal Naval Volunteer Reserve, killed on 10 September 1915 at Gallipoli. The window by Christopher Whall (1849–1924) shows an armoured archangel Michael slaying the dragon in the central light and a bare-headed St George with a red cross on his shield in the window to the left. The right-hand side is occupied by St Hubert, patron saint of Belgium, implying that the war was fought in a just cause in response to the German invasion of that country.

The memorial of the Plymouth Division Royal Marines deploys a secular version of the monster-slayer. William G. Storr-Barber's figure represents a nude athlete slaying the German eagle whose feathers give the human a winged appearance. The plinth is flanked by stone everyman figures, kitted out to represent service on land and sea. The monument is inscribed with a quotation from *Pilgrim's Progress*: 'So he passed over and all the trumpets sounded for him on the other side'. The reverse of the British War Medal by William McMillan shows the mounted figure of St George trampling the German eagle shield underfoot. Gothic in the twentieth century still provided a language to express the creative tensions between chivalry and horror, enchantment and disenchantment.

Jutland

In spite of unprecedented firepower, the decisive major fleet action so widely anticipated failed to materialize. The war turned out to be, in large part, a bloody conflict with German commerce raiders, above all U-boats. Jutland was the largest battle of the war, one which both sides claimed to have won. Afterwards the German High Seas Fleet remained in port, although the British lost more ships: fourteen as opposed to eleven and double the number of men. A marble wall memorial in the baroque style stands in St Michael's church, Brooksby, Leicestershire, since the seat of Admiral of the Fleet Earl Beatty was formerly nearby at Brooksby Hall. Beatty commanded the battle-cruiser squadron which made first contact with the enemy and sustained the preliminary stages of the conflict. The memorial commemorates: 'Our friends, Officers and Men who died gloriously for their King and Country in the Battle of Jutland …' The central dedication panel is surmounted by the Beatty coat of arms with military trophies in the traditional style placed below. The flanking panels list eight of the more senior officers killed in the battle: Rear-Admiral Sir Robert Keith Arbuthnot, Captain Stanley Venn Ellis, Rear-Admiral the Honourable Sir Horace Lambert Alexander Hood, Captain Arthur Lindesay Cay, Captain Charles Fitzgerald Sowerby, Captain Cecil Irby Prowse, Captain Thomas Parry Bonham and Captain Charles John Wintour. The style of the monument could not have been more characteristically eighteenth-century but these men were not shot down on their quarterdecks. Their ships were lost with all hands or with only a handful of survivors. Magazine explosions, following a hit on a turret roof and flash fires in the turret and shell-handling rooms, killed most of them.

The view of Jutland as a significant episode in a glorious maritime history is implied in a four-light window in the cloisters of Chester Cathedral. It forms part of a larger, post-war scheme by Archibald Nicholson (1871–1931) and Frederick Eden (1864–1944) showing saints grouped according to the month of their feast days throughout the church's year. The windows also have contemporary dedications, and April (which shows St Leo, St Alfege, St Anselm and St George) also commemorates Robert Armstrong Yerburgh, local MP, President of the Navy League and advocate of British naval supremacy during the arms race with Germany. Below the saints, baroque cartouches surround a galleon with the date 1588, and a contemporary cruiser with the date 1916 below (the date of Jutland and also the year of Yerburgh's death) (fig. 42). The League's badge and motto are shown at the top of the third light above St Anselm. That the parallel is drawn with the Spanish Armada rather than Trafalgar suggests Jutland averted a national threat rather than defeated it outright.

Heroes

Individual heroism was overwhelmed in the face of mass slaughter wrought by twentieth-century weaponry. Official commemoration was not hierarchical: the decision was made to mark individual war graves with uniform headstones, distinguished by their inscriptions. Four Victoria Crosses were awarded to men who served at Jutland, three of them posthumous. Commander Loftus William Jones in *Shark*, leading a division of four destroyers, found himself

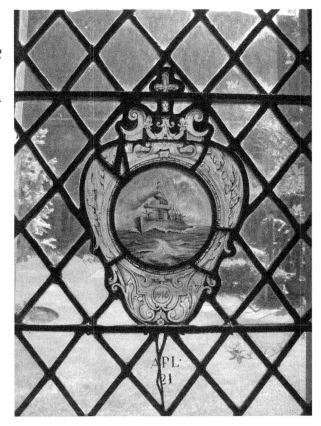

42. *Window commemorating Robert Armstrong Yerburgh MP, by Archibald Keightley Nicholson and Frederick Charles Eden, at Chester Cathedral (detail).* © *Author.*

opposed by three enemy battle-cruisers. Although wounded twice, Loftus Jones kept up resistance, helping to man a gun and ordering the ensign re-hoisted. Although he was among those who successfully abandoned ship, he later succumbed to loss of blood and exposure. Local subscribers erected a memorial at Fiskebäckskil in Sweden near where his body was washed up. It was transferred to Kviberg Cemetery, Göteborg, in 1961, where it lies under the standard Commonwealth War Graves Commission headstone carved with the fouled anchor and the Victoria Cross.[3] He has a memorial at St Peter's church, Petersfield, Hampshire, near that of his naval father, a modest brass plaque within a rope twist border. It bears the ship's badge of HMS *Shark*.

Major Francis John William Harvey VC, whose prompt action in ordering the magazine of HMS *Lion* to be flooded saved Beatty's flagship, was buried at sea. His name is among those on the sea-mark memorial at Chatham; a

---

[3]   David Harvey, *Memorials to Courage: Victoria Cross Headstones and Memorials* (1999), vol. 1, p. 379.

stark contrast to the substantial public memorial commemorating his direct ancestor Captain John Harvey, killed during the Battle of the Glorious First of June in 1794.

The only one of the four Jutland VCs to become a posthumous national celebrity was 16-year-old John Cornwell who, though wounded, remained standing awaiting orders at his gun on the cruiser HMS *Chester*, while most of the rest of the gun crew had been killed. His sacrifice made no practical contribution to the outcome but his extreme youth caught the public imagination. The image of 'Jack' Cornwell at his gun by Fortunino Matania, published in *The Sphere*, became a national icon and national fundraising for naval charities was conducted in his name. After initial burial in a mass grave at Grimsby, his body was transferred to Manor Park Cemetery, London, and re-interred on 29 July 1916 with much ceremonial in the presence of local dignitaries. A substantial if conventional memorial marks the grave. A cross standing on a rock, with an anchor, also commemorates Cornwell's father, who died shortly afterwards. The inscription includes a translated quotation from Ovid: 'It is not wealth or ancestry but honourable conduct and a noble disposition that make men great.' Cornwell had been a delivery boy, his father a tram driver.

The two British commanders at Jutland, John Rushworth Jellicoe and David Beatty, were acknowledged and rewarded but hardly idolized. They both have discreet monuments in the crypt of St Paul's near Nelson, and busts by Sir Charles Wheeler and William McMillan in Trafalgar Square were unveiled in 1948.[4] However, the prospect of what Corelli Barnett calls a 'Steam-driven Trafalgar' had failed to materialize.[5]

Outgunned

The German navy, lacking the far-flung imperial bases of the British, were still prepared to carry on the war in isolation, far from home. When it started, Admiral Maximilian von Spee's East Asia squadron abandoned its base in Tsingtao, China, and travelled east across the Pacific threatening the trade routes on the west coast of America which lay on its path home. Confused instructions from the Admiralty resulted in Sir Christopher Cradock encountering Spee's five ships in November 1914 off Coronel, Chile, where the British were 'Outnumbered and outclassed in ships, outranged in guns

---

[4] The memorials had been voted by the House of Commons in December 1935 and May 1936 (*Hansard*, 21 November 1938) but their installation was delayed by the outbreak of war. New fountains were also part of the scheme as indicated by an inscription on the paving between them.

[5] Corelli Barnett, *Engage the Enemy More Closely* (1991), p. 5.

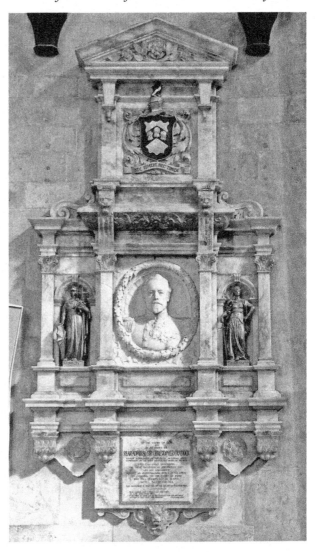

43. *Memorial to Sir Christopher Cradock, by Frederick William Pomeroy, at York Minster.* © *Bart O'Brien.*

and hopelessly overwhelmed by weight of metal'.[6] The result of the action was the loss of the cruisers *Monmouth* and *Good Hope*, Cradock's flagship, both with all hands: 1570 men died, as against just three Germans wounded. Cradock's memorial at York Minster was funded by public subscription and unveiled in 1916. The work of Frederick William Pomeroy (1856–1924), it is a neo-classical wall tablet in alabaster with a marble portrait bust of Cradock flanked by gilded figures representing Loyalty and Courage (fig. 43). Like the memorial to Cradock in Concepçion, Chile, it bears a quotation from

6   Inscription of the memorial to Cradock at Gilling West, North Yorkshire.

Maccabees I: 'God forbid that I should do this thing, to flee away from them …' *The Times*'s special correspondent describes him like Captain Oates as 'A very gallant Gentleman',[7] but the defeat, however chivalrous the language that described it, shattered the Navy's reputation for invincibility.

Von Spee, having expended much of his ammunition on Cradock, was intercepted by an avenging Royal Naval squadron off the Falkland Islands in December 1914 and even more conclusively sunk, in what turned out to be the only decisive British victory of the war. Of von Spee's two armoured and three light cruisers, only one of the latter (the *Dresden*) escaped, but was cornered and scuttled herself three months later. In 1927 the ex-chairman of the Falkland Islands Company (which owned much of the land there) and a committee of persons who also had financial interests in the islands erected a triumphalist Cornish granite monument overlooking the harbour at Port Stanley. This celebrates the islands' salvation from attack by von Spee. The work of Frank Ransom, it is surmounted by a ship on a globe and a seven-foot-high figure of Victory looks out to sea in the direction of the battle. On the back is a representation of piled shells surmounted by a ship's wheel and a lifebelt, flanked by flags. The ships which took part in the battle are shown on panels to the side.

Submarines

The Navy was, in truth, embarking on a new sort of warfare. It rapidly became apparent that the submarine, until then deprecated by conservative officers as 'underhand, unfair and damned un-English' (Admiral Sir Arthur Wilson's 1901 phrase), could be effectively deployed as a commerce raider and against unwary warships, particularly by the Germans. On 22 September 1914, in the North Sea, a squadron of admittedly old protected cruisers, *Aboukir*, *Cressy* and *Hogue*, was sunk at a stroke and with great loss by *U-9* , as it headed home from an otherwise fruitless patrol. The British blockade of Germany was essentially carried out by surface warships but British submarines were used in the Baltic and the Dardanelles campaign and for coastal patrol. Losses of men were heavy in proportion to the numbers employed. Rather than being sunk in action with surface ships, many of these vessels were damaged or destroyed in surface shoot-outs with other submarines, in encounters with mines or in accidents such as collisions or strandings. The National Submarine War Memorial on the Victoria Embankment, with sculpture by Frederick Brook Hitch (1877–1957), owes something to the sinister gothic fantasy of the German medals designed by artists such as Karl

7 *The Times*, 17 June 1916, p. 8.

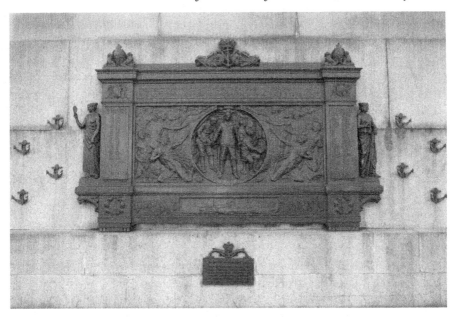

44. *National Submarine War Memorial, by Frederick Brook Hitch, at Victoria Embankment, London.* © *Author.*

Goetz and Walther Eberbach, which made sardonic comment on the war at sea (fig. 44). The circular central panel of Brook Hitch's memorial represents a section through a submarine containing the captain and crew in high relief. This effectively conveys the notoriously cramped conditions in these vessels. The commanding officer, placed at the centre of the composition, wears the Admiralty special-issue clothing of leather boots and roll-neck sweater. Figures of hostile mermen in lower relief, giving them an unearthly appearance, fill the remainder of the rectangular panel. They are attempting to trap the submariners in nets. Anti-submarine nets were an all-too-literal hazard.[8] The memorial is flanked by female figures representing Truth and Justice. The panel at the base, showing a submarine in relief, was modified by 1959 to add the dates of the Second World War and the names of the submarines lost in that conflict were also added.

Submarine accidents continued during peacetime. In 1939, ninety-nine men were lost in HMS *Thetis* during trials in Liverpool bay (the normal crew had been supplemented on this occasion by shipyard employees and additional naval officers). Although the vessel was only partly submerged and was later successfully salvaged, all but four of the occupants died of carbon

---

[8] The medal by E. Zehle commemorating the return of the submarine *Deutschland* in 1916 shows a beaver breaking through nets.

monoxide poisoning while abandoning ship. Forty-four of the casualties were buried in a common grave at Maeshyfryd Cemetery, Holyhead. A memorial there was dedicated on 7 November 1947, taking the form of a granite stele carved with a cross in the form of a sword, plunging into waves with the Admiralty anchor on the plinth below. The conception owes something to Sir Reginald Blomfield's cross of sacrifice, while the execution with simplified lines and high relief is a popular form of modernism. The names of the casualties are on a slate slab in front.

A Merchant Navy

The U-boat war against British shipping was to change the nature of the merchant service. The prize laws which had protected the life of the merchant captain, if not his investments, were to break down under the pressure of this new form of conflict. Submarines could neither take on board the crews of the vessels they sunk and remain operational, nor could they put a prize crew on board captured vessels. Armed resistance by merchant ships and by the naval crews of Q-ships (armed vessels disguised as merchant ships) escalated the conflict further. At the beginning of 1917 the German government announced the blockade of the British Isles by unrestricted submarine warfare. After the belated introduction of regular convoys later that year, the 'British Mercantile Marine' – its customary formal style at the time – came to be recognized as a 'Merchant Navy', a term which slipped increasingly into use, though it was only in 1922 that George V granted it as the merchant service's official title in recognition of its wartime role.[9] Employed under naval officers on armed cruisers and naval auxiliaries, not to mention merchant vessels at risk from attack by U-boat, civilian seamen had ceased to be non-combatants.

The Mercantile Marine Memorial stands in Trinity Square Gardens between Trinity House and All Hallows-by-the-Tower. The original part of the memorial was designed by Sir Edwin Lutyens and takes the form of a pavilion with a barrel-vaulted interior. The names of the merchant seamen are inscribed on bronze plates which clad the exterior, broken up by ridges to suggest joints in the structure. The inscription reads: '1914–1918 to the glory of God and to the honour of 12,000 of the Merchant Navy and fishing fleets who have no grave but the sea'. The structure parallels those erected on the battlefields to those missing in action whose bodies were not identified.

Sir William Goscombe John's Engine-Room Heroes memorial at the Pier Head, Liverpool, was originally intended to commemorate the engineers, firemen, trimmers and greasers of *Titanic*, who kept the lights and the pumps running while the lifeboats were launched. War broke out before the

---

[9]   A.G. Course, *The Merchant Navy: A Social History* (1963), p. 278.

unveiling of the memorial in 1916 and the loss of life in this one accident was overwhelmed by casualties of the conflict. The dedication of the memorial was widened to cover all fatalities sustained among engine-room crew in the performance of duty (fig. 45). The memorial takes the form of an obelisk terminating in a flame. The top is surrounded by four lightly draped women

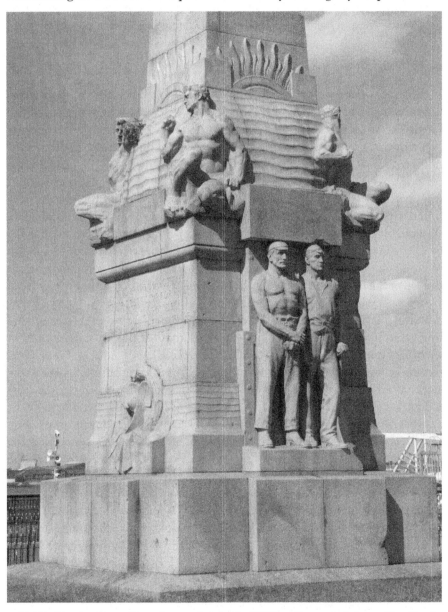

45. *The 'Engine Room Heroes' memorial, by Sir William Goscombe John, at Pier Head, Liverpool. © Author.*

joined by the breeches-buoys they hold, which represent the sea. Crouching figures at the corner of the base represent the elements. Below, are four full-length figures; the two facing west represent two engineers holding a spanner and a stoking-hatch lever. On the east side, two stokers hold, respectively, a cloth and a shovel. Rough and somewhat slovenly, the lower ranks of the engineering department frequently worked and lived in bad conditions. Goscombe John depicts them in an appropriately primitivist, modern style.

Martyr

In London's Liverpool Street Station, a memorial illustrates the ambiguous military status of merchant personnel. Charles Fryatt was a master of the Great Eastern Railway vessels which shuttled between eastern ports and the Netherlands. Congratulated and presented with a gold watch by the Admiralty in 1915 for a (probably ineffectual) attempt to ram *U-33*, his ship, the SS *Brussels*, was boarded a year later leaving the Hook of Holland and Fryatt was interned, tried by court-martial on 27 July 1916 and, on the Kaiser's immediate personal endorsement, shot that evening as an illegal combatant. A standard 'British Mercantile Marine' uniform for officers was established by Order in Council on 4 September 1918 and further regulated by legislation the following year.[10] The new cap badge appears, flanked by olive branches, at the top of the headstone erected by his shipping company over Fryatt's grave at Dovercourt where he was reburied in 1919, after a service in St Paul's Cathedral. The inscription, which describes him as 'Illegally executed', is surrounded by rope in high relief, tied in figure-of-eight knots at the top corners, and in a carrick bend at the base; the words 'PRO PATRIA' are enclosed in a laurel wreath below. The symbolism perfectly embodies the mercantile marine's new status as an arm of the state. Fryatt's fate also aroused sympathy in the Low Countries. A memorial erected at Bruges in 1922 marks the site where Fryatt and twelve others were executed by the Germans for espionage or assisting the enemy. A series of pillars terminating in stylized flames runs along the wall which still bears the marks of the bullets. Fryatt's pillar was erected by the English Convent, a local religious community. Another memorial was placed at Liverpool Street by the Netherlands Section of the League of Neutral States, on the anniversary of Fryatt's death. At the London site, a marble wall tablet bears a bronze portrait roundel, probably by the Dutch sculptor Willem Frederik Hendrik van Golberdinge (1877–1963), though the artist's initials are unclear.

---

10 British Mercantile Marine Uniform Act, 1919 [9 & 10 Geo. V]. A further Order in Council of 13 December 1921 brought the 1918–19 provisions in line and appears to have prompted George V's formalization of the title 'Merchant Navy' shortly afterwards (1922).

Things to come

Another new force emerged in naval warfare. From 1915 the Royal Navy controlled the Royal Naval Air Service (later to be merged with the Royal Flying Corps to form the Royal Air Force). By the end of the war, aircraft were being used to sight, if not sink, submarines. Seaplanes were initially used to operate at sea. Memorials at St Lawrence's church, Bradfield, Essex, commemorate the first pilot to land on the deck of a warship at sea. Commander Edwin Harris Dunning, after having performed this feat twice, was killed while attempting a third run on 7 August 1917. Two windows were presented in his memory with a dedication plate and an alabaster wall memorial in baroque style. The Dunning arms and crest are placed in the segmental pediment (he was the son of Sir Edward Harris Dunning). The memorial quotes a prescient letter to his next of kin:

> The Admiralty wish you to know what great service he performed for the Navy. It was in fact a demonstration of landing an Aeroplane on the deck of a Man-of-War whilst the latter was under way. This had never been done before; and the data obtained was of the utmost value. It will make Aeroplanes indispensible to the Fleet, & possibly revolutionise Naval Warfare.

The brass plate dedicating the windows has a border of leaves and acorns, broken by the Dunning arms at the base. An inscription in gothic script proclaims Dunning: 'a verray perfight [*sic*] gentil knight'. Above is shown the cap badge of the Royal Naval Air Service, the unofficial badge of HMS *Furious* and, in the centre, a scene based on a photograph, showing the Sopwith Pup biplane landing on her deck.

Total war

Passengers as well as merchant seafarers fell prey to submarine warfare during both world wars. Most notoriously, the RMS *Lusitania* was torpedoed by *U-20*, ten miles south of the Old Head of Kinsale, southern Ireland, and sank in eighteen minutes with the loss of 1198 passengers and crew on 7 May 1915. The loss of American passengers in the disaster was a factor in bringing the United States into the war. The most substantial memorial stands in the main square at Cobh (formerly Queenstown), County Cork, now in the Republic of Ireland. It was commissioned ten years later, by a committee of United States citizens who lost relatives in the disaster. An Irish American sculptor, Jerome Connor (1874–1943), was commissioned to produce the work, in particular the figure of the angel that now stands on top. By 1937 the memorial had still not been completed and money ran out. There had also

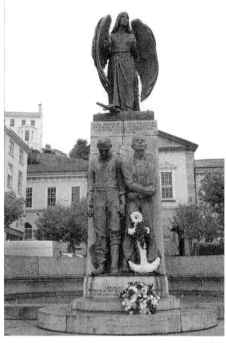

46. *The* Lusitania *memorial, sculptor Jerome Connor, at Cobh, Ireland.* © *celtjan (CC BY-SA 3.0).*

been differences between Connor and the local council over the placing of a Gaelic inscription on it and the council proposed to withdraw their permission for it to be sited in the town.[11] Eventually, in 1967, the project received a grant from Ireland's Arts Council and the memorial was finished.[12] Considering that over this long period Ireland had become an independent state and one that had remained neutral during the Second World War, the design and wording of the monument was something of a diplomatic minefield. The memorial consists of an over-life-sized figure of an angel on a plinth; two mourning fishermen stand below (fig. 46). The inscription reads:

TO THE MEMORY OF ALL WHO PERISHED BY THE SINKING OF THE LUSITANIA MAY 7 1915 AND IN THE CAUSE OF UNIVERSAL AND EVER-LASTING PEACE. LABORARE EST ORARE. TO ALL WHO HELPED IN THE RESCUE, GAVE AID AND COMFORT TO THE SURVIVORS AND BURIED THE DEAD.

The headstone of 3-year-old Alfred Scott Witherbee, in the nearby Old Church Cemetery, reads by contrast: '... victim of the Lusitania, foully murdered by Germany'. The loss of the child wrecked his parents' marriage.

---

11 *The Times*, 6 September 1937, p. 14.
12 *The Guardian*, 31 October 1967, p. 4.

City of Benares

By the beginning of the Second World War, advances in air power saw British civilians under threat of air attack. The potential for devastation created considerable anxiety during the last years before the 1939–45 war and government policy was to evacuate non-essential civilians from cities. A government scheme was set up to ship children to temporary homes in the dominions under the auspices of the Children's Overseas Reception Board (CORB). Attempts to mitigate civilian casualties resulting from submarine warfare by allowing surrendered merchantmen to evacuate their passengers once again proved impractical.[13] On 17 September 1940 the *City of Benares*, carrying ninety child evacuees to Canada, was torpedoed by *U-48* in the Atlantic, shortly after her naval escort had left to join another incoming convoy. As nearby vessels would be vulnerable to attack if they attempted to pick up survivors, only thirteen of the CORB children survived the delay until they were rescued, with many dying of exposure in waterlogged boats.[14] They were being escorted mainly by women teachers and clergymen. Michael Rennie, who was training for ordination at Keble College, Oxford, dived in repeatedly to drag children out of the water, before himself succumbing to the cold on 18 September. Rennie is commemorated by a painting at St Jude's, Hampstead Garden Suburb, where his father was vicar. By Walter P. Starmer (1877–1961), it forms part of a general scheme of painted murals within this Lutyens church and is placed in a lunette above St George's altar. There are cherubs in the upper border and shields of arms in the corners. The painting shows a sinking lifeboat filled with children. Rennie is seated in the bows with his arm around a boy and girl, pointing to the horizon (fig. 47).

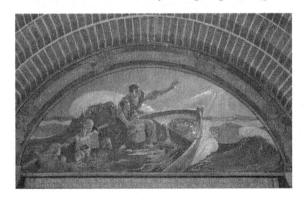

47. *Michael Rennie, by Walter Percival Starmer, a mural at St Jude, Hampstead Garden Suburb. © The Parish Church of St Jude-on-the-Hill, Hampstead Garden Suburb.*

---

[13] The London Naval Treaty, 22 April 1930, and the London Protocol, 1936.
[14] Figures from Ralph Barker, *Children of the Benares* (1987), p. 145.

The highest civilian casualties suffered at sea in fact occurred at the end of the Second World War. During Operation Hannibal, in 1945, German vessels evacuating troops and civilians from Courland, East Prussia and the Polish Corridor came under attack from Allied aircraft and submarines. The resulting sinking of the *Wilhelm Gustloff* involved the highest loss of life in a single incident and casualties from the *Goya* were also very heavy.

Gardens of remembrance

The casualties of the First World War were commemorated by a surprising amount of neo-gothic design, in spite of some disapproval from more progressive opinion: 'We all know how much our churches have been injured by ugly brasses and stained glass windows.'[15] Writing in 1919, Edward Warren thought, 'the frank acceptance and portrayal of contemporary arms, costumes, ships, aeroplanes, and machines of war, affords an endless opportunity for effective and historically valuable presentment'.[16] By the end of the Second World War even the formerly 'modern' memorials were in a style that had gone out of fashion and were in a neglected condition. Portrayal of weaponry was out of favour: 'the multiplying of memorials (bad sculpture, bad lettering, worst of all, tanks, guns and other weapons) should be discouraged'.[17] So much for Charles Sargeant Jagger's now much-admired Royal Artillery Memorial at Hyde Park Corner. In this frame of mind, it was decided to extend the naval memorials at Portsmouth, Plymouth and Chatham and add new names. The architect of the additions was Sir Edward Maufe (1883–1974), with additional sculpture by Charles Wheeler (1892–1974) and William McMillan (1887–1977), and also Esmond Burton at Portsmouth. The plan was different at each site but each includes Portland stone figures of heroic seamen in duffle coats and sea boots.

Maufe also designed the extension to the Mercantile Marine Memorial in the form of a sunken garden, somewhat reminiscent of the plan of a ruined church. The idea of memorial gardens was popular with members of war memorial committees.[18] The enclosure is guarded by pylons carved with the Merchant Navy badge and by figures of a merchant officer and seamen, again by Charles Wheeler. The greatly increased roll of names (listed under their ships) is divided by panels carved with rather frivolous figures from classical myth, representing the seven seas (fig. 48).

---

[15] Arthur Clutton-Brock, *On War Memorials* (1920), p. 9.

[16] Edward Warren, *War Memorials* (1919).

[17] *South Wales Argus*, 28 April 1944.

[18] NMM CHT/7/5, A.E.M. Chatfield, 1st Baron Chatfield, War Memorial Advisory Council.

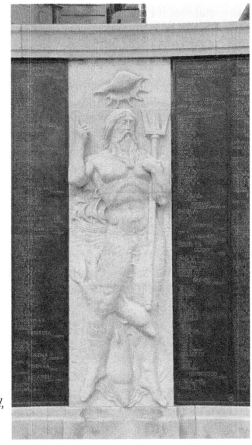

48. *The Mercantile Marine Memorial, sculptor Charles Wheeler, at Trinity Square, City of London. © Author.*

New memorials were erected by the Imperial War Graves Commission to those with no known graves but the sea. At Liverpool Pier Head, a circular column has reflective lenses at the top to suggest a beacon: a celestial and terrestrial globe flank the head of the steps to the base. This commemorates merchant naval personnel who died while serving with the Royal Navy.[19] The architects were Stanley Harold Smith and Charles Frederick Blythin, the sculptor George Herbert Tyson Smith (1883–1972). The Fleet Air Arm memorial is at Lee-on-Solent and that of the Royal Naval Patrol Service (RNPS) is at Lowestoft. A fluted column surmounted with a golden galleon or Lymphad under sail, this is a more immediately appealing design than Liverpool's stark, modernist beacon and Lee-on-Solent's column. The names of the missing are placed on a wall behind it. The architect of the Lowestoft

---

19 This memorial is specifically to merchant seamen who signed the T124 agreement under which they were subject to naval discipline while retaining their Merchant Navy rates of pay.

memorial was F.H. Crosley and the sculptor again Tyson Smith. Many men from the local fishing industry served in the RNPS which manned small craft such as minesweepers. All these memorials were designed to be visible from passing ships.

The idea of a 'green' memorial was most completely realized in the National Memorial Arboretum, which primarily commemorates military casualties since the Second World War. Begun in 1997 at Alrewas, Staffordshire, it has a Merchant Navy Convoy and a Navy Wood. Sited well away from centres of population (and almost as far from the sea as one can be in England), the Arboretum accords with the twenty-first-century taste for land art, sculpture parks and green burial.

Victors

The post-war period took a more positive view of its naval heroes. Military chapels had been set up in cathedrals following the First World War, cementing links with local regiments. The maritime equivalents were mostly established after the Second World War, establishing links between towns and the naval vessels named after them. The bell of HMS *Canterbury* (of 1915) hangs in the cathedral of the same name and is struck at six bells; HMS *Sussex's* bell is at Chichester.

Two of the major Royal Naval leaders of the Second World War died during the 1960s – Andrew Browne Cunningham, Viscount Cunningham of Hyndhope, in 1963, and Sir Philip Louis Vian in 1969. The former – 'ABC' – is regarded as the greatest British naval commander of the war: Cunningham, as commander-in-chief in the Mediterranean, had faced an alliance of German and Italian forces, and 'No British Admiral has ever had to contend against more dreadful odds.'[20] The Second World War was beginning to assume a crucial place in British national identity; a crusade, a time of unprecedented unity, a last hurrah. Furthermore, it provided an arena where heroic action was not necessarily overwhelmed by high explosive. The ecclesiastical authorities at St Paul's and the Admiralty Board began to cooperate in establishing a hall of naval heroes around Nelson's tomb, containing memorials to Cunningham, Vian and Admiral of the Fleet Sir Dudley Pound (1877–1943). The Admiralty Board agreed that the area should be redecorated and the lighting improved. 'It was further agreed that henceforward and as a matter of regular routine, a party of naval ratings should attend the Cathedral at six monthly intervals to do whatever is needful by way of scrubbing and polishing to keep this location of naval memorials in good

---

[20] NMM DCK/43/3, Admiral Sir John Hamilton's address on the unveiling of a memorial to Cunningham in Malta, 1967.

order.'[21] A plaque to Cunningham was erected at St Paul's Anglican Cathedral, Valletta, on 28 April 1967, and a bust by Franta Belski was unveiled in 1967 in Trafalgar Square, next to Jellicoe and Beatty.

The Siege Bell

Veterans' associations were the moving force behind the continuing erection of memorials in the years following the Second World War. The most successful and most challenging project of this type was the placing of the Malta Siege Bell at the entrance to Grand Harbour, Valletta. This was commissioned by the George Cross Island Association to commemorate the 7000 lives lost in the successful defence of the island. The artist was Michael Sandle, then Professor of Sculpture at Karlsruhe, and the chief manager and diplomat on the commissioning body was Admiral of the Fleet Terence Thornton Lewin (Lord Lewin) – a veteran of 'Operation Pedestal', the critical relief of Malta in 1942. The two men established and retained amicable relations in spite of Sandle's creation in 1986 of the *Belgrano Medal – a Medal of Dishonour*, showing Margaret Thatcher as a death's head. Lewin had been Chief of the Defence Staff and a member of the British war cabinet during the Falklands Conflict of 1982, when the decision was taken to sink the Argentine cruiser. Sandle had, in previous work, used the sculptural language of commemoration in a provocative fashion.[22] There were also many practical problems owing to the components of the memorial being made or built in three countries (England, Germany and Malta), the fact that it involved moving parts and that it was sited on exposed sea rocks overlooking the harbour. This location necessitated a modification in the design and additional granite cladding. The concept was supposedly inspired by an existing bell at Vittoriosa (Birgu), the bell which had alerted the island to the approach of the Turkish siege force in 1565 and which was rung after its eventual defeat. The original model showed the new bell suspended in a cupola resembling the conning tower of a U-boat with, in front of it, a funeral effigy[23] carried on a base resembling the bows of a ship. The conning tower was replaced with a more classical cupola to blend in with a nearby memorial 'temple' to Sir Alexander Ball (the post-Napoleonic Royal Naval governor of Malta), and the ship's bows were modified (fig. 49). The bell, its design based on the 500-year-old Maria Gloriosa bell at Erfurt, was decorated with a figure of the Virgin Mary within

21 NMM GTN/8/7 (3).
22 See *A Twentieth Century Memorial* in the collections of the Tate Gallery. This combines a Micky Mouse figure with a machine gun in response to the Vietnam War.
23 NMM LWN/3/10/1, Michael Sandle, 3 September 1990: 'There is a precedent for such a figure and masonry, and that is Lutyens's superb memorial to the Great War in Manchester.'

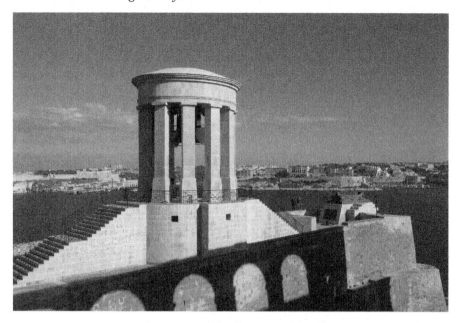

49. *The Siege Bell Memorial, by Michael Sandle, at Valletta, Malta. © Frank Vincentz (CC BY-SA 3.0).*

an aureole of flames in tribute to the Santa Maria Convoy (as the Maltese called 'Operation Pedestal', the surviving convoy having arrived on the Feast of the Virgin). It was inscribed: 'Obumbrasti super caput meum in die belli MCMXL-MCMXLIII' ('Thou hast covered my head in the day of battle', Psalm 140:7). The emblem of the George Cross Island Association was placed on the other side.

The memorial and its associated book of remembrance was opened during a royal visit by Queen Elizabeth II in 1992 on the fiftieth anniversary of the Santa Maria Convoy, with the help of an additional £100,000 contribution from the British government which wished to ensure friendly relations with an independent Malta. It looked (and remains) splendid, and became a successful tourist attraction. Unfortunately, two years later, Lord Lewin's patience was further tried when the wooden headstock, on which the bell was hung, gave way. Naval efficiency established that the contractor was liable for the repair and today it is hung from a stronger, if less aesthetically pleasing steel headstock which was substituted for the wooden one.

Johnny Walker

In 1998 another veterans group, the Captain Walker's Old Boys' Association, also commissioned a memorial. Frederick John Walker had been a successful and somewhat ruthless naval commander who had specialized in anti-submarine warfare. After initially sinking U-boats that attacked the convoys he was protecting, he was given command of the second support group which had an active remit to hunt and destroy them. He sunk more submarines than any other commander and thereby contributed to the successful outcome of the Battle of the Atlantic. The full-length statue on Liverpool Pier Head, by Tom Murphy, shows the gaunt Walker, balanced on the deck of his ship clutching his binoculars. He had been understandably popular at the time of his premature death in 1944 and, towards the end of the century, there was a revival of interest in Liverpool's wartime past. Not only had the city's seamen run the gauntlet of enemy blockade to get supplies through from North America but it had also been heavily bombed and suffered decline. By the 1990s it was seeking economic regeneration based on its culture and heritage. The Pier Head, now a UNESCO World Heritage Site, is the public face of the revived Liverpool waterfront and is the main showcase for the city's public sculpture.

Glass

The damage caused by enemy bombing to the towns and cities of Great Britain encouraged the commissioning of replacement stained glass in the post-war period. St Mary's church, Dover, very much in the firing line, installed new commemorative windows. One particularly attractive example, dedicated in 1980, commemorates the air-sea rescue service introduced by the RAF in 1941, in many ways a positive outcome of the war in the air. The window consists of two lancets and a roundel which contains the Royal Air Force badge. The upper part of the lights is decorated with stars, the lower part with water. A central scene crossing both lancets shows a downed airman in a life-raft, the nose of his sinking plane in the foreground. A plane and a motor launch speed to the rescue (fig. 50). The dedication reads:

IN . MEMORY . OF . ALL RANKS . OF . THE . ALLIED AIR . FORCES . AND AIR - SEA . RESCUE . & . MARINE / CRAFT . SECTIONS . OF . THE . ROYAL . AIR - FORCE WHO . PERISHED . IN . THE SEAS . THROUGHOUT . THE WORLD . DURING . THE . SECOND WORLD . WAR .

The design includes the badge of the Royal Air Force Coastal Command.

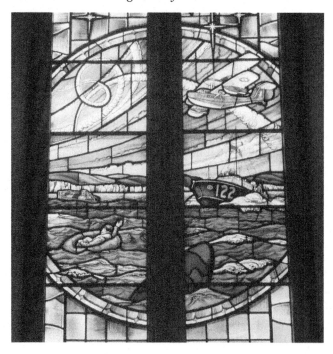

50. *Royal Air Force Coastal Command, window at St Mary's Church, Dover. © Author.*

Entirely secular commemorative windows of this type had long become an acceptable feature in church interiors.

The most influential stained-glass designer in the immediate post-war period was Hugh Easton (1906–65), who designed many of the new windows in St Dunstan's and All Saints, Stepney. A rating kneeling at the feet of a crucified, clean-shaven Christ commemorates sailors who lost their lives in the Second World War. This type of composition, associating death in battle with the death of Christ, Easton referred to as 'visions' and they were used in many of his commemorative windows. Easton's work is in a neo-baroque style which became very popular in the second half of the twentieth century.

The Falklands Conflict

The long period of uneasy peace during the second half of the twentieth century was broken by a series of small wars. The Navy and Merchant Navy played a crucial role in the Falklands campaign of 1982, and six ships – HMS *Ardent*, *Sheffield*, *Coventry* and *Glasgow*, the Royal Fleet Auxiliary *Sir Galahad* and the requisitioned merchantman *Atlantic Conveyor* – were lost. Memorials to the conflict were erected at St Paul's Cathedral, Plymouth, Cardiff and Portsmouth – the Plymouth memorial being specifically maritime. The most well-known is a statue by Philip Jackson of 'The Yomper', depicting a Royal Marine and unveiled in 1992 by Margaret Thatcher (fig. 51), whose steely

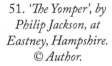

51. '*The Yomper*', by
Philip Jackson, at
Eastney, Hampshire.
© *Author*.

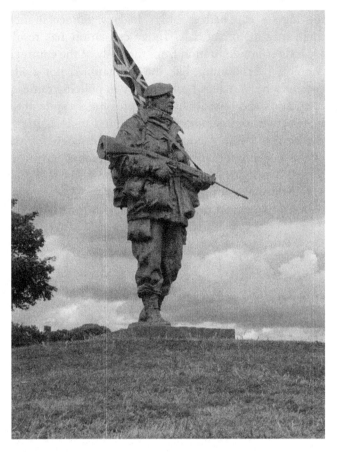

determination as Prime Minister ten years before was key to the defeat of the Argentine military regime's ambitions. It stands at the entrance to the Royal Marine Museum at Eastney. The Marines had to cross the islands carrying ('yomping') most of their kit, following the loss of the helicopters carried in *Atlantic Conveyor*. The statue is based on a photograph of Corporal Peter Robinson and is similar to a type of hyper-realistic sculpture popular for military memorials in the United States.[24]

Remembrance today

During the twentieth century, flamboyant individual tombs came to be seen as somewhat eccentric but a restrained display of personal heraldry was considered perfectly tasteful. A maritime identity could be indicated by the choice of devices and supporters. In an age of commercial and corporate branding,

[24] Erika Doss, *Memorial Mania* (Chicago, 2010).

the logo – cap badges, ships' badges, service branch badges – appeared frequently on memorials. Today cremation has resulted in a tendency to separate commemoration from the body of the commemorated: the National Memorial Arboretum, like the cenotaph, is not a site of burial. The Navy currently has a reduced role, mainly in policing duties and combined-service operations, and is under financial pressure. In spite of this, there is an increasingly active commemoration of war and its casualties. As part of this trend, the British Legion led a successful campaign for the revival, from 1995, of the two-minute silence on 11 November (Armistice Day in 1918) and formal Merchant Navy Day commemoration services were started in 2000. The dwindling numbers of Second World War veterans and the search for national identity in times of change both contribute to this movement.

5

Commerce and philanthropy: mercantile commemoration

Maritime trade and warfare have always been closely interrelated. Apart from defending coasts from invasion and projecting military power overseas, the role of navies is to protect sea-borne commerce, and the naval costs of doing so have generally been met through taxation on the profits of that trade. Until the early nineteenth century, crews, and to a lesser extent, officers, might have experience of service in both merchantmen and warships. Seamen tended to be reluctant naval recruits, pressed in wartime from incoming merchant ships in which they were often better paid, and resentful of harsher naval discipline. Large merchant ships, East Indiamen in particular, carried guns to fight off attacks by pirates or, more commonly, privateers. A tablet in the church of King Charles the Martyr in Falmouth commemorates an American passenger, Captain John Navarre Macomb of New York, who died of wounds sustained defending HM packet *Princess Charlotte* from attack by a French privateer, *La Vénus*, in 1810.[1] Such packets were privately owned or hired vessels which carried passengers and mail on behalf of the Post Office. During that year *Princess Charlotte* was constantly engaged in carrying government despatches from Lisbon, a vital source of information on the progress of the Peninsular campaign against the French, which may explain her determined resistance to this attack.

A peaceful occupation?

There were, of course, peaceful and beneficial outcomes from maritime trade, generally seen in a positive light by the mid-eighteenth century (or at least its profits were so regarded). However, in remarking that 'There are few ways in which a man can be more innocently employed than in getting money', Samuel Johnson was mocking some of the social attitudes of his

---

[1] *Hampshire Telegraph and Sussex Chronicle*, 19 November 1810.

time. Military rank and achievement, allied to notions of aristocracy, patriotism and disinterested public service made possible by inherited wealth, had long had a cachet denied to more entrepreneurial activities. There was also a dark side to trade. Demands currently continue for the removal of Edward Cassidy's 1895 statue, at Bristol, of Edward Colston (1636–1721), merchant and philanthropist of that former slave-trading city – in which trade he was also involved as a member of the Royal African Company. Memorials which allude to personal wealth gained through commerce have therefore tended to deploy a degree of spin. New wealth would also come under scrutiny in a religious context, so fair-dealing and philanthropy are emphasized in epitaphs.

Those who merely gained a modest living from the sea might have their occupation commemorated by their families on memorials whose iconography gives maritime symbols a religious twist. Largely excluded from the discussion of imagery that follows are the great majority of mercantile memorials dating from the nineteenth and early twentieth century. These mass-produced grave markers may only indicate occupation (or shipping line) in a brief inscription and by the choice of religious text.

The iconography of trade: peace and plenty

Trade had its own iconography. It frequently appears in the context of a cessation of hostilities, celebrating the benefits of well-negotiated peace treaties. The memorial to Sir Benjamin Keene (1697–1757) which stands in St Nicholas's chapel, King's Lynn, takes the form of a marble sarcophagus with lion's-head terminals and paw feet (fig. 52). A relief on the side shows the giant seated figure of Peace treading the weapons of war beneath her feet and indicating ships being laden with cargo to her right, where a view of a port includes a quayside and a crane. The other side shows a profile portrait of Keene, and the plinth is carved with garlanded ox skulls in the manner of a Roman altar. Robert Adam is believed to have been the designer. Keene, son of a former mayor of King's Lynn, negotiated a successful commercial treaty with Spain in 1750 and ensured her neutrality during the early years of the Seven Years War until 1762. Spain was an important trading partner but British incursions into her extensive empire were a constant source of dispute between the two nations. This imagery celebrating the trading benefits of peace is shown in other decorative arts of the period, such as a French waistcoat panel in the collections of the National Maritime Museum, celebrating the Eden Treaty of 1786 between England and France. The design shows a British seaman, seated on a bale of Indian cottons, toasting the treaty with his French equivalent, seated on a barrel of Bordeaux wine.

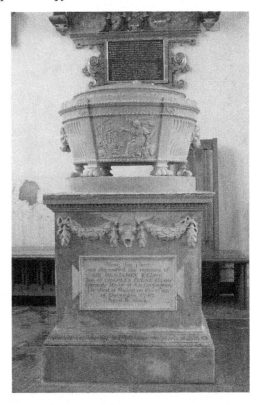

52. *Sir Benjamin Keene, by Robert Adam, at St Nicholas' Chapel, King's Lynn.*
© *Author.*

Insurance and the afterlife

The memorial to Nicholas Magens at Brightlingsea similarly displays cargo imagery (fig. 53) and is one of the most opulent celebrations of maritime trade in England. Magens was not strictly a seafarer; his interests were in insurance. He amassed a large fortune as a merchant and underwriter, which amounted to about £100,000 at the time of his death. He also published on these topics[2] and the memorial at Brightlingsea erected by his widow claims: 'His extensive knowledge in Commerce renders his death a Public as well as a private Loss. His Writings eminently display his shining Abilities and will perpetuate his Name to the latest Posterity.' Born in the Duchy of Holstein in about 1697, Magens became a naturalized Briton and purchased the manor of Brightlingsea in 1763, requesting to be buried in the church there. His memorial is in marble by Nicholas Read and was erected in 1766. No expense was spared. On its left, the angel stands before bales of goods holding a scroll bearing the inscription; to the left a cherub holds a large cornucopia spilling

---

2   Nicholas Magens, *An essay on Insurances ... to which is annexed some brief hints to Merchants and Insurers concerning the risks to which navigation is exposed in the time of war* (1755).

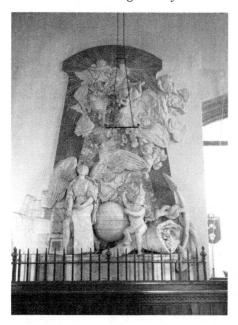

53. *Nicholas Magens, by Nicholas Read, at Brightlingsea, Essex. © John Salmon (CC EY-SA 2.0 UK).*

fruit and coins. The stern of a ship, an anchor and a globe are also included in the composition. The globe shows the Pacific, with Australia omitted, and California shown as an island. A host of cherubs' heads in clouds are depicted above, with an angel blowing the last trump. The wreath and scales shown on the pyramid behind symbolize both God's final judgment on Magens's life and his fair trading during it. The epitaph and the contemporary press are in agreement over Magens's kindness and generosity: he left several bequests to London hospitals.

Life as a voyage

A badly flaking limestone headstone at St Edmund's church, Southwold, erected about 1772 to members of the Steele family, follows the imagery of the seventeenth-century Dutch marine painters in comparing life to a voyage (fig. 54). The carving above the inscription is going the way of all flesh but the surviving central portion depicts a female angel in a low-cut bodice blowing a trumpet. Below her a herring buss under bare poles weathers a rough sea and, to the right, are shown the symbols of mortality – a skull and hour-glass: the battle of life followed by death and resurrection.

English epitaphs which make the comparison even more explicitly are found on high-status seventeenth-century memorials to merchants and others with a more tenuous connection to the sea. That to John Millett at St Bartholomew's church, Smithfield, London, who died in 1660 (fig. 55), runs as follows:

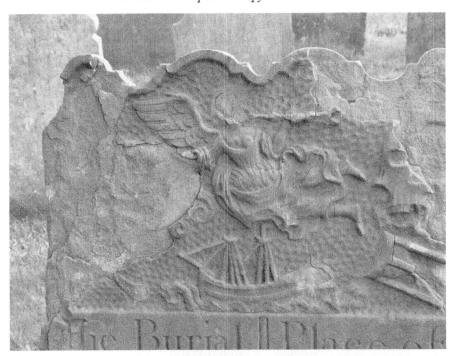

54. *Gravestone of the Steele family, at Southwold, Suffolk.* © *Author.*

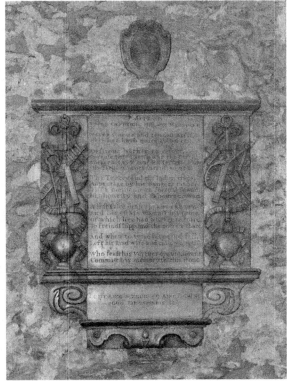

55. *Memorial tablet, John Millett, at St Bartholomew, Smithfield, City of London.* © *National Maritime Museum, Greenwich, London. By kind permission of St Bartholomew the Great, West Smithfield, London, L8028.*

EPITAPH
VPPON CAPT: IOHN MILLETT MARRINER
Many a storme and tempest past,
Here hee hath quiet anchor cast.
Desirous hither to resort,
Because this Parish was the Port,
Whence his wide soul sett forth: and where
His fathers Bones intrusted are.
The Turkey and the Indian trade;
Advantage by his dangers made;
Till a convenient fortune found,
His honesty and labours crown'd.
A iust faire dealer he was knowne;
And his estate was all his owne.
Of which hee had a heart to spare,
To friendshipp and the poore a share,
And when to tyme his period fell,
Left his kind wife and children well.
Who least his Virtues dye unknowne,
Committ his memory to this stone.

Pride in an emergent English literature gave way by the end of the century to an increased use of Latin, but vernacular verse remained in use at the popular level, where a variety of less dignified epitaphs might make literary play with the trade of the deceased. Variants of the following most common maritime example are found at many sites in England and as far afield as Calcutta:

Though Boreas' blasts and Neptune's waves
have tost me two and fro. Yet in spight of
both by God's decree I harbour here below
where I do now at anchor ride with
many of our fleet yet once again
I must set sail our Admiral Christ to meet.[3]

During the nineteenth century, verse (by then regarded as rather 'common') was often replaced by suitably maritime passages from the bible such as 'They

---

[3] Recorded at Southwold, commemorating Philip Church (d. 1754) in *The Register of English Monumental Inscriptions*, vol. 2 (1914), p. 114. The earliest version of the lines on a surviving stone (and so far recorded) may be on that of 1692 for a drowned sailor, William Morris, at Blessed Virgin Mary parish church, Hambleton, Lancs.

that go down to the sea in ships' (Psalm 107:23), or from contemporary literature, such as Alfred, Lord Tennyson's poem *Crossing the Bar* (1889).

Navigation

Navigational instruments are a recurring motif. They represent the means by which the mariner found his way to his destination, making possible European trade with distant regions and indicating contemporary advances in technology. John Millett's epitaph is flanked by carved panels in alabaster, with cross-staves, dividers and rulers suspended from ribbons, and terminating in globes at the base of the panels. The cross-staff was used to determine latitude, by measuring the height of the Sun at midday, and was in time replaced on memorials by the more up-to-date octant or sextant, performing the same function.

The more prestigious monument to Thomas Smythe (d. 1625), merchant adventurer and first governor of the East India Company, at Sutton-at-Hone, has an effigy of Smythe on a tomb-chest between columns, with globes in relief at his head and feet. The panels with reliefs of navigational instruments are placed behind the pillars supporting the pediment. Smythe promoted voyages to search for a North-West Passage to Asia and is commemorated by Smith Sound in Baffin Bay. This tomb is worthy of the merchant prince he became. However, his involvement with overseas trade was primarily financial and political, although he made a voyage to Archangel in 1604 as special ambassador to the Tsar of Russia, and obtained a grant of additional privileges to the Muscovy Company. Smythe promoted trade with Asia and colonies in Virginia and Bermuda from his base in the City of London, eventually retiring to his house at Sutton Place, Kent.

From those large KINGDOMES where the SVNN doth rise;
From that rich new found=world that westward lies
From VOLGA to the flood of AMAZONS:
From vnder both the POLES an all the ZONES;
From all the famous RYVERS LANDES & SEAS
Betwixt this PLACE and our ANTE=PODES:
He gott intelligence, what might be found
To give contentment, through this massie ROVND.
But finding earthly things did rather tire
His longing SOVL then answer her desire:
To this obscvred VILLAGE he with drewe
From hence his Heaunlie VOIAGE did persue
Here, sumd vp all.
And when his GALE of Breath
Had left becalmed in the PORT of DEATH

The Soules frail BARKE (and safe had landed her
Where FAITH his FACTOR and his harbinger Made place before)
He did (no doubt) obtain
That wealth wch here on earth wee seek in vain

Transport

Ships appear on sepulchral memorials from headstones to monuments – not necessarily symbolizing the carrier of the soul to the afterlife but perhaps indicating a pride in the deceased's career. Maritime iconography on the headstones of those with a more modest involvement in sea trade survives in the smaller ports which were not overwhelmed by industrial development. David Simpson, shipowner, erected a headstone in Arbroath in memory of his two sons. John was lost at sea in November 1824 aged 27 (vagueness in the date suggests the vessel foundered). Above a verse is carved a small, decked vessel, cutter-rigged, probably a coastal trading ship. The dedication is on the reverse.

The memorial to Edward Quayle (d. 1862) at Kirk Braddan, Isle of Man, shows the early introduction of steam to power mail- and passenger-carrying services around the British Isles. 'For twenty years Commander in the service of the Isle of Man Steam Packet Company … as a sailor he was prompt, fearless, faithful and brave as a man, he felt and acted like a man.' The company is still trading to this day, celebrating its 180th anniversary in 2010. Quayle's memorial, a conventional draped urn on a tall plinth, has a pediment carved with a paddle steamer.

Shipbuilders are not neglected. Thomas Fearnie of Arbroath (d. 1813) has a headstone erected by his brother, Alexander. It is inscribed with the hull of a merchant ship in a manner suggesting a plan of the vessel, with a biblical quotation below: 'The carpenter stretcheth out his Rule, he marketh it out with a line, he fitteth it with planes, and he marketh it out with the compass' (Isaiah 44:13).

A shipwright's tools – an adze, an axe and a caulking mallet – are carved in relief on the memorial to Charles Voast (d. 1853) at nearby Kirk Maughold. The smack *Mona Castle* in which Voast traded between the Isle of Man and Liverpool is shown above the tools, with a realistically carved swag of rope draped around the obelisk below the vessel (fig. 56).

The most common symbol of a seagoing life is the anchor.[4] Fouled with

---

[4] The anchor as a religious symbol is discussed in more detail by David J. Stewart, *The Sea Their Graves: An Archaeology of Death and Remembrance in Maritime Culture* (Gainesville, Fl., 2011).

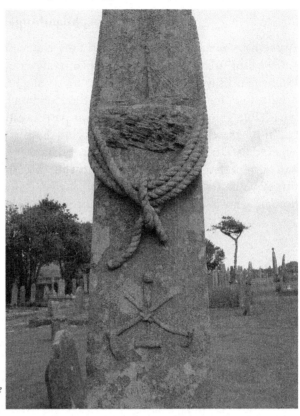

56. *Gravestone of Charles Voast, at St Maughold's Church, Kirk Maughold, Isle of Man.* © *Author.*

a piece of rope it served (and serves) as the badge of the Admiralty and thus might be used in a naval context. As a symbol of the virtue Hope, it fitted into any commemorative context, not necessarily a maritime one. With its attendant female personification, it was particularly popular during the period of the French Revolutionary and Napoleonic Wars. On patch boxes, jewellery and china, the hopeful woman appeared with her anchor (and without Faith, and Charity) gazing out to sea awaiting the return of her loved one – most notably on the porcelain service commissioned from the Worcester porcelain factory for HRH the Duke of Clarence in 1792. (Having then just ended his serving career as a naval officer, he would eventually ascend the throne as the 'sailor king' William IV in 1830.) This version of the image, showing Hope holding a small anchor and pointing to a departing warship to the left, also appears on a now otherwise illegible headstone at Deal. Another variant is carved on the headstone of William Turner, mariner (d. 1807), at St Margaret's church, King's Lynn: here the seated woman appears with her anchor but without the ship. In its most common and in its latest manifestations, the anchor features on its own, sometimes realistically carved as a piece of contemporary ship's equipment.

Trade and philanthropy

As we have already seen, there was a long connection between philanthropy and wealthy urban merchants. Christianity never entirely approved of riches: 'And again I say unto you, it is easier for a camel to go through the eye of a needle, than for a rich man to enter the kingdom of God' (Matthew 19:24). Charitable giving played an important part in establishing a positive reputation for merchants such as Thomas Smythe and passing it down to future generations. The Thomas Smythe Charity that benefits the poor of Tonbridge and surrounding parishes survives to this day. The objects of this philanthropy became more secular after the English Reformation, with the epitaph becoming a way of publicizing and encouraging charitable activity.

Churches and chantries

The pre-Reformation pattern of charity is exemplified by William Canynges of Bristol (1402–74), one of several merchants responsible for the rebuilding of St Mary Redcliffe there.[5] Saying masses for the souls of the deceased was something that the living could do for the dead and altars and tombs might share the same small chantry chapel. Canynges founded two chantries with chaplains in this church and, following the death of his wife, took holy orders and eventually became Dean of Westbury. He had traded with south-west Europe, the Baltic and Iceland, exporting cloth and importing fish and eventually moving into building ships and transporting other merchants' cargo. St Mary Redcliffe contains a restored effigy of Canynges and his wife, Johanna, within a canopy inscribed with an exhortation to pray for their souls: Canynges is clad in the robes of Mayor of Bristol (fig. 57). A second effigy, in the same church, believed to show Canynges in priest's vestments, was moved from Westbury when this collegiate church was dissolved. The only visual reference to his maritime activities is the merchant's mark painted on the front of his tomb – one of many such in this church. Canynges's mark combined the numeral 4 (derived from the Christian *Chi Rho* symbol), a + sign and a heart. This would have been used to identify bags and bales of cargo, sometimes stamped on a lead seal.

---

[5]   The last (Protestant) gothic cathedral built in England was completed as late as 1978 in Liverpool. Gilbert Scott's mighty tower was paid for by William, 1st Baron Vestey, and his brother Edmund Vestey in memory of their father and mother Samuel and Hannah. The Vesteys were the owners of Blue Star Line and major shippers and retailers of frozen meat and other produce. The edifice was nicknamed 'the Vesteys' fire escape'.

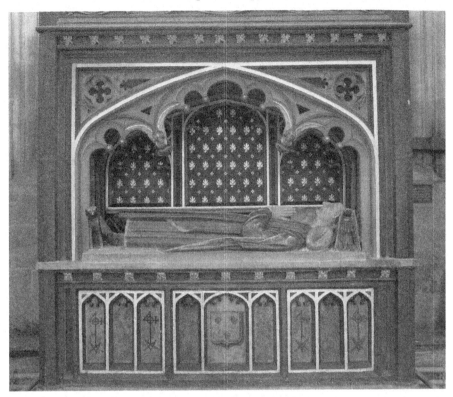

57. *William Canynges, at St Mary Redcliffe, Bristol.* © *Author.*

Improving this world

Thomas Ferres (1568–31) was one of Hull's biggest benefactors. In a manner typical of post-Reformation philanthropy, he became involved in funding municipal good works, from highway repairs to a university scholarship. These were now seen as a proof of grace (the new Protestant theology emphasized salvation by faith rather than salvation by works). Ferres got rich quick during an eighteen-year career as master of a coasting vessel, a circumstance to which not entirely creditable stories are attached. He served as Mayor of Hull from 1620 and warden of Hull Trinity House (a body whose charitable activities extended beyond navigation). In 1859, Trinity House erected a monument to Ferres in Holy Trinity church, Hull, by Thomas Earle (1810–76). The inscription, as befits the era of 'self-help', notes that: 'Born in a humble and obscure station, he raised himself to distinction and honour.' A bust of Ferres on a plinth observes an angel raising a cup to the lips of a seated seaman. Ferres had left an estate to Trinity House, the income to be used for repairing a chapel and aiding poor and infirm sailors.

The local paper interpreted it thus: 'The monument represents an old seaman, who having been shipwrecked, has swam [*sic*] on shore and fainted from exhaustion. A figure of Benevolence is supporting him and pouring into his mouth a draught to restore him to animation. Contemplating the figure of Benevolence is a fine bust of Mr Ald. Ferres, through whose instrumentality, Benevolence is supposed to be doing a Christian work.'[6] Is the author quiz-zically thinking of the administration of strong drink to revive those feeling faint?

The public good

William Hogarth's portrait of Thomas Coram (1668–1751) shows him as the epitome of the kindly, rough-diamond, merchant captain. Coram made his money as a shipbuilder and master, transporting naval stores. Although involved in philanthropic projects such as James Oglethorpe's new American colony of Georgia, and other schemes in the New World, Coram is best known for his creation of London's Foundling Hospital, for abandoned children. At this time donors began to pool their efforts to establish institutions based on the joint-stock company, with the aim of improving society, and Coram was a keen mercantilist who believed in building up the wealth of the nation through colonial trade. The Foundling Hospital was based on similar institutions on the continent and was inspired by Coram's response to the dead and dying abandoned children he saw in south London. He distributed all his wealth during his lifetime and, dying poor, was buried in the vault under the Hospital chapel with the following epitaph in the south cloister:

CAPTAIN THOMAS CORAM
Whose Name will never want a Monument
So long as his Hospital shall subsist,
Was born in the year 1668;
A Man eminent in that most eminent virtue,
The love of Mankind;
Little attentive to his Private Fortune,
And refusing many Opportunities of increasing it,
His Time and Thoughts were continually employed
In endeavours to promote the Public Happiness,
Both in this Kingdom and elsewhere;
Particularly in the Colonies of North America;
And his Endeavours were many times crowned

---

6   *The Hull Packet and East Riding Times*, 1 July 1859.

With the desired Success.
His unwearied Solicitation for above Seventeen Years together
(Which would have baffled the Patience and Industry
Of any Man less zealous in doing Good),
And his application to persons of distinction, of both sexes
Obtained at length the Charter of the Incorporation
(Bearing date of 17th of October, 1739)
FOR THE MAINTAINANCE AND EDUCATION
OF EXPOSED AND DESERTED YOUNG CHILDREN
By which many thousands of Lives
May be preserved to the Public, and employed in a frugal
And honest Course of Industry
He died the 29th March, 1751, in the 84th year of his age;
Poor in Worldly Estate, rich in Good Works,
And was buried, at his own Desire, in the vault underneath this
Chapel (the first here deposited), at the east end thereof,
Many of the Governors and other Gentlemen
Attending the funeral to do Honour to his Memory.
Reader,
Thy Actions will show whether thou art sincere
In the Praises thou mayest bestow on him;
And if thou hast Virtue enough to commend his Virtues,
Forget not to add also the Imitation of them.[7]

The Hospital building was sold to a property developer and demolished in 1926, while the children it housed were moved first to Redhill, Surrey, then to a new building at Berkhamsted. Coram was reburied in the church-yard of St Andrews, Holborn, in 1961. His new tomb, designed by Lord Mottistone,[8] is just inside the entrance with the arms of the Hospital on the front.[9] A solitary weeping putto figure in the style of Henry Cheere, standing in a niche above, was salvaged from the ruins of a City church bombed in the Second World War. Back on the original Hospital site, part of which is now a children's playground, a statue of Coram by William McMillan (1887–1977) stands outside the Foundling Museum and the headquarters of the Thomas Coram Foundation for Children (fig. 58). It is based on the Hogarth portrait and was erected by the Foundation governors in 1963 to replace the

---

7   Frederick Teague Cansick, *The Epitaphs of Middlesex* (1872), vol. 2, p. 235.
8   Henry John Alexander Seeley, 2nd Baron Mottistone (1899–1963), an architect special-izing in the restoration of historic buildings.
9   The charge is a naked babe below a moon and stars, the supporters Nature and Britannia holding a cap of liberty. The crest is a lamb. The motto reads simply 'HELP'.

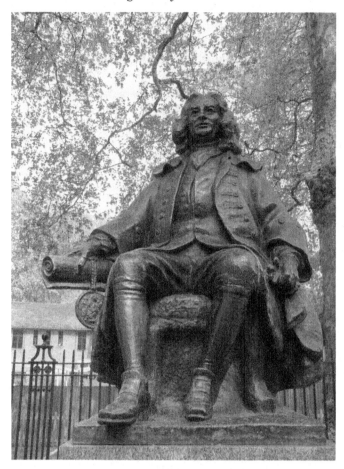

58. *Statue of
Thomas Coram, by
William McMillan,
at Bloomsbury,
London. © Author.*

earlier statue by William Calder Marshall (1813–94) placed in front of the
original building in 1856 but now at Berkhamsted.[10] The inscription claims
him somewhat anachronistically as a 'Captain in the Merchant Navy' and a
'Pioneer in the Cause of Child Welfare'. The Foundation now concentrates
on supporting children within the family. In both statues, and in Hogarth's
portrait, the captain holds the charter of his foundation.

Adventurers and the profit motive

The prominence given to charitable activity on the memorials of the wealthy
should not distract us from the primary aim of sea trade, which was to make
profits for investors. We have seen our merchants involved with a number of

---

[10] Made in stone instead of bronze as an economy measure, Marshall's statue followed the
removal of the Foundation to Berkhamsted in 1927.

corporate bodies. The medieval church disapproved of usury and therefore loans, but a profit on loans could be acceptable as a compensation for risk, and voyages were certainly risky. Partnerships were acceptable as a way of raising capital and sharing risk. During the sixteenth century these expanded into joint-stock companies with shareholders. One of the earliest, the Russia Company, in 1555 secured itself a legal monopoly giving it the sole right to trade with Russia. The East India Company, founded in 1600, was organized along the same lines. The late-medieval merchant companies were associations aimed at regulating trade and, as we have seen, they were and still are heavily involved with charity.

Merchant commander Martin Pring of Bristol, who died in 1626, commanded the last voyage of trade and exploration to set out in Elizabeth I's reign for northern Virginia, securing modern fame as discoverer of Plymouth harbour there. He was involved in other colonial ventures and was later employed by both the Society of Merchant Venturers of Bristol and the East India Company, acting as master of the *New Year's Gift* on the latter's first joint-stock voyage in 1613–14 and commander of the fifth in 1617. These exploits involved him in armed conflict with the Portuguese and Dutch respectively. He was also a freeman of the Virginia Company, holding land there, a brother of Trinity House, and in 1623 was elected a member of the Society of Merchant Venturers of Bristol (his former employers), a body which held a monopoly of the trade with that city. His career combined merchant, explorer, naval commander and privateer.

Pring has a painted alabaster wall memorial at St Stephen's church, Bristol (fig. 59). At the top, within a broken pediment, is the shield of arms of the Bristol Merchant Venturers: its supporters recline in relief at the base – a mermaid with an anchor and a satyr with a scythe. The emblems of mortality, a crossed pick and spade behind an hourglass, are placed between them. The inscription is placed on a black oval tablet with the usual life-as-a-voyage theme.

> His painefull, skillfull trauayles reacht as farre
> As from the Artick to th'Antartick starre.
> Hee made himselfe A shippe, Religion
> His onely compass, and the truth alone
> His guiding Cynosure, faith was his sayles
> His Anchour hope, A hope that neuer fayles.
> His fraught was Charitie, and his returne
> A fruitful practise: In this fatall vrne
> This shippes fair Bulck is lodg'd but ye ritch lading
> Is housd in heaven A hauen never fading

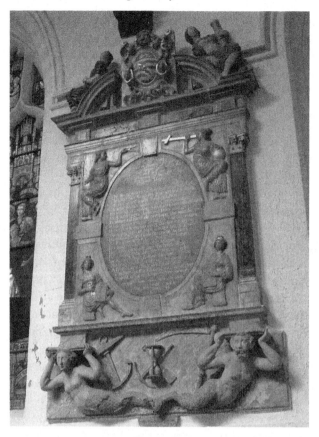

59. *Martin Pring, at St Stephen, Bristol.* © *Author.*

Pring had indeed travelled as far as Japan and North America and, on occasion, made a profit. Personifications of Prudence and Fortitude, virtues necessary for survival in this hazardous maritime world, are carved reclining on the pediment as described in the inscription: 'Prudence and fortitude ore topp this toombe'. The mermaid and satyr also represent, respectively, Hope and Time. The inscription is surrounded in relief by female figures representing grammar, mathematics, navigation and astronomy: Navigation holds a globe and dividers, Astronomy a globe and a backstaff.[11]

Sweet teeth

St Peter's church, Bristol, remains in ruins after being destroyed by wartime bombing. The tomb of Robert Aldworth (d. 1634) was comparatively little damaged but remained exposed to the elements until 1958, when it was

[11] Jean Wilson, 'Ethics Girls', *Church Monuments: Journal of the Church Monuments Society*, vol. 13 (1998), p. 93.

removed. By then it was irretrievably damaged.[12] Aldworth, Mayor of Bristol in 1609, had been another prominent member of the Society of Merchant Venturers. Its heraldic satyr decorated Aldworth's house, which stood near St Peter's and was another casualty of the Second World War. Aldworth's pioneering sugar refinery (the first in Bristol) stood adjacent. His monument, fourteen feet high, incorporated two kneeling effigies of Aldworth and his wife under two of three arches supported by Corinthian columns: the third arch was filled with a later inscription tablet to other members of the family. Figures representing Faith and Charity stood at the top with the arms of the Bristol Merchant Venturers. The panels on the base of the plinth were carved with three ships, with Aldworth's merchant's mark between them, and the guild badges of three barrels for a trader in rum and five sugar loaves for a sugar boiler. During the early seventeenth century this sugar would have been imported from Spanish and Portuguese colonies, but England, like other European nations, aspired to produce such tropical imports on its own territories.

The Atlantic slave trade ... and its Manx connections

By the end of the seventeenth century sugar was imported from large, slave-cultivated plantations in the British West Indies, part of a triangular trade which sent out home goods to exchange for enslaved Africans, rounded up under European encouragement by West African middlemen on that coast. Dire conditions on the plantations kept up the demand for imported slaves, in spite of the heavy mortality of the infamous 'middle passage' (the outward, transatlantic leg of a triangular voyage). The economic tentacles of sugar reached into all corners of national life, even the financial interests of the most philanthropic merchants. The trade in slaves had begun in the sixteenth century and remained a legal monopoly of the Royal African Company until 1698, when it was opened up to other private merchants. After that it spread from London to Bristol and Liverpool, and other regional ports. But by the end of the eighteenth century there was an increasing campaign for abolition, and however 'respectable' the trade had previously been it was not an activity one wished advertised on one's memorial.

There are always exceptions. When Manxman Hugh Crow died in 1829, he left £200 to his executors for 'the expenses attending the preparing for printing and publication a sketch of my life'.[13] To their embarrassment, this turned out to be an unabashed account of his career in the slave trade, in

---

12 Reece Winstone, *Bristol in the 1920s* (Chichester, 1971), pl. 33.
13 TNA PROB11/1756/417. Crow left £50 towards the purchase of a burial plot, preparation of a vault and the erection of a tomb.

which 'mind your eye, Crow' nevertheless shows himself in a good light.[14] He had prospered and bought a cottage between Maughold and Ramsey, which he improved as a small Georgian house and renamed Crow Villa. The semi-independent status of the Isle of Man made it an entrepôt for the East Indian cloths and other trade goods which were picked up by Liverpool vessels outward bound for Africa, and thus avoided customs duties.

Hugh Crow made his career in Liverpool but is buried in Maughold churchyard with a neo-classical tombstone in Welsh slate, inscribed: 'Captain CROW commanded the ships WILL, CERES, MARY and KITTY'S AMELIA with much credit to himself ... he also fought several actions with the enemy for which he received repeated marks of approbation of the merchants and underwriters of London and Liverpool. An honest man's the noblest work of God.' It also commemorates his brother William Crow, the commander of the slaver *Charlotte*, who drowned in the West African port of Bonny (now in Nigeria) on 3 February 1800.

Lancashire slave traders

On the mainland, the slave trade also thrived briefly in Lancaster. The first ship sailed in 1736 attracting the least well-established local merchants into the business. Thomas Hinde (1720–98) made four voyages to Africa in the *Jolly Batchelor*, building up his share in the vessel and eventually retiring as a merchant. With the slave trade everywhere else in decline, he moved his operations to Liverpool in the 1780s, where the family remained active in the trade until abolition. Hinde's memorial in Lancaster Priory, a plain marble wall tablet in the shape of a sarcophagus with anthemion acroteria, commemorates his family members but makes no mention of anything else. Another slave captain is commemorated on a slate ledger behind St John's church in Lancaster. John Nunns died on 4 October 1807 in the last year of the trade and within a few days' sail of Trinidad, in command of *The Johns*. The crews and commanders of slavers were very vulnerable to the mosquito-borne diseases of the tropics. The oddly named ship was originally the embodiment of a partnership between John Lowther, John Nunns and John Cumpsty. The partners together had owned four vessels, *The Johns* making six consecutive voyages to Africa.

Lancaster remains the largely Georgian city it was then. Liverpool, however, in spite of the dire warnings of the anti-abolitionists, continued to develop and prosper. As the port area industrialized, so the Georgian churches in the city centre lost their congregations and were redeveloped with the loss

---

[14] A joke – said to be an instruction from the owner of his ship – in reference to the fact that Hugh Crow had only one eye.

of their memorials. Most of those that remained were destroyed in Second World War bombing. St James's, Toxteth, still survives and St Nicholas was rebuilt but without its wall tablets. This removed almost all memorials associated with the slave trade, though some were recorded beforehand. The now notorious inscription to Captain Thomas Hughes, who died in 1777 aged 45, is variously attributed to St James's or St Nicholas: 'He was many years a Commander in the Africa Trade which office he filled with great industry and integrity. An affectionate husband and a tender father, an honest man.'

After the slave trade

Liverpool's continuing prosperity was in part due to continuing trade with Africa. The West African place names on seamen's gravestones along the north-west coast of England are an indicator that this was so. A certain amount of illicit slaving still went on well into the nineteenth century but most African trade was in legal goods, a trend already growing before abolition as traders could see the way the wind was blowing. This traffic in dyewoods, beeswax and skins was dominated by former slave traders who had the necessary West African contacts. From 1820 it shifted increasingly to palm oil and timber. The former was used in machine lubrication, before the introduction of mineral oil, and in the manufacture of soap and candles, laying the foundations of the later big shipping and manufacturing companies such as the Elder Dempster Line and Lever Brothers. This continuing African trade explains the perhaps otherwise puzzling inscription on a headstone which stands outside St George's church, Douglas, Isle of Man: 'ERECTED IN MEMORY OF WILLIAM CLAGUE. Carpenter of this Town who died at Bonney on Board of the Oscar; 3rd of August 1837. Aged 46 Years. on his 19th voyage to Africa.'

Lessons

The memorials erected to abolitionists such as Wilberforce, or to former African servants by their masters, fall outside the scope of this book. The 2007 bicentenary of abolition in a multicultural society saw a variety of responses, mostly rather uncomfortable ones. The first memorial to the victims of the slave trade was erected in 2005 at Lancaster by the Slave Trades Arts Memorial Project, a group of local teachers and academics. The memorial by Kevin Dalton-Johnson, a British/Jamaican artist, employs mixed media in a rather edgy popular style. It is made of Peakamoor stone in the shape of a ship's side, with decks of clear acrylic with the words 'wealth', 'rum', 'mahogany', 'cotton', 'sugar' and 'slaves' written on them. The top is inlaid with coins, the bottom with the well-known plan of the slave ship *Brooks* (or commonly but wrongly,

Brookes). The acrylic blocks are attached by steel bars to a stone slab and a steel plate listing twenty Lancaster voyages, with details of captain, name of ship and the number of slaves embarked. Thomas Hinde, in the inappropriately named *Jolly Batchelor*, is at the top of the list and John Nunns at the bottom. The whole stands on a plinth surfaced with an inlaid mosaic of the Atlantic triangular trade, with three-dimensional moulded figures of enslaved Africans placed on it.

Similar memorial initiatives were implemented in London, the original centre of the slave trade, including the commemoration of two abolitionists who were also seafarers. A sculpture by Michael Visocchi was unveiled by Archbishop Desmond Tutu in 2008 at Fen Court in the City, incorporating columns suggesting sugar cane and Lemn Sissay's poem 'The Gilt of Cain' (fig. 60). The memorial is near that of John Newton (1725–1807), a slave-trading captain but later clergyman and hymn writer (not least of 'Amazing Grace'), whose autobiography is one of religious conversion. His lowest point, as described in the epitaph he wrote for himself, was as an 'Infidel and Libertine, A servant of slaves in Africa'. Newton's conversion came in stages and he made four slaving voyages after escaping his own personal African servitude. Later in life, when he had given up the sea, he lent his personal support to abolition, writing a tract entitled *Thoughts upon the African Slave Trade* in 1788. For Newton and his fellow evangelicals it was all about a personal relationship with God, faith rather than works: 'Custom, example and interest had blinded my eyes. I did it ignorantly ...'[15]

A memorial to Olaudah Equiano (d. 1797), whose autobiography under his European alias of Gustavus Vassa revealed the horrors of the middle passage to a wide readership, was unveiled in St Margaret's, Westminster, in 2009. Enslaved in his youth, Equiano worked as a seaman before finally buying his freedom. He was baptized in St Margaret's in 1759. The wall tablet by Marcia Bennett Male deploys appropriately elegant lettering to good effect in a manner reminiscent of the title-page of a book.

Voyaging East

The Atlantic, with its triangular trade routes linking Europe, Africa and the Americas, was not the only arena of European trade. The products of South Asia and the Far East offered an even more enticing prospect. The Honourable East India Company, set up as a joint-stock operation to trade in spices with Sumatra and Java, was granted a charter and legal monopoly by Queen Elizabeth in 1600. Facing European rivalry in the East Indies, it obtained

---

[15] *The Works of the Rev. John Newton* (Newhaven, 1824), vol. 4, p. 72.

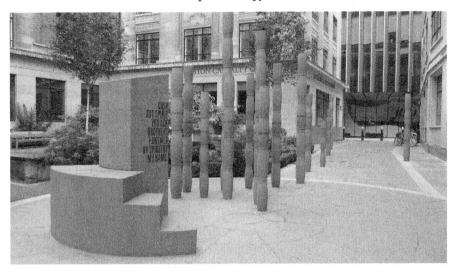

60. *'The Gilt of Cain', by Michael Visocchi, at Fen Court, City of London. © Author.*

a toehold in India. There, the company established factories (as its trading posts were known), eventually becoming a state within a state. Its maritime service, which manned the great armed merchantmen trading to India and China, was second in prestige only to the Royal Navy. From 1781, the officers wore uniform and this was resented by the Navy proper: 'there was no service equal to it, or more difficult to get into, requiring great interest'.[16] However a memorial at St David's chapel, Llanwrtyd, proclaims:

> Sacred to the memory of John Lloyd, eldest son of Rees Lloyd of Dinas and Captain of the Honbl. East India Company's ship MANSHIP who left this, his native parish at the age of sixteen, without friends or interest, but by good conduct and perseverance acquired both: and after 32 years of active naval service and 12 voyages to India in the course of which he twice suffered shipwreck and cruel imprisonment in the hands of Tipoo Sultan of Mysore, returning to display the same active and enterprising spirit in promoting the welfare and cultivating the resources of his native country. He died Feby. 1818, aged 70.[17]

[16] Robert William Eastwick, *A Master mariner: being the life and times of Captain Robert William Eastwick* (1908), p. 41.
[17] *Chowkidar* (British Association for Cemeteries in South Asia), vol. 6, no. 6 (autumn 1993), p. 115.

Officers could carry a considerable quantity of their own privately traded goods in Company ships and prospered accordingly. Until 1796 the position of captain could be purchased, inherited or sold. They are commemorated by the same sort of marble wall tablets as the more junior naval officers of the later eighteenth century, enlivened by accounts of shipwreck or naval actions.

From 1686 the East India Company ran its own local navy in the East, the Bombay Marine, initially deployed against the fleets of local rulers on that (western India) coast, whom the British referred to as Angrian pirates. William James, a commander in this force, captured four Maratha forts at Suvarnadrug in 1755. Returning to England he was awarded a baronetcy and became a director and later chairman of the East India Company. After his death in 1783 his wife erected a castellated folly on Shooter's Hill, Kent (but now in the Royal Borough of Greenwich). As with many such structures it was within distant sight of their home and has a commemorative inscription to him on it: though hardly a replica of the forts he captured, it became known as Severndroog Castle and, now a charming feature in tall woodland, stands to this day.

Many Company servants did not return home. Job Charnock set up a settlement at Sutanuti in Bengal, later known as Calcutta, where the European burial ground is now known as South Park Street Cemetery. Its mud-brick and plaster memorials have not weathered well but the inscriptions were recorded in *The Bengal Obituary or a record to Perpetuate the Memory of Departed Worth*, published in 1851. The British, sensing perhaps the impermanence of their presence in India, were scrupulous inscription recorders. Charnock's Moghul-style three-storied tomb is one of the earliest there. There are also many memorials to members of the Bengal Pilot Service, as the port of Calcutta was situated 126 miles from the sea, up the Hooghly River.

The 'country trade'

The Bengal Obituary records two men – Richard Welsh and George Silverlock – who died from injuries sustained during the explosion of three barrels of gunpowder on 19 March 1813. Both were officers of the 'country' ship *Eliza*. Country ships traded in the coastal waters of India and neighbouring countries. They were privately owned, sometimes with Asian proprietors, and from 1790 operated under licence from the East India Company. Robert William Eastwick (1772–1865) left both a lengthy epitaph on his memorial in All Saints church, Lower Edmonton, and a ghosted autobiography. His wall tablet is in conventional, neo-classical, naval style with guns, four flags and an anchor carved above the inscription. A small shield of arms is placed at the top of the black limestone mount. The epitaph stresses his very brief period in Royal Navy and East India Company ships, and his other public services.

Eastwick had influence in the shape of his wife's rich uncle, who on two occasions found him a position on an East Indiaman. He initially concluded that he did not have the necessary capital to flourish and could not live on the pay. A second opportunity arising, he made one voyage but, not wanting to start again as a junior, left the vessel in Bombay and spent much of his subsequent career in country ships, with some involvement in the opium trade. He was shipwrecked three times and lost three fortunes. The Angrian pirates were still a problem and Eastwick's commercial activities were threatened by French privateers based in the Ile de France (now Mauritius). During the cruise from there into the Bay of Bengal by the 42-gun French frigate, *La Forte*, early in 1799, trade was paralysed and the cost of insurance rocketed. Eastwick's was one of eight country ships captured by *La Forte*, as he was returning to Calcutta and looking out for a pilot: 'I cannot describe my feelings of mortification as I saw the boarding party put foot on my deck.'[18] He was not insured.

Defending trade

During the night of 28 February 1799, *La Forte* fell in with the British 38-gun frigate *Sybille*, herself a captured French ship. As she had doused her lights, the French mistook her for another merchantman until engaged by her at close range. Captain Beaulieu of *La Forte* was killed and the English captain, Edward Cooke, mortally wounded, dying at Calcutta on 23 May. Eastwick was freed but the Navy declined to recapture his ship and he had to borrow the capital to buy another vessel from contacts that trusted him.

Cooke was buried at South Park Street Cemetery, where his grave is marked by a stone column. In 1806 the East India Company erected, in Westminster Abbey, a monument commemorating this fallen defender of British trade in India (fig. 61). The action is shown in relief on the base, flanked by an Indian elephant and Bengal tiger. Above in higher relief, Cooke clasps the flag and points heavenward, supported by a muscular kneeling seaman, while in the sky above, Victory offers a wreath. The artist was John Bacon junior.[19]

Filling a vacuum

In 1833, the East India Company finally lost its remaining trade monopolies. The Green and Wigram families then owned the well-known shipbuilding

---

[18] Eastwick, *A Master mariner*, p. 134.
[19] The design is in the Victoria and Albert Museum (VAM8417.7), reproduced in John Physick, *Designs for English Sculpture, 1680–1860* (1969), p. 177. Bacon also produced a version for a military memorial.

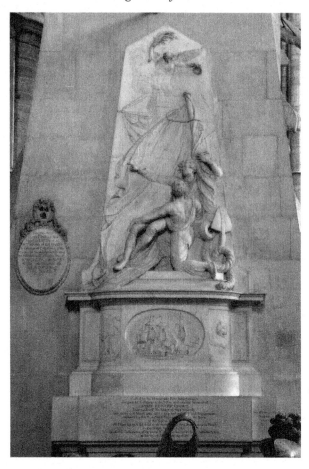

61. *Captain Edward Cooke
RN, by John Baker junior,
at Westminster Abbey.
© Dean and Chapter of
Westminster.*

yard at Blackwall which had built East Indiamen for the company since the
mid-seventeenth century. After 1834 the Green family moved into the vacuum
left by the demise of the Company as a commercial monopoly, continuing
as shipbuilders and owners trading to India and Australia. Richard Green
gradually took over both the building and managing of ships from his father,
George (d. 1849), and both took an active interest in charitable activity in the
East End, in particular the Sailors' Home and Poplar Hospital. Following
Richard's death in 1863, his associates set up a committee to erect a statue of
the local benefactor in bronze on a granite plinth (fig. 62). The sculptor was
Edward William Wyon (1811–85) who had already made a bust of Green
for the family. The shipowner is shown seated, with an open book in his lap
(probably the Bible, which is how his pious father was also twice painted).[20]

---

[20]   See NMM BHC2725 and PAH5558: both are buried at Trinity chapel, Poplar, which
George built.

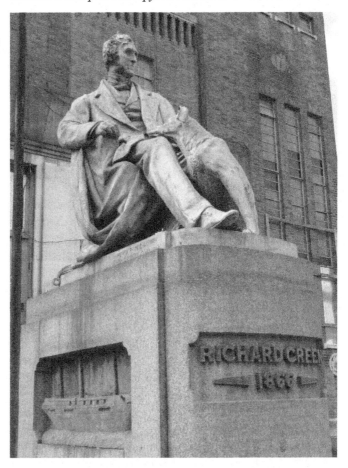

*62. Richard Green,
by Edward William
Wyon, at Poplar,
London. © Author.*

Unmarried, his companion is his Newfoundland dog, Hector, who rests his head on his master's knee and gazes adoringly into his face. Two bronze reliefs are set into the base, one of 'the first ship which Mr Green dispatched after the East India Company's charter became extinct; and on the other side of the pedestal a like bas-relief of a frigate which he was building for the Spanish Government at the time of his death'.[21] The former vessel was *Seringapatam* (1837, the first of Richard's so-called 'Blackwall frigates'); the latter, the *Arapiles*, was launched in 1864. Like all of Green's ships to that date, she was wooden but was altered during building to a broadside ironclad.

---

[21] *Illustrated London News*, 19 May 1866, p. 494.

Steam and Suez

A bronze statue stands in Railway Street, Chatham, clutching a map and pointing to the north, frequently wearing a traffic cone on its head. The inscription on the plinth identifies the subject as: 'Thomas Waghorn [1800–50] founder of the overland route ...'

The last years of the East India Company's monopoly saw the advent of steam-powered ships and their challenge to sailing vessels on the long-standing route to the East via St Helena and the Cape of Good Hope. This was first navigated by the paddle steamer *Enterprise* in 1825 but proved beyond normal practicalities for the time. The overland route favoured by merchants in Bombay was initiated in 1829 by the Bombay Government. Steam services ran between Bombay and Suez carrying passengers and mail. There was a second steam link through the Mediterranean, and in the middle a desert crossing by camel train. Waghorn had had a short career as a junior naval officer and a stint in the Bengal Pilot Service, during which he noted the efficacy of steam in improving access along the Hooghly to the port of Calcutta. He promoted various schemes to link Britain and India by steam vessel (initially via the Cape) and eventually set up as an agent, organizing passengers' journeys through Egypt, across the desert to Suez. A difficult character but a brilliant publicist, Waghorn's business ventures ultimately failed and he died with only £200 to his name in 1850.

Waghorn nevertheless impressed the builder of the Suez Canal, Ferdinand de Lesseps, who, when it opened from 1869, had a bronze bust of him by sculptor Vital Dubray erected, overlooking its southern entrance at what was then Port Tewfik. There it remained until destroyed during the Suez crisis of 1956. De Lesseps was also on the statue committee which met at the Mansion House, London, in 1884, with a proposed budget of £3000 for a British monument to him. This was shortly after the British occupation of Egypt in 1882 and Waghorn had acquired the status of neglected genius and 'explorer' or 'pioneer' of the route; neither claim really standing up to scrutiny. The statue by Henry Hugh Armstead (1828–1905) was erected in Waghorn's native Chatham in 1888 and unveiled by Lord Northbrook. The projected site was changed during the planning stage, with the result that the figure no longer pointed east, as originally intended, but north.

The age of sail was then drawing to a close. Old monopolies had been abolished in the name of free competition, great Victorian steam-shipping lines like P&O circled the globe, supplied by colonial coaling stations and carrying the mail and passengers formerly the preserve of the Post Office packets. The memorials to their employees show some pride in the corporate culture which these firms had adopted from the Navy but little quirkiness or individualism.

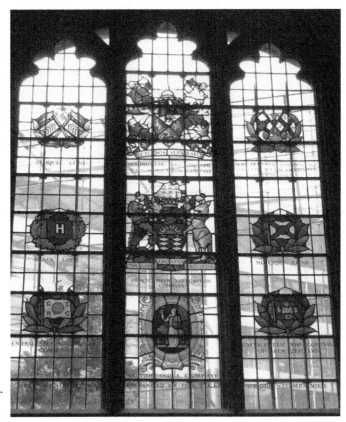

63. *Armorial window showing the badges of the companies in the P&O Group, at All Hallows-by-the-Tower, City of London.* © *Author.*

Decline

By the 1970s old-established, family-owned British shipping companies were falling prey to takeovers and 'flagging out'. From the 1970s onwards there was a rapid decline in British-owned and crewed merchant tonnage, although even today London remains a centre of marine services such as insurance and ship-broking. A mariner's chapel was established in All Hallows-by-the-Tower when it was rebuilt following damage in the 1940s London blitz, conveniently close to the Merchant Navy Memorial on Tower Hill. An armorial window displays the full coats of arms of the Peninsular and Oriental Steam Navigation Company and the Oriental Steam Navigation Company; and they are flanked by the cap badges of smaller companies in the P&O group (fig. 63). P&O was eventually to move out of deep-water shipping to become a port and ferry operator and in 2006 was taken over by Dubai Ports World, under whom it continues to operate as a subsidiary.

Corporate identity is ever-shifting. In London, architectural sculpture, setting in stone the nature of a business in the walls of its head office, has given way to anonymous steel and glass. Free-standing sculpture still thrives at street level. The iconography of commerce also changed during the nineteenth century. In the decorative scheme of the Albert Memorial (completed in 1875), Commerce is shown accompanied by Agriculture, Engineering and Manufacture to reflect Britain's new role as an exporter of goods. Britain's present-day service economy still requires a shipping sector, as most goods continue to be imported by sea. In spite of this, present-day British-owned and flagged commercial shipping is a low-profile industry, its UK-based seafaring personnel dwindling in numbers. Philanthropy by entrepreneurs is still a popular way to enshrine individual memory, with an emphasis on cultural and artistic patronage. Much continuing maritime commemoration is nostalgic in tone but the spectacular tragedy of marine disaster can still catapult shipping into public consciousness once more.

6

Lost at sea: maritime accidents

Whatever the motives for travel by sea, it was a dangerous undertaking: death in various types of accident was all too common for seafarers and passengers until recent times. Statistics published in 1885 revealed merchant seafaring as the most hazardous occupation in Britain. Some vessels foundered, sometimes without trace, in mid-ocean; some were wrecked on shore, or sank following collision or explosions. The advent of steam brought its own hazards, but sailing ships were even more dangerous. Seafarers might be killed in personal accidents on board or in the loss or capsize of small boats. Although major passenger disasters such as the loss of the *Herald of Free Enterprise* (1987) still occur, safety on UK merchant ships improved throughout the twentieth century with advances in technology and procedures.[1]

During the eighteenth century, the loss of naval vessels was commemorated by a series of important monuments. These were prestigious ships whose officers might be drawn from the social elite. Although, in a disaster, the elite were literally in the same boat as everybody else, early commemoration was about significant individuals dying in a common catastrophe.

Storm

An early shipwreck memorial at St Mary and St Lawrence church, Great Waltham, Essex, commemorates Hugh Everard, who went down with the *Restoration* when it was wrecked and lost with all hands on the Goodwin Sands, during the Great Storm of 26–27 November 1703 (Old Style) (fig. 64). Hugh was the second son of Sir Hugh Everard whose family had owned the nearby manor of Langleys for 200 years and had established the church as their mausoleum. Five naval ships in all were lost on the Goodwins that night in weather of exceptional ferocity at the cost of around 1086 lives.[2]

---

1 Stephen E. Roberts, 'Fatal Work-Related Accidents in UK Merchant Shipping from 1919 to 2005', *Occupational Medicine*, vol. 58, 2008, pp. 129–37.
2 William Laird Clowes, *The Royal Navy: A History from the Earliest Times to 1900*, vol. 2, p. 389.

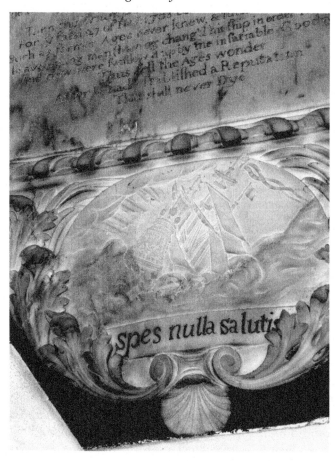

64. *Hugh Everard, at
Great Waltham, Essex
(detail). © Author.*

Among the casualties, Everard's commemoration is exceptional.[3] Only about 15 at the time of the disaster, he had already killed his first man: 'A Descent being made into Spain, His choice and request put his courage upon action, Being the third yt landed, and ye Spaniard horse coming upon them, The Commander fell by his hand, And ye sword of the man of war grac'd the side of ye young stripling.'[4] His reputation, it claimed, would never die. The memorial adopts that standard feature of the shipwreck memorial, the relief of the sinking vessel, with 'Spes nulla salutis' (no hope of safety) inscribed below. Above the inscription, a hand in relief clasps a sword and a trumpet proclaims Everard's bravery to the passing reader. The fortunes of naval war were not

3   Admiral Basil Beaumont, another casualty (in his flagship, *Mary*), has a more modest memorial at Stoughton, Leicestershire.
4   This refers to the landing at Rota, 15 August 1702, part of a general and unsuccessful attack on Cadiz.

kind to the Everard family. A second younger son, Morton Everard, died on the *Hampshire*, Captain Henry Maynard, during an attack on a convoy escort by the French in 1709. The eldest son, Sir Richard, succeeded to the baronetcy in 1705/6, but had to sell his debt-encumbered estate, which was bought by a wealthy City merchant in 1710. He became Governor of North Carolina, and during the next generation the title died out.

Navigational error

Sir Cloudesley Shovell (1650–1707) had been caught at the mouth of the Thames during the Great Storm but had kept his ship, *Triumph*, from dragging her anchor and being blown onto the Galloper Sands by ordering her mainmast to be cut down, thereby reducing wind resistance.

In autumn 1707 he was in command of a squadron of twenty-one British ships returning from service in the Mediterranean. On 21 October they had reached the shallower water at the entrance to the Channel but the weather was foggy and they were uncertain of their precise position. Visibility was still bad the following evening when they found themselves in all-too-close proximity to the rocks of the Isles of Scilly. Most of the fleet escaped but Shovell's flagship *Association*, with the *Eagle* and *Romney*, were lost with all hands excepting a quartermaster from *Romney*. Francis Percy and twenty-three or twenty-four people escaped in a boat from the wreck of the fireship *Firebrand*. Shovell may also have left his ship in the same way before she broke up, as his body (surprisingly little damaged in view of the surrounding rocks) was washed up at Porth Hellick Cove. The bodies of his stepsons Sir John and James Narborough were found nearby, with that of the captain of *Association* and a pet dog. Initially buried with the other casualties above high-water mark, Shovell's body was disinterred three days later, identified, disembowelled on the Scillies, embalmed at Plymouth and returned to London for final reburial in Westminster Abbey.

Queen Anne paid for the funeral, only three naval commanders since the Restoration having been previously accorded this honour. The admiral's monument was made, on the orders of the Queen, by Grinling Gibbons and his workshop (fig. 65). The inscription is within a curtained baldachino with a crest on top. There are two columns on either side above which are cherubs holding shields of arms. The reclining figure of Shovell is placed below the inscription tablet, wearing Roman armour and periwig and wrapped in a cloak. Drops of laurel and oak are visible behind the columns. On the base, a relief shows the wreck of *Association*, the ship being under reduced canvas and wearing the Union flag at the main, denoting Shovell's rank as Admiral of the Fleet. The sterns of five ships, representing the remainder of the squadron, are seen making their escape to the left. The scene is flanked by panels with naval trophies. The

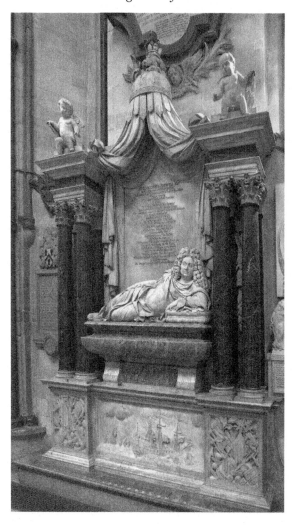

65. *Sir Cloudesley Shovell,
by Grinling Gibbons, at
Westminster Abbey.* © *Dean
and Chapter of Westminster.*

design pretty much follows that adopted by Gibbons for previous monuments erected to members of the nobility, notably that of the first Duke of Beaufort (1629–1700) at Great Badminton. The oak and laurel branches shown on the right-hand trophy panel are deeply undercut in Gibbons's characteristic style.

Although the death of Sir Cloudesley after a distinguished naval career was the occasion of general grief, only a couple of years later his monument displeased the writer Joseph Addison (1672–1719). In an essay published in 1711 in which he wanders the Abbey musing upon mortality, he singles it out for especial criticism:

Instead of the brave rough *English* admiral, which was the distinguishing character of that plain gallant man, he is represented on his tomb by the figure of

a Beau, dressed in a long periwig, and reposing himself upon velvet cushions under a canopy of state. The inscription is answerable to the monument; for instead of celebrating the many remarkable actions he had performed in the service of his country, it acquaints us only with the manner of his death, in which it was impossible for him to reap any honour.[5]

Addison here objects to the aristocratic character of the memorial, and its failure to project Shovell, 'a brave man of humble birth', as a national hero. It also sets Shovell's navigational error in stone, although the designs of the two trophy panels, which almost exclusively show weaponry, to an extent counterbalance the disaster in the centre.

The Narborough brothers were buried near where they died in the Old Town church, St Mary's, with some of the other officers. Their mother Elizabeth, wife of Admiral Sir John Narborough senior, erected a monument at St Clements, Knowlton, in Kent. This more modest marble tomb chest has two weeping cherubs flanking the inscription tablet, which has two flaming urns on top. A copy of the Gibbons relief in Westminster Abbey is placed below, flanked by two coats of arms.

> Great was the Loss of these two Young Gentlemen whose
> Obliging Conversation, Constant Friendship & Religious
> Duty were the admiration of all that knew them. They were
> Ingenious, Virtuous, Pious,
> Happy in their inclinations, Happy in their Fortunes,
> Unhappy only in their Fate.
> The Ardency of their Affection had this Peculiar in it,
> That their Mutual Impatience of living long Asunder
> was the great Occasion of their Dying both Together.
> The elder in the 23rd and the younger in the 22nd Year of their Age.

It ends with the Latin phrase 'Nescit Naufragium Virtus' (virtue does not know shipwreck).

Francis Percy (who as previously mentioned survived the disaster) served forty-seven years in the Navy, also surviving an explosion in the *Carlisle* in 1700 and being dangerously wounded in 1704. He died, a gouty 67, in 1742, and is commemorated by a marble wall tablet at St Margaret's, Rochester, listing his various exploits and carved with skulls, cherubs' heads and garlands (common imagery at this period).

---

5   Joseph Addison, *Spectator*, 30 March 1711.

On the rocks

The Westminster Abbey memorial to Sir John Balchen (1670–1744) echoes that of Shovell in depicting his flagship, *Victory*, breaking up on the rocks of the Channel Islands on 7 October 1744. The relief is placed on a white marble sarcophagus, flanked by naval trophies, this time including many navigational instruments, with the Balchen arms above. The memorial, erected in the spring of 1746, in addition commemorates the death of Balchen's son George, also a naval officer, who died in the West Indies in 1745. The monument was commissioned by his widow Susannah from Peter Scheemakers (1691–1781) who produced Abbey memorials to Captain Aubrey Beauclerk and Admiral Sir Charles Wager at much the same time. The tone of the epitaph is more aggrieved than patriotic:

> … in the Year 1744 being sent out Commander in Chief of the Combined Fleets
> of England & Holland
> to cruise on the Enemy was on his return Home in his MAJESTY'S Ship the
> VICTORY,
> lost in the Channel by a Violent Storm, From which sad Circumstance
> of his Death we may learn that neither the greatest Skill, Judgement or Experience
> join'd to the most firm unshaken resolution can resist the fury of the winds
> and waves, and we are taught from the passages of his Life which was fill'd
> with Great and Gallant Actions but ever accompanied with adverse Gales of
> Fortune, that the Brave, the Worthy, and the Good Man meets not always his
> reward
> in this World. Fifty Eight Years of faithfull and painful Services he had pass'd
> when being just retired to the Government of Greenwich Hospital to wear out
> the Remainder of his Days, He was once more, and for the last time call'd
> out by his KING & Country whose interests he ever preferr'd to his own and
> his unwearied Zeal for their Service ended only his Death which weighty
> misfortune to his Afflicted Family became heighten'd by many aggravating
> Circumstances attending it, yet amidst their Grief had they the mournful
> Consolation to find his Gracious and Royal Master, mixing his concern with
> the General lamentations of the Publick, for the Calamitous Fate of so Zealous
> so Valiant and so able a Commander …

A few years previously, Balchen had expressed annoyance over the prestige enjoyed by other officers and their gains in prize money. During the spring of 1744 he had been appointed Governor of Greenwich Hospital and awarded a generous pension. On 1 June he took up active command again, aged 74, in order to relieve a fleet of store ships blockaded in the River Tagus by a French squadron under Admiral de Rochambeau. The French withdrew in the face of Balchen's superior force and, its mission accomplished, Balchen's squadron returned to England. The flagship *Victory* became separated from the rest of the fleet during a gale in the Channel and disappeared. Her loss took place at night and there were neither witnesses nor survivors. Wreckage identified as belonging to the ship was washed ashore on Alderney in the Channel Islands but no bodies were recovered. The actual site of the wreck was not discovered until 2008, off Torbay and outside territorial waters.

Lady Balchen was awarded a royal pension of £500 per annum in early November and the epitaph expresses suitable gratitude for the concern of the monarch. The press, which had been keenly following Sir John's movements during 1744, subjected his widow to distressing misinformation in the weeks following his death. The *Daily Advertiser* twice reported that Sir John had arrived safely, first in Portsmouth and later in Plymouth, and the *Daily Gazetteer* falsely reported the death of Lady Balchen herself in its 12 November edition – 'aggravating Circumstances' indeed.

Toll for the brave

Other hazards threatened the sailing navy. Ships' gun decks were not partitioned, were liable to ingress of water if the gun ports were open, and were filled with heavy cannon on wheeled carriages. This could potentially lead to a catastrophic loss of stability.

Early on 29 August 1782 the 100-gun *Royal George* was anchored at Spithead, heeled over to enable a plumbing repair on the high side of the ship, with stores being loaded through open gun ports near the water on the other side. Rising wind sent water into the open decks and the ship capsized with the loss of about 900 lives, including visiting women and children. Rear-Admiral Richard Kempenfelt (1718–82), of whom she was flagship, went down with her. Commemoration of this event, not least in William Cowper's poem 'On the Loss of the Royal George' ('Toll for the brave …'), shows a new interest in the other casualties of the disaster, perhaps stimulated by the growth of evangelical religion and humanitarianism towards the end of the century. A widows and orphans fund was set up, to which Gustavus Adolphus Kempenfelt, brother of Richard, contributed 200 guineas. *The Gentleman's Magazine* records a memorial marking the grave of thirty-five unnamed casualties in St Mary's churchyard, Portsea, erected by the parish: 'Reader, with solemn thought, Survey the grave And reflect on the untimely death of thy fellow mortals: and whilst As a man, a Briton and a patriot, Thou readest the melancholy narrative, Drop a tear for thy Country's Loss.'[6] This memorial by

---

6   *Gentleman's Magazine*, May 1783, pp. 357–58.

James Hay is now lost. It showed a pyramid in relief, flanked by flaming urns, with reliefs of naval trophies on either side of the base. A plainer memorial stood nearby whose now illegible inscription identified it as: 'A testimony of sympathy for the unfortunates who perished by the sinking of the HMS Royal George, August 29 1782. Erected by one who was a stranger both to officers and the ship's company.'[7]

The disaster continued to resonate in the collective memory. The Westminster Abbey memorial to Kempenfelt was erected with a bequest from his brother, Gustavus Adolphus, who died in 1808 and is buried nearby in the family vault in St Margaret's, Westminster.[8] The sculptor was John Bacon junior and the design, carried out in white marble, shows an original variation on the sinking vessel theme (fig. 66).[9] A broken column stands on an inscribed plinth with the family arms on the base. On the column, a relief shows the masts of the ship sticking out of the water – still with Kempenfelt's flag as Rear-Admiral on the mizzen mast. Above it, his soul rises upwards towards an angel who offers a heavenly crown and a palm branch. An evangelical Christian, Kempenfelt supported the reintroduction of Christian observance in the fleet. The memorial also acknowledges the philanthropy of his brother, Gustavus.

The wreck lay in relatively shallow water, with masts originally poking above the surface, and was a hazard to navigation. Some guns were salvaged in 1782 and most of the remainder were recovered between 1834 and 1836 by Charles Anthony Deane, using pioneering air-pumped diving helmets to achieve this task. Three years later the remains of the wreck were blown up. Some of the wood was used to make commemorative souvenirs – typically book covers, dummy books and small boxes.

In the same boat

Personal accidents also claimed many lives during the age of sail. Many involved small boats which were swamped or overturned in sailing accidents. The capsizing-boat scenario is shown, with a certain grim humour, on the gravestone of Edward Collins at Warblington, Hampshire. It shows, in relief, an empty boat with the face and hat of the drowning Collins to the right. The incident took place in Emsworth Harbour on 17 August 1785.

Another such accident was commemorated in a wall tablet erected in 1825 by the officers and crew of HMS *Nimrod* at St Nicholas's church, Carrickfergus, Northern Ireland. A Swedish warship had put into Belfast Lough

---

7   www.memorials.inportsmouth.co.uk/churches/st_marys/royal_george.htm (accessed 27 October 2009).

8   TNA PROB11/1477.

9   During 1808 Bacon passed the daily running of his workshop to Charles Manning.

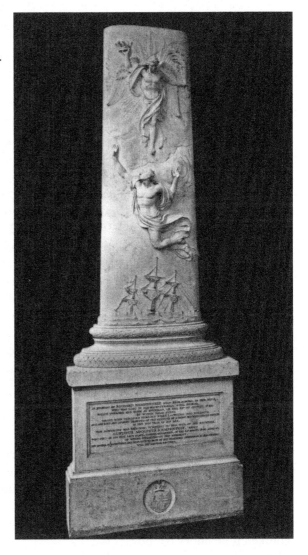

66. *Rear-Admiral Richard Kempenfelt, by John Bacon junior, at Westminster Abbey.* © *Dean and Chapter of Westminster.*

in bad weather on 15 August 1825. James Everard wrote a commemorative memoir of his son (also James), which described the events that followed:

Both from etiquette and the desire to afford any assistance that might be wanted – a boat with an officer was sent from the Nimrod: that officer was my son. Besides himself in the Boat was a midshipman and six crew and the Coxswain. The Swede was some distance from the Nimrod. The Nimrod's Boat left under her canvas; and having got sufficiently near the [ship] luffed up into the wind in order to take in the sail: to accomplish which quickly, two or three men were already standing up in the boat – to haul it down – it was a lug-sail.

At that instant a heavy sea struck her, and their weight added to the force of the sea in the same direction, caused the Boat to upset; and she turned keel upwards. The last words my son was remembered to have been heard to say, were speaking to the men "Sit down". He was an excellent swimmer, but I believe much encumbered by his Boots, Cloak etc.

Everard junior and three crew members drowned.[10]

Another memorial by a bereaved father is the stained-glass window at St Mary's, Marlborough, Wiltshire to Alfred Henry Manders (aged 14) and nine other merchant service cadets from the training ship HMS *Worcester*, who were drowned in a sailing accident near Erith in 1865. The window, by the studio of Michael O'Connor, London, shows four suitably maritime scenes from the New Testament: the Ascension, Our Lord saving Peter on the Sea of Galilee, Christ asleep during the storm and the shipwreck of St Paul. The drowned boys are shown in white robes in the upper lights. Three boats, each with twenty-two boys on board, were going on a trip up the Thames from Greenhithe to inspect the Southern Outfall Sewer Works, now more commonly known as the Crossness Pumping Station. It had recently opened, in April 1865, and then as now was regarded as a masterpiece of engineering. Nearing their destination, attempts to retrieve a boy's cap which had been lost overboard resulted in the boat tipping over to one side. This combined with the wind catching the sail and the boat capsized.[11]

Trips and slips

Falls from rigging and into holds were another common cause of maritime death and injury. Their depiction is a rarity, with the exception of a well-known gravestone at Bosham in West Sussex. It commemorates Thomas Barrow, who drowned on 13 October 1759 following the breaking of a hawser (fig. 67). It is carved with a sloop in profile, with a figure falling into the sea below a broken rope under her bowsprit.

A more typical memorial is the plain gravestone at Kirk Braddan, Isle of Man, to 'RALPH FOREMAN of Douglas Mariner who on the 12 May 1820 by an accidental [*sic*] fall fell into the hold of the Douglas, a trader, to Liverpool which occasioned his premature death in a few days after aged 44 years'.

Another accident is commemorated by an inscription on a mourning ring in the National Maritime Museum collections.[12] A lock of plaited fair hair

---

10 NMM MSS/89/060.
11 *Morning Chronicle*, 2 March 1865.
12 NMM JEW0179.

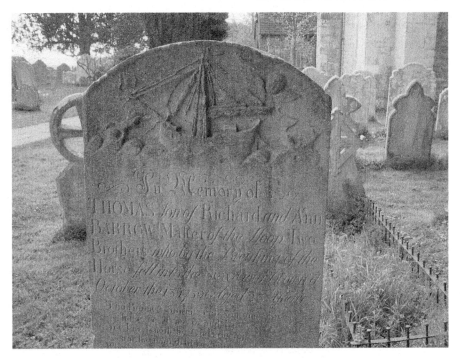

67. *Gravestone of Thomas Barrow, at Bosham, West Sussex.* © *Rina Prentice.*

is contained under glass within the bezel and the white enamel band which surrounds it is inscribed in gold letters: 'SACRED TO THE MEMORY OF' and 'OB[iit] 8 JULY 1817 AET[atis] 20'. Engraved behind the bezel and round the inside of the ring are the words: 'In memory of John Malcolm Stevens 2 mate who on heaveing [*sic*] the log was knocked overboard by the Spanker Boom of the Ship Lord Cranstoun' and 'Jamaica to—Lat 46 10N Long 30W'.

Missing

Some vessels foundered at sea as opposed to being wrecked on shore. If there were no survivors, not only would the deceased have no known grave but even their date of death would be unknown. The memorial to Sir Robert Chamberlayne in the church of St Bartholomew the Great, Smithfield, London, has a kneeling effigy in armour under a canopy held back by angels. The Latin inscription records:

Eventually he reverently approached the Holy Land and the Sepulchre of our Lord, and found also (alas) his own [sepulchre] of what kind or on what shore is unknown, dying in the year of the Virgin Birth 1615. A Batchelor, far from his own people he perished by the inclemency of the weather or of man between (as far as can be guessed) Tripoli and Cyprus ... He is covered by heaven though he has no tomb.

Sir Robert had faced the hazards of sea travel as a passenger.

More typical subjects of later memorials to the 'disappeared' were merchant seamen on long sea passages particularly across the Atlantic. The most likely cause of disappearance in mid-ocean was severe weather or ice. Their deaths start to be recorded in the late eighteenth and nineteenth centuries, at a period when mass-produced gravestones could be afforded by those of modest means. A typical gravestone in the church of Holy Trinity, Salcombe, commemorates:

WILLIAM WILLS

FATHER OF THE ABOVE

SUPPOSED TO HAVE BEEN

LOST WITH ALL HIS CREW IN THE SCHOONER 'FIDGET'

ON THE COAST OF LABRADOR

IN THE MONTH OF OCTOBER

1857

AGED 25 YEARS

The gravestone of Samuel Toms at Upland Road Cemetery, Guernsey, shows the sinking of his vessel, the *Alice* of Guernsey: she was lost with all hands, probably during a severe gale on 22 October 1882, during a return trip from Newcastle laden with coal. A carving above the inscription shows the brigantine, the mainsail on her foremast torn, being overwhelmed by an enormous wave.

With an interest as much in loss of property as loss of life, *Lloyd's List* provided reports of casualties and shipping movements from 1734. By the nineteenth century it was collating information on vessel movements, based on sightings at sea and arrivals and departures from port. It took full advantage of advances in communications such as merchant flag-codes and later the telegraph. Other less specialized newspapers also provided this sort of information, of keen interest to readers in the days before wireless.

The clerical response

The loss of the body at sea was not viewed as an obstacle to salvation. 'At the appointed hour "The sea shall give up its dead" coral tombs, and the giant caverns of the unfathomed ocean, will resign their charge and at the sound of the last trumpet "Corruption will put on incorruption, and this mortal be clothed in immortality."'[13]

Shipwreck narratives sometimes mention clergymen leading prayers among the passengers. Some notable nineteenth-century poetry was inspired by these accounts, in particular John Greenleaf Whittier's 'The Swansong of Parson Avery' and Gerard Manley Hopkins's 'The Wreck of the Deutschland'. *The Book of Common Prayer* includes a section on 'Prayers to be used in Storms at Sea' including 'Short Prayers in respect of a Storm'. In addition to asking 'Save Lord, or else we perish', the Anglican Church considered it important that sins were repented before death. The memorial to the Reverend John Morell Mackenzie, lost in the wreck of the steamship *Pegasus* at Bamburgh on 20 July 1843, says: '... in death amid circumstances of a particularly appalling character he afforded a striking example of the power of that religion which he professed to compose and elevate the mind in the prospect of an imminent entrance into the world of spirits'. *The Times* of 25 July 1843 included a report by a survivor named Baillie: 'I saw Mr M'Kenzie on the quarter-deck praying with several of the passengers on their knees around him. Mr M'Kenzie seemed calm and collected. All the passengers were praying too, but Mr M'Kenzie's voice was distinctly heard above them all.'

Cast ashore

Coastal shipwrecks, requiring the burial of unidentified dead washed up on shore, represented a different sort of challenge to local clergy. Kin would normally be expected to pay for burials. However, the vessel might only be identifiable through a name on a piece of flotsam or by the few survivors who reached the shore safely, and identifying the dead could be an even bigger problem. The unpleasant realities of shipwreck can be glimpsed through the writings of the celebrated Robert Stephen Hawker (1803–75), a notable if minor romantic poet and vicar of Morwenstow, north Cornwall, between 1834 and 1875. He found himself in a maritime accident-blackspot but an area largely occupied by farmers. The shipwrecked seamen were likely to be foreign to the area, but the burden of life-saving, burial of the dead and general cleaning up fell on the local people, with a few inevitable disputes over salvage and pilferage of flotsam belonging to the crown. Hawker gave Christian

---

[13] Thomas B. Barker, *Abney Park Cemetery* (1869), p. 28.

burial to over forty seamen. He was a high churchman and regarded burying the dead as one of the seven acts of mercy. 'This decency of sepulture', he wrote, 'is the result of a fairly recent statute, passed in the reign of George the Third. Before that time, it was the common usage to dig, just above highwater mark, a pit on the shore, and therein to cast, without inquest or religious rite, the carcasses of shipwrecked men.'[14] The Burial of Drowned Persons' Act of 1808 did offer something in the way of financial compensation to Hawker's helpers, which he added to from his own limited purse. Once an inquest had passed the usual verdict of 'wrecked and cast ashore', Hawker could bury any subsequent crew members of the same vessel that might turn up. Battered by the rocks, they might come ashore over many days in a mutilated condition. Many were tattooed with religious symbols, and their initials, to try to ensure identification and Christian burial.

> On his broad smooth chest was tattooed a Rood, that is to say ... our blessed Saviour on His Cross, with on the one hand his Mother, and on the other St. John the Evangelist, underneath were the initial letters of a name P.B. ... The greater number of my dead sailors ... were so decorated with some distinctive emblem and name: and it is their object and intent, when they assume these pictured signs, to secure identity for their bodies if their lives are lost at sea ...[15]

It was a harrowing task and also involved the vicar in extensive correspondence with embassies, relations and shipowners. PB was subsequently identified and turned out to be Danish. In Hawker's churchyard, the graves of drowned seamen from *Alonzo* and *Caledonia* were marked by an upturned boat and a figurehead.

Secular charity

Hawker, however, was not quite the innovator he claimed to be. On Guernsey during 1848 and 1849, a subscription started by the Guernsey United Tradesmen's Club was able to raise funds for the dependants of eight crew members of *Sea Witch* of London, wrecked on 24 November 1848 on a reef in Portifer Bay. With the assistance of the three survivors, a full account of the accident was published in the local paper, *The Guernsey Star*, and republished in the *Glasgow Herald* on 4 December 1848. Charitable funds also provided a high-quality tomb of Portland stone, placed over the grave of the eight men in the churchyard of St Michel du Vale (fig. 68). Inscribed in English and French,

---

14 Robert Stephen Hawker, *Footprints of Former Men in Far Cornwall, etc.* (1948), p. 122.
15 Ibid., p. 134.

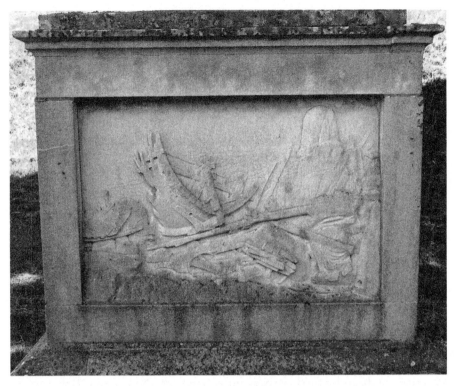

68. *Memorial to the crew of* Sea Witch, *lost 1848, designed by George S. Reynolds, at St Michel du Vale, Guernsey.* © *Author.*

it records the names of all the men who died. Designed by George S. Reynolds and executed by local mason William Randell,[16] its relief does not show the usual depiction of the ship striking the rocks but the scene the morning after. Most of the vessel is in pieces excepting the bows, which are wedged perpendicularly in a cleft in the rocks. All of the three survivors were in this part of the vessel and managed to avoid being washed away by clinging to the bowsprit.

The dangers of innovation

From the mid-nineteenth century, the Royal Navy saw rapid technical change. The evolving designs of naval vessels were depicted in wool embroideries by their ratings and on memorials to a series of famous peacetime disasters, since few British vessels saw action at this period. The most notable

---

16 The 1851 census lists him as 'Statuary and Mason Master 19 Alley Street, St Peter Port'.

was the loss of HMS *Captain* on 7 September 1870. Her design was the subject of a heated controversy between the cautious chief constructor of the Navy, Edward James Reed (1830–1906), and Captain Cowper Phipps Coles (1819–70), a naval officer and inventor who was developing schemes for placing naval guns in turrets, so the gun could be turned and not the ship. Coles, with the support of the press and Parliament, was enabled to implement his ideas for the design of an ironclad which combined low sides and turrets with a full spread of canvas. As built, she was even lower in the water than originally intended and although her sea trials were successful, she was 'stiff': that is, she was stable at small angles of heel but not larger ones. The ship eventually capsized during a stormy night off Cape Finisterre with only eighteen survivors out of a crew of over 500. Her loss effectively marked the end of the sailing navy. Reed's *Devastation* of 1869, designed without sailing rig, proved to be the prototype for future battleships. During a period of rapid technological change, safety had to be scientifically calculated.

Among the casualties of the disaster was Coles himself, on board as a guest of the ship's commander, Captain Hugh Talbot Burgoyne VC. William Ashmore, the captain's valet, was among those drowned in their bunks. He had worked for the family of Rear-Admiral W. Walker as a page and then entered the Navy as captain's servant. His death left a widow, Annie Ashmore, and two children. She was awarded a year's pay from Greenwich Hospital funds and a further six months' pay from the Captain Relief Fund, Portsmouth. She preserved the paperwork and more personal mementoes of her husband including *carte de visite* photographs of them both (fig. 69). Jane Carlyle wrote in 1859: 'Blessed be the inventor of photography ... by which even the poorest can possess themselves of tolerable likenesses of their absent dear ones.'[17] Mrs Ashmore also kept a memorial card – an embossed paper representation of a neo-classical monument personalized by the addition of a printed epitaph.[18] After a period in which she returned to live with her parents, Annie remarried William H. Northcott, a colour-sergeant in the Royal Marines.

The surplus money from the relief fund was to be used to erect a memorial which the committee decided should take the form of a stained-glass window in Westminster Abbey. This was to be accompanied in another part of the building by a brass plaque with the names of all the deceased: the distinction between a memorial and a window-dedication plate could be ambiguous. It was at this point that Rear-Admiral Alfred Ryder, who was organizing the erection of the memorial, began to fall foul of the Dean of Westminster, the Reverend Arthur Penrhyn Stanley. The Dean had an ongoing space problem

[17]   Quoted in Huw Lewis-Jones, *Face to Face: Polar Portraits* (Cambridge, 2008), p. 27.
[18]   NMM ADL/Z/4.

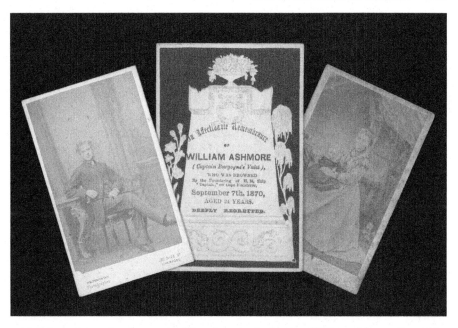

69. *Memorial card and* carte de visite *photographs showing William Ashmore, lost with* HMS Captain *in 1870, and his wife Annie.* © *National Maritime Museum, Greenwich, London, ADL/Z/4.*

and said that he wanted to leave room to commemorate those who might fall in battle in any future wars. He turned down the proposed brass plate as too big, in favour of 'a small tablet on the floor commemorating the principal names and the numbers of those who were lost'.[19] Ryder approached the Dean and Chapter of St Paul's Cathedral who were happy to install his large brass plate (fig. 70). The window by Clayton and Bell, with its maritime scenes from the Old and New Testament, remains in the Abbey, its explanatory text on the floor where it is somewhat difficult to find. Ryder's negotiations with the Dean and Chapter of St Paul's were more straightforward and the changes they suggested were comparatively minor. They vetoed the inclusion of the Noah's Ark in association with the ship. The crew were said to have 'died' rather than 'perished' and the ship 'foundered' rather than 'capsized' – a term they found too technical.

The completed brass plates on the north side of the nave are most impressive. They have rope twist borders and shell decoration. The first plaque has a profile portrait of the ship and quotes the verdict of the court-martial on its

---

[19] Quoted in Arthur Hawkey, *Black Night off Finisterre: The Tragic Tale of an Early British Ironclad* (Shrewsbury, 1999), p. 170.

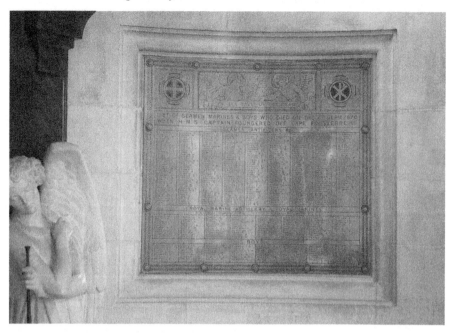

70. *Brass to the officers and crew of* HMS Captain, *lost 1870, at St Paul's Cathedral.*
© *National Maritime Museum, Greenwich, London & the Chapter of St Paul's
Cathedral, London, L7777.*

loss, which sharply criticized the role of public opinion expressed in Parliament in overriding professional opinion. Reed had resigned in July 1870, a couple of months before the disaster. The officers who died as a result of it are listed below. The second plaque names casualties of other ranks, above which two angels hold a scroll which reads: 'The sea shall give up her dead'.

The middle classes erected family memorials to officers lost in the disaster and in particular to the ten midshipmen. Admiral Ryder's nephew, Edward Dudley Ryder, is commemorated by a window in St Ann's church, Portsmouth, one of a series of Ryder memorials in this building.

Passengers

The naval officer in command of a vessel would be court-martialled if it were lost. If he perished in the disaster, as Burgoyne did, the most senior survivor would face the court. The seaman, to a degree, was seen as the author of his fate and belonging to a separate community from the rest of society. Passengers involved in maritime catastrophes were hapless victims, literally out of their element, particularly if they were women.

In January 1786 the East Indiaman *Halsewell* sprung a leak in a gale in mid-Channel, lost a mast and drove on shore at the base of a 200-foot Dorset cliff. Captain Pierce, his two daughters, two nieces, the other female passengers and their servants remained in the stern of the vessel and went down with it. Some of the crew and the troops on board managed to reach the cliff face or a cave at its base. Once someone had climbed the cliff and raised the alarm, local Portland quarrymen hauled seventy-four to safety, others having been swept off the rocks by the sea or falling to their deaths. The destitute surviving seamen had to walk back to London, though the landlord of the Crown Inn at Blandford gave them each 2/6d and a meal. The story made the newspapers, and two of the surviving officers – Henry Meriton and John Rogers – published a narrative of the event. The memorial to the 16-year-old passenger Charles Beckford Templer at St Michael's church, Shute, in Devon, follows the conventional pattern, with a bas-relief showing the ship driven on the rocks and the Templer on the apron. The numerous prints of the disaster, notably by Robert Dodd and after paintings by John Hoppner and Thomas Stothard, begin to explore new imagery and other responses.

> Capt. Pierce a little while before the ship went down, called Mr Meriton into the cuddy, where his two daughters, two nieces and three other beautiful young ladies were clinging round him for protection, and on being told, that it was impossible for the ladies to escape, he nobly resolved to share their fate, and holding in each hand a beloved child, in a few minutes fell a sacrifice to the devouring waves.[20]

In Stothard's small painting showing this scene (fig. 71) the natural forces menacing the distraught passengers are visually excluded from the interior of the cabin. Robert Dodd, by contrast, produced an image of the disaster which focuses on the seamen and troops struggling for survival on the cliffs, while the terrified passengers impotently meet their fate in the background.

Troopships

At the end of the Napoleonic War, 'the inhabitants' of Mylor in Cornwall erected a headstone to mark the burial place of the 200 unnamed men, women and children lost in the wreck of the troop transport, *Queen*, which went ashore at Trefusis Point on 14 January 1814. The stone was embellished with a carving of the dismasted vessel crashing on the rocks but the casualties are

---

[20] *London Recorder or Sunday Gazette*, 15 January 1786. The passage is a slightly adapted abbreviation of that in the Meriton and Rogers account, which calls the cabin the 'round house', as was more usual on Indiamen.

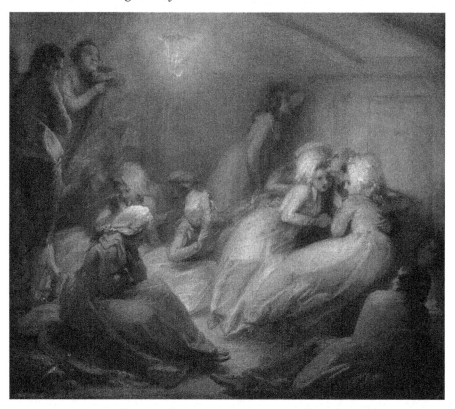

71. The Wreck of the Halsewell, Indiaman, 1789, *oil painting by Thomas Stothard.*
© *National Maritime Museum, Greenwich, London, ZBA4537.*

not mentioned by name. Like the *Royal George* memorials, this philanthropic gesture would have been encouraged by contemporary sensibility, patriotism and press coverage.

By mid-century, a disciplined response was expected from the military in these situations; self-control in the face of disaster, as opposed to the distressing helplessness witnessed in those who perished in the *Queen*. When the horse transport *Europa* caught fire on 1 June 1854, 200 miles from Plymouth, the conduct of officers and men was reported 'most exemplary'. As other vessels were nearby, and most of the ship's boats were launched, only twenty-one lives were lost. Lieutenant-Colonel Willoughby Moore and the men of the 6th Dragoons who died are commemorated in York Minster. The list of names below the memorial includes all casualties excepting three non-military persons – two sailors and 'Mrs Parsons, woman'. The master, William

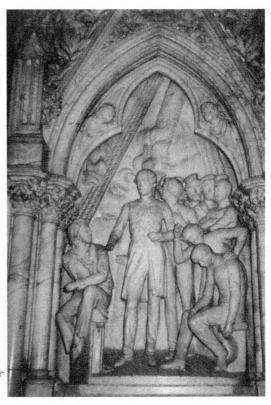

72. *Memorial to Lieutenant-Colonel Willoughby Moore, lost in the* Europa *1854, by John Birnie Philip, at York Minster.* © *Conway Library, The Courtauld Institute of Art, London.*

Gardner, had been the last to leave the ship. He reported that: 'The noble old lieutenant-colonel, I regret to say, perished in the wreck. Several troopers implored him to leave the ship in the boats, but he would not leave his men and shared their terrible fate.'[21] The gothic-revival memorial by John Birnie Philip (1824–75) draws its inspiration from medieval carvings of Christ and the apostles (fig. 72). Within a gothic architectural frame, the colonel stands on the deck of the burning vessel, surrounded by those of his troops who could not be taken off in the boats. He is extending a hand to reassure a seaman.

Women and children first

The 'women-and-children-first' principle began with the wreck of another troopship, the steam frigate *Birkenhead*, which struck an uncharted rock near Cape Town on 26 February 1852. Fortunately, most of the women

---

[21] *Daily News*, 17 June 1854.

and children accompanying the troops had disembarked at her last point of call. There is a memorial at the Royal Hospital, Chelsea, erected by order of Queen Victoria, and regimental memorials to those lost from the 74th Highlanders at St Giles's Cathedral, Edinburgh, and from the Suffolk Regiment at Bury St Edmunds – the latter deploying the usual sinking-ship relief. The weather was calm and the accident took place only about two miles from shore but the steamer sank in about twenty minutes, with some troops drowned in their hammocks or killed by the falling funnel. After the horses had been pushed overboard, the remaining seven women and thirteen children were transferred to one of the three serviceable boats, in charge of a man. Preserving admirable discipline, the remaining troops refrained from rushing the boats (filled, in fact, mainly with other men) and remained with the vessel until she sank. Some were picked up from the rigging and others swam to shore through the kelp, but many died of exposure or were taken by sharks. Although the women and children had played a comparatively minor part in the original event, by 1906, when *A deathless story or the 'Birkenhead' and its heroes* by Addison and Matthews was published, the loss had become an exemplary story of British heroism, which also gave rise to 'the Birkenhead drill' as an expectation for male, or at least soldierly, comportment in parallel cases. The frontispiece reproduced Thomas M.M. Hemy's famous picture of the wreck, painted in about 1892. It shows the troops lined up on the deck, a drummer in the foreground, while the last remaining women and children await their places in a boat.

Titanic

One of the biggest and certainly the most famous civil disaster at sea was the foundering of the RMS *Titanic*, on 15 April 1912, following damage by ice on her maiden voyage. After a last-minute swerve to avoid the iceberg, the ship scraped past it, resulting in an extended gash along the side of the vessel, through which the sea gradually flooded her compartmentalized interior. In spite of just over two hours and thirty minutes in which to abandon ship, only a third of the passengers survived. The greater size of iron and steel vessels increased the potential number of fatalities in any accident. Steam had brought timetables, intense competition between companies and new maritime hazards. The formerly fatalistic personal attitude towards shipwreck had been replaced by an expectation that technology could provide safety for the traveller, but experience proved a costly teacher until effective regulation caught up and began to ensure it. New technologies, such as wireless, also proved only as effective as their operational procedures. These were both areas in which the *Titanic* episode was a significant watershed. The press provided a flicker of light in its disaster narrative by describing inspirational heroism in passengers and crew. A microcosm of the society of its time, the *Titanic* story embodied class, gender and national divisions, and at the same time engendered solidarity within these groups.

Chivalry

'Women and children first' – as we have already seen, a comparatively recent tradition – is embodied in Gertrude Vanderbilt Whitney's statue at Washington, dedicated to 'The brave men who perished in the wreck of the Titanic April 15 1912. They gave their lives that women and children might be saved. Erected by the women of America.' The fundraising was organized by the well-connected ladies of the Women's Titanic Memorial Fund, inspired by the deaths of some distinguished first-class passengers on the ship such as John Jacob Astor (1864–1912): chivalry was after all an aristocratic concept. The unfortunates in third class were not seen at the time as particularly heroic. The fund was specifically to erect a memorial. Whitney's original model shows a frail semi-draped male body with outstretched arms, reminiscent of the crucifixion. It has affinities with the Dover War Memorial by Reginald R. Goulden and Kathleen Scott's statue 'Youth' at the Scott Polar Research Institute, all ultimately deriving from Rodin. It is said to resemble Whitney's brother Alfred Vanderbilt, lost in the sinking of *Lusitania*, and the pose was memorably adopted by the heroine of James Cameron's film, *Titanic* (1997). Not erected until 1931, its scaling up to an eighteen-foot version in granite, carved by John Horrigan, is not altogether happy.

Its inscription is inclusive but a greater proportion of women and children were saved from among first-class passengers, compared to third-class, and of course some men also survived. That the women were given any priority, however partial, was only possible because the ship sank relatively slowly. It was also only necessary because of the inadequate provision of lifeboats, although *Titanic* carried more than were required by the Board of Trade, while some of them lowered in the early stages of the disaster had empty places. The conception and execution of the project owed much to the current campaigns for political rights for women, although an alternative view saw equality as the right to drown heroically with the men. Following the wreck of the passenger steamer *Stella*, on 30 March 1899, commemoration of stewardess Mary Rogers was promoted and funded by Annie Byams and Frances Power Cobbe, respectively a radical and a suffragette. One of two stewardesses lost in the wreck, Rogers had refused a place in the lifeboat, and put her duty before her right to escape.

The cable ship *Mackay-Bennett* was chartered to retrieve bodies of those who had died of exposure in the water when the *Titanic* went down. Passengers and crew with no place in a lifeboat stood very little chance of survival.

Bodies in poor condition which could not be identified were buried at sea; the rest were mostly interred at Halifax, Nova Scotia. Private memorials to *Titanic* casualties are not uncommon in the United Kingdom and British memorials are for the most part modest, middle-class affairs to individual passengers or families. All the casualties of the disaster were commemorated in 1913 by a tower in the shape of a lighthouse, erected by public subscription. It formerly stood on the roof of the Seaman's Institute in New York and is now at the South Street Seaport Museum.

Be British

The British officers and crew of *Titanic* are represented in memorials ranging from grand public affairs to modest local commemorations. Sneaking off in a boat was now unacceptable and opprobrium was heaped on Bruce Ismay, the Chairman of the White Star Line, the ship's owners, who belatedly took a place in a lifeboat. At least the captain, Edward Smith, had gone down with the vessel. Accused of reckless navigation by the Union of Seamen, he was posthumously exonerated by the Board of Trade inquiry. A popular hero immediately after the wreck, his exhortation to the passengers to 'Be British' became a song title, though many of them were not British at all. Smith's reputation thereafter gradually declined. He was commemorated by a bronze statue at Lichfield (chosen at the time as a generally accessible point for pilgrimage by rail in his native county of Staffordshire) sculpted by Kathleen Scott (fig. 73). A relief on the plinth shows the transport medal with South Africa clasp that Smith received after two voyages carrying troops during the Boer War. There is also an allusion to Smith's commission in the Royal Naval Reserve and a Staffordshire knot, to indicate his birth at Hanley, in the Potteries. The inscription does not include the word 'Titanic' but that he was master of the ship was subsequently added to the plinth, an indication of how what starts as something 'everyone knows' can soon be forgotten.[22] Smith is also commemorated in a window in the Anglican Cathedral in Liverpool, near Mary Rogers.

The builders

Belfast was hard hit by the disaster but felt it did not reflect favourably on Harland & Wolff, the company that built the ship. A memorial was erected by the sculptor Thomas Brock (1847–1922), who adopts the standing female classical figure with a wreath, which she extends over the half-submerged

---

[22] Ann Savours, 'Kathleen Scott's Statue of Captain Smith of the *Titanic*', *Mariner's Mirror*, vol. 95, no. 4 (November 2009), pp. 478–83.

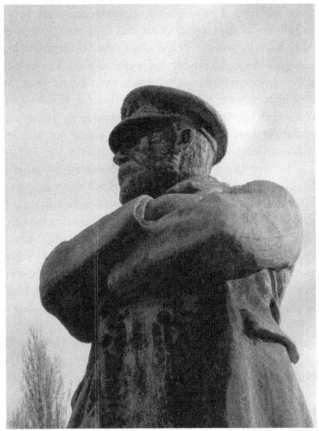

73. Edward Smith,
the master of Titanic,
by Kathleen Scott, at
Lichfield.
© *Pieter van der Merwe.*

figure of a drowning man supported by two women. It was unveiled in 1920 and bears the names of Northern Irish crew members and members of Harland & Wolff's guarantee group headed by the ship's designer, Thomas Andrews (1873–1912), who went down with her. The publication of Walter Lord's book, *A Night to Remember* (1955), and the film that followed in 1958 vastly enhanced the reputation of Andrews, who emerged as one of the heroes of the disaster. As at Southampton, *Titanic* is now exploited in Belfast as an ongoing source of tourist income.

Officers and crew

A duty of sacrificial heroism fell upon even the lowliest member of the crew. An inscription on the grave of trimmer Everett Edward Elliott at Halifax, Nova Scotia, says: 'Each man stood at his post while all the weaker ones stood by and showed once more to all the world how Englishmen should die.' There is also a new emphasis on trade union and professional solidarity, since labour and professional organizations were very active at this period.[23] While watches stopped at around 2.15 a.m., when they entered the water, were found on many of the passengers' bodies, the lower ranks of the ship's company by contrast carried a union card. Crew members of all ranks are commemorated in Southampton, their home port. Some, such as stewards and bakers, were involved in the floating-hotel aspect of the vessel, others worked in the engine rooms – the trimmers, firemen and stokers. Such is the enduring interest in *Titanic* that the name occurs even on the memorials of survivors who died long after the disaster.

The engineering department operated in a crucially important and particularly hazardous zone. They kept the pumps working and the lights blazing until the last moment: some engineering crew survived but none of the officers. The memorial to the engineer officers stands in East Park, Southampton, erected by their fellow officers and other subscribers. It was produced by Whitehead & Sons with the figures sculpted by Ferdinand Victor Blundstone and Romeo Rathmann. The design follows the traditional neo-classical pattern of commemoration for military heroes. A female figure representing Victory stands on the prow of a ship and holds out wreaths over panels in relief on either side, on which engineer officers go about their work. They are also commemorated on a bronze plaque by George Alexander (1881–1942), originally at the Institute of Marine Engineers in London and (at time of writing) on loan to the National Maritime Museum (fig. 74). The top depicts the head of Neptune between polar bears; the sinking ship is below, within a broken pedestal. Two reliefs of engineers flank the inscription.

The band

Although less crucial than the engineers, the band were more conspicuous. They played ragtime tunes until the end to promote calm. Whether the last number was 'Nearer my God to Thee' or 'Autumn', it was the former hymn which became inseparably associated with the disaster. The body of bandmaster Wallace Hartley was recovered, identified and repatriated to the mill town of Colne in Lancashire where he was born. The funeral procession was attended by an estimated 30,000 spectators, bands from neighbouring towns and local civic dignitaries. The monument on his grave incorporates a broken column, the music of 'Nearer my God to Thee' (in the version by Sullivan favoured by Methodists) with Hartley's violin in relief (fig. 75). An additional memorial fund was set up and a bronze bust of Hartley by the Bromsgrove Guild was unveiled at Colne in 1915.[24] A contributor to the

---

[23] Trimmers fed coal from the bunkers to the firemen, keeping the residue stably distributed.

[24] The Guild was an association of artists and craftsmen who also produced the Liverpool

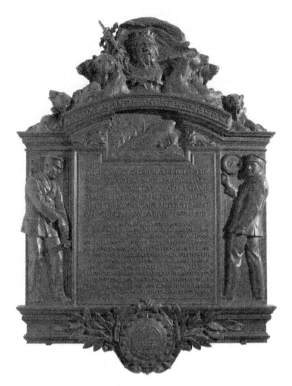

74. *Memorial to the engineer officers of* Titanic, *by George Alexander.* © *National Maritime Museum, Greenwich, London. On loan from The Institute of Marine Engineering, Science and Technology, LOA1369.*

Colne and Nelson Times had decried the original suggestion of a fountain by saying that 'Surely there has been enough water in this sad affair without introducing any more …'[25]

The Amalgamated Musicians Union, Southampton branch, erected a memorial to all the *Titanic* bandsmen at Southampton, which combined a mourning figure with the bow of the ship. Destroyed in the Second World War, a replica on the Municipal Mutual Building was unveiled in 1990. There is another plaque in St Mary's church at Southampton and, unexpectedly, a broken column erected by the citizens of Broken Hill, New South Wales, to 'The heroic bandsmen of the Steamship Titanic who playing to the end, calmly faced certain death whilst women, children and their fellow men were being rescued from the wreck of that ill-fated vessel'. It also gives the casualty figures. Politics in Broken Hill were left-wing, hence this commemoration of heroic workers. The Victorian Band Association in the city of Ballarat (north-west of Melbourne, Australia) also put up a bandstand on which the ship in profile forms the weathervane.

Liver Birds and helped to fit out the interior of *Lusitania.* One of their sculptors, Leopold Weisz, was also a casualty of the *Titanic* disaster.
25 Quoted in Yvonne Carroll, *A Hymn for Eternity* (Stroud, 2002), p. 122.

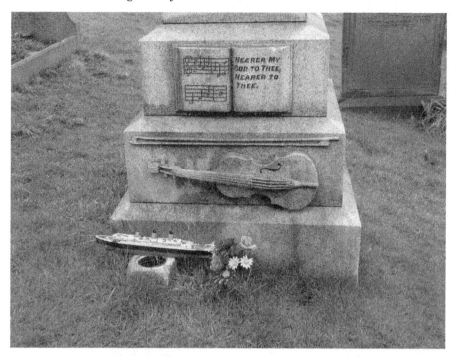

75. *Gravestone of Wallace Hartley, the bandleader of* Titanic, *at Colne, Lancashire.*
© *Author.*

Titanic commemoration saw a new expression of group solidarity among employees and professionals. Some of the iconography deployed had been associated with military memorials and was to be used again for the same purpose from 1914. The survival of these *Titanic* monuments is ensured because it is a disaster continually revisited by successive generations, conscious of social gains since it occurred, nostalgic for lost glamour and uneasy about threats to civilization, stability and wealth. The increasing list in the first-class smoking room, well re-imagined in both the 1958 and 1997 films of the disaster, never fails to chill an audience.

Herald of Free Enterprise

In spite of advances in safety at sea, vessels are still lost. The capsize of the car ferry *Herald of Free Enterprise* in 1987 was one of a series of transport accidents that occurred during a period of economic deregulation and privatization under Margaret Thatcher's long rule as Conservative Prime Minister in Britain (1979–90). At the time there was fierce competition between cross-Channel ferry firms, following the government decision to break up

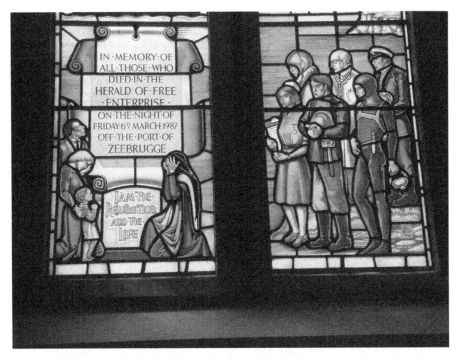

76. *Window commemorating those lost in the* Herald of Free Enterprise, *at St Mary, Dover (detail). © Author.*

an unofficial cartel between companies. Car ferries have the same design problem as eighteenth-century warships: vulnerable openings in the hull and a large amount of undivided internal space containing heavy equipment on wheels. There have been a series of disasters involving these vessels, mostly in severe weather, but the need to transport vehicles across the sea economically means they continue to operate. The *Herald* sailed from Zeebrugge on 6 March 1987 with her bow doors open, and water washing into her car deck compromised stability. Within ninety seconds she turned over just outside the harbour with the loss of 193 passengers and crew. Had she not remained on her side and partly above water on a sandbank, the casualties would have been even worse. It seemed a completely unnecessary accident and it became apparent that the blame did not lie solely with the unfortunate crew member responsible for closing the doors. A coroner's inquest jury returned a verdict of unlawful killing and there were attempts to prosecute the owners, P&O European Ferries, for manslaughter. A correspondent to the *Guardian*, Dr James Hemming, wrote on 12 March of 'the cruel irony that this ill-fated vessel, the Herald of Free Enterprise was itself the victim of the over-eager pursuit of profit, the rush inseparable from hurried turn rounds inevitably results in cutting corners'.

Commemoration centred on the ferry's home port of Dover, where the main memorial is a window and book of remembrance at St Mary's church. A depiction of Christ stilling the waters occupies the upper part of the two-light window by Frederick Walter Cole (1908–98). Members of the Belgian medical and emergency services stand in the lower part of the right-hand window looking left toward the dedication which has a mourning family shown below (fig. 76). Above is the ship, floating serenely upright in her red and white Townsend Thoresen livery. P&O, which had taken over Townsend Thoresen shortly before the accident, hastily changed the name of the company and the livery. Another window by Goddard & Gibbs in the church of St Margaret of Antioch at St Margaret-at-Cliffe commemorates three local men who died in the disaster and shows Christ walking on the water with the White Cliffs of Dover and the ferry in the background. The third memorial in the Dover area is at St Paul's church, and takes the form of a wall painting on the rear wall of the baptistery by Dr Henry Campbell FRSA (1917–2010). It shows the baptism of Christ with the bows of the ship placed below the figure of St John. The intention of the fresco is to show both death and new life through water.

The sculptural sinking ship has gone the way of skulls on tombstones, a too sharp reminder of mortality, no longer seen as edifying. The sinking ship itself remains a reality.

7

Maritime explorers: Drake to Shackleton

Explorers are often commemorated by public memorials erected long after their death. They became a popular subject for municipal statuary and other commemoration during the nineteenth and twentieth centuries. The whole concept of 'explorer' is generally speaking a post-Renaissance, European one. The search for identity by the settlers of the lands he discovered was one good reason to celebrate the explorer as a founding father. As scientific research assumed increased importance in the wake of the Enlightenment, those who died in the quest for knowledge were seen as martyrs to a worthy cause. The return of the traveller to tell his tale and its eventual publication were essential in establishing a posthumous reputation. Records and narratives are all-important. Although Sir John Franklin's much-commemorated 1845 expedition might be seen as an exception to this rule – there were no survivors and only a couple of official documents were recovered – a narrative of sorts was established by the findings of the search expeditions. Statues have even been erected to figures verging on the mythical, such as the eleventh-century voyager Leif Ericsson in Reykjavik, or the tenth-century Maori, Kupe Raiatea, in Wellington. Even in those cases, oral traditions had put a name to a discovery. Most human migration went unrecorded.

Sea dogs

The earliest British circumnavigations were military incursions into Spanish spheres of influence in quest of plunder or military and commercial advantage. No contemporary memorials survive to Sir Francis Drake (who was buried at sea in 1596) or to Walter Ralegh (executed in 1618), although his body still lies in St Margaret's, Westminster. Such men were immortalized by a series of published voyage narratives and would be referenced as patriotic heroes during future periods of conflict. Busts of Ralegh and Drake by Peter Scheemakers were included in the 'Temple of British Worthies' at Stowe, designed for Richard Temple, first Viscount Cobham, by William Kent and erected in 1734–35. This was a time of trade disputes with Spain, eventually resulting in the War of Jenkins's Ear.

During the early part of the nineteenth century the Elizabethan privateers had their place in published national histories. Their freebooting activities were sometimes questioned, sometimes excused, but were not unduly glorified. They only gained more widespread popularity during the zenith of the British Empire. They were rehabilitated as 'sea dogs' after the publication of Charles Kingsley's *Westward Ho!* in 1855 and his contemporary, James Anthony Froude's *History of England from the Fall of Wolsey to the Spanish Armada*. Both authors had West Country origins and contributed to a local cult of Drake. This exaggerated his role in the defeat of the Armada and down-played the circumnavigation (1577–80) that had so impressed his contemporaries: it was only the second such voyage and Drake was the first leader to complete one, since Magellan had been killed on the way. Sailing round the world during the nineteenth century was not such an impressive achievement. Nevertheless, the cultural significance of both explorers and historical anniversaries had been growing since the late eighteenth century, a period when citizens of the United States had rediscovered Columbus. In 1880 the Reverend W.S. Lach-Szyrma suggested, in *The Western Daily Mail*, that a memorial should be erected to celebrate the tercentenary of Drake's achievement. Fundraising for a statue in Plymouth proved initially slow. However, the proposal was appropriated during a public meeting by the neighbouring small town of Tavistock, Drake's birthplace and already a tourist destination. A somewhat acrimonious rivalry existed between the two towns but Tavistock, the smaller settlement, had a wealthy patron in Francis Charles Hastings Russell, ninth Duke of Bedford (1819–91), who owned the mineral rights to the local Great Consols Mine. A generous response from the Duke enabled the town to spend £4000 on a bronze statue by Joseph Edgar Boehm (1834–90), one of the most fashionable sculptors of the day.

The swaggering figure of the circumnavigator that resulted holds a compass over a globe.[1] The granite pedestal by John Pethick of Plymouth is decorated with bronze reliefs showing the knighting of Drake by Queen Elizabeth in 1581,[2] his legendary game of bowls before the Armada, and his burial at sea off Panama with the body wrapped in a sail rather than in the lead coffin mentioned by contemporary accounts. Plymouth swallowed its pride and, for £1000, ordered a copy without the reliefs (fig. 77), which was unveiled with due ceremony on the Hoe in 1884. The festivities and speeches of the day

---

[1]   The plaster studio model for the statue has been at Buckland Abbey since 2002, after being discovered in 1999 in shrubbery near the eighteenth-century Belvedere on Haldon Hill, Exeter, during grounds restoration work.

[2]   She is said to have passed the sword to the French Ambassador; the game of bowls is also a later and somewhat embroidered anecdote; Bruce Wathen, 'Making Drake' (unpublished thesis), University of Exeter, 2001, pp. 99–100, 120.

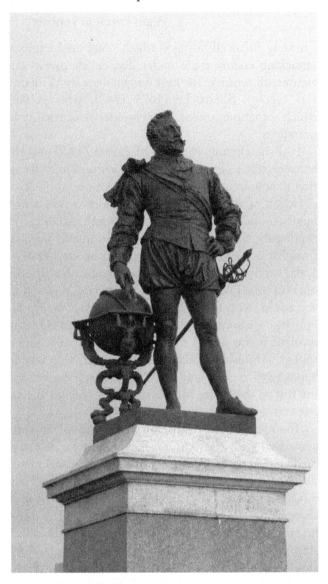

77. *Francis Drake, by Joseph Edgar Boehm, on Plymouth Hoe.*
© *Author.*

dwelt on Drake's achievements as Mayor of Plymouth, his improvement of the town's water supply, his support of Protestantism and his repelling of foreign invaders. Mr Rouse, a local ironmonger, was clearly aware that the Plymouth naval base was still vital to the economy of the town: he linked imperial exploits, ancient and modern, by decorating his shop with a large picture of the recent Royal Naval bombardment of Alexandria, captioned 'All honour to our British sailors, the descendants of Sir Francis Drake'.[3]

3   *Western Daily Mercury*, 15 February 1884.

A government venture

Privately financed voyages which combined exploration with privateering (attacking enemy trade under licence for profit) continued into the early eighteenth century. The best known were by William Dampier (1651–1715) and George Shelvocke (1675–1742), who publicized their adventures, which sometimes crossed the boundaries of legality into piracy, in published narratives.

It is the circumnavigation of Anson (1740–44) that marks the boundary between these older, uncontrolled ventures and the age of scientific exploration to come. Commodore George Anson (1697–1762) commanded a naval squadron of six warships and two store vessels sent by the British government to raid the Pacific coast of South America. He was also ordered to capture the Spanish vessel that sailed annually from Acapulco, carrying silver from Mexico to the Philippines. Only about 500 of his original crew of over 1,900 survived the hazards of the voyage, notably scurvy and shipwreck, and only his own ship, the 60-gun *Centurion*, completed the voyage. However, he succeeded in capturing the Manila galleon, *Nuestra Señora de Covadonga*. The immense treasure from the prize was paraded through the streets of London; most of it was added to the public purse and reissued as British currency, though Anson also became rich from it. This was a propaganda coup that appealed to the patriotic ethos of the times. Anson's voyage stimulated British interest in exploring the Pacific, even though his expedition was in many respects a disaster.

The memorials of those fortunate enough to survive show a wish to be associated with the venture. The gravestone of Captain Arthur Lusk, who died on 9 April 1808, aged 94, at Ballywalter in County Down, mentions that he 'circumnavigated the globe with Lord Anson'.[4] Matthew Michell (1705–52) has a marble wall memorial at Chilterne in Wiltshire that also claims his share of the glory: 'In the years 1740, 41, 42 … He sailed round the world under Commodore Anson.' The dates discreetly indicate that Michell lost his ship, *Gloucester*, and took passage back to England from Macao, missing the capture of the *Covadonga*. The inscription says that 'The constant Dangers which accompany a Maritime Life, wrought in Him the most reverential Awe of the Deity.' One of Anson's lieutenants in *Centurion*, Philip Saumarez (1710–47), was killed in action a few years after his return. His memorial in Westminster Abbey says somewhat modestly that he 'was commanding officer of the said ship when she was driven from her moorings on the island of Tinian'. The ship left Anson and most of the crew marooned on shore and

---

4   TNA ADM33/371. In *Centurion*'s pay book as able seaman and appointed coxswain, 22 June 1741.

Saumarez battled for nineteen days with a quarter of her normal complement to bring her back to rescue them.

The voyage had succeeded at least partially, in carrying out its nearly impossible objectives. Anson himself, after distinguished fighting service, rose to become First Lord of the Admiralty. At the time of his death in 1762, his elder brother and heir, Thomas Anson, was in the course of erecting a triumphal arch on his own estate at Shugborough in Staffordshire, designed by architect James 'Athenian' Stuart and based on the arch of Hadrian in Athens (fig. 78). One of a number of such monuments in the park around the house, it was converted to a memorial to Admiral Lord Anson and his wife Elizabeth by the addition of sculpted portrait busts by Peter Scheemakers. The

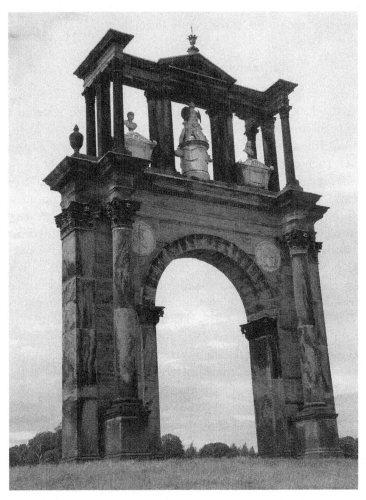

78. *George Anson, First Baron Anson, at Shugborough, Staffordshire.*
Triumphal arch designed by James Stuart. © Author.

military trophies that stand between them, on a pedestal decorated with the protruding bow and stern of a Roman war galley, imply that military success is founded on naval supremacy. Two medallions on the façade of the arch celebrate Anson's victories and naval reforms. The second medallion is based on the reverse of a medal struck in 1747 to celebrate Anson's victory that year at the First Battle of Finisterre and his circumnavigation of 1740–44.[5] The family deliberately chose to commemorate the achievements of Anson in the decorative scheme of the house and grounds, rather than by erecting a grand monument at his place of burial at Colwich. The prize money from the capture of the *Covadonga* transformed the Shugborough estate and gained Thomas Anson control of the parliamentary seat at nearby Lichfield. The triumphal arch dominates the surrounding landscape from the brow of its hill as a reminder of the source of the family fortunes.

Elizabeth Cook's family tragedy

Between the voyage of Anson and those of Captain Cook (1768–80), a major change took place. Cartographical and related scientific research (though 'scientific' is of later coinage) assumed a more important role in voyages of exploration, although economic and military objectives were also firmly on the agenda. Their organization had also improved considerably.

Captain James Cook (1728–79) led his three voyages of Pacific discovery with exemplary efficiency, although latterly the strain of command began to tell. Through his insistence on obtaining fresh food whenever possible, he prevented scurvy. He surveyed the north-west coast of America, the east coast of Australia and many of the island groups of the Pacific, and circumnavigated New Zealand. His ships carried scientific specialists who made important contributions to natural history, astronomy and ethnology. His leadership ethos was one of Enlightenment rationalism and humanity, and in the two hundred years following his death on Hawaii, his admirers projected agendas of their own onto his reliable, prosaic figure.

The Cook family memorial at St Andrew's church, Cambridge, records Cook's death, 'killed by the Natives of *Owyhee*' in 1779, as the first event in the destruction of a naval family. It was erected by his widow Elizabeth, who died in 1835 aged 94, having outlived her husband by over fifty years and all their six children. Three died before the age of 5 while their father was at sea. Of their three sons, Nathaniel was lost in the *Thunderer*, when that vessel sank with all hands during a hurricane in the year after his father's death. Hugh Cook, who was destined for the church, died aged 17 while a student

---

5   Patrick Eyres, 'Neoclassicism on Active Service: Commemoration of the Seven Years War in the English Landscape Garden', *New Arcadian Journal*, 1993, pp. 94–100.

at Cambridge in 1793, possibly of scarlet fever. Their last son, James, died less than a month later, apparently drowned following the loss of a ship's boat during bad weather. There were certain suspicious circumstances, as his body was found on the Isle of Wight with a head wound and the pockets emptied of valuables, while no trace was found of the boat's crew. Elizabeth Cook remained profoundly affected by the loss of her entire family. Her husband, 'one of the most celebrated Navigators', is listed first in the Cambridge inscription but is otherwise given no particular prominence. The ambitious memorial by R.J. Wyatt that she erected to her cousin, Rear-Admiral Isaac Smith, and his family, at Merton, is similarly even-handed. The iconography and text indicate Hope (shown as a kneeling woman extending an open hand) giving way to resignation. The Cambridge wall tablet is more decidedly naval in character with sprays of olive and oak, naval trophies, and a female mourning figure holding a chart. It includes a version of the Cook arms – a star above a globe with the crest of an arm holding a Union flag. These were granted to the family in 1785.[6]

Elysian fields

Cook's reputation grew from the time of his first Pacific voyage. The officers' journals were published in 1773, edited by John Hawkesworth.[7] Although the exciting story he produced was popular with the public, Cook took editorial control of the second voyage account in order to provide a more accurate and less sensational narrative. As early as 1778, the year before his death, Cook was celebrated by a monument erected in the grounds of Stowe (fig. 79). Standing on a small island in a lake in the Elysian Fields, it takes the form of a stone globe on a plinth, carved with an antique profile portrait intended to represent the explorer.

The news that Cook had been killed in Hawaii inspired the usual contemporary responses to a heroic death. Anna Seward wrote 'An Elegy on Captain Cook'. Johan Zoffany and John Webber produced paintings of the event and Philippe-Jacques de Loutherbourg (1740–1812) an apotheosis which formed the backdrop to a pantomime performed at the Theatre Royal, Covent Garden, in 1785 entitled *Omai or a Trip Round the World*: for this de Loutherbourg, a pioneering *metteur en scène*, devised all the scenery and costumes. Thomas Banks (1735–1805) made a speculative design for a public monument and

---

6 TNA PROB 11/1847/09: Elizabeth Cook left the churchwardens of St Andrews £1000 to keep unobliterated and in repair 'the monument and inscription which I have caused to be put up in the said church to the memory of my dear deceased husband Captain Cook and family'.

7 John Hawksworth, *An Account of the Voyages undertaken … for making Discoveries in the Southern Hemisphere* (1773).

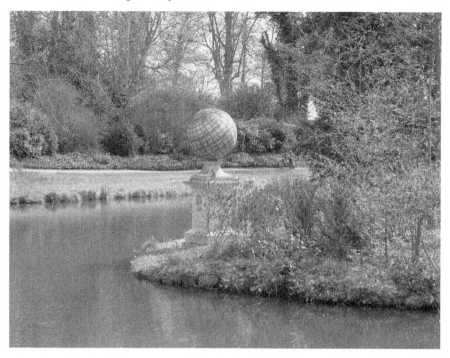

79. Captain James Cook RN commemorated in the grounds of Stowe, Buckinghamshire.
© Author.

exhibited the model at the Royal Academy in 1780. It was never erected but its intended appearance is known from a contemporary print.[8] The body of Cook is shown as a heroic nude, stretched across a globe, mourned by Britannia who ties a laurel branch to his obelisk. Putti representing Castor and Pollux, stars used as guides by mariners, point out his place of death in the Pacific. The skirmish with the Hawaiians is shown in relief on a sarcophagus. The stretched-out, naked figure relates to Banks's preoccupation with Homeric illustration. Ancient Greek references are similarly deployed in Zoffany's depiction of the Hawaiians.[9]

Just as the South Pacific was being seen through a classical prism at this time, landowners were landscaping their parks into a semblance of Arcadia. In a few cases the tomb in the view ('Et in Arcadia ego') was that of Cook. There was no body to bury: the remains that the Hawaiians handed back to John Gore, Cook's first lieutenant, had been buried at sea. Comptroller of the Navy and later Governor of Greenwich Hospital, Admiral Sir Hugh

---

8 Julius Bryant, *Thomas Banks, 1735–1805, Britain's First Modern Sculptor* (2005), p. 48.
9 Mrs Cook's executor presented the unfinished Zoffany painting of the death of Cook to the Naval Gallery at Greenwich in 1835, though her probable ownership of it was only from after 1827: it is now in the NMM (Greenwich Hospital Collection).

Palliser (1723–96) erected a memorial on his estate at Chalfont St Giles, with a lengthy inscription by Admiral the Hon. John Forbes (1714–96), originally printed in the preface to the published journals of Cook's last voyage. This takes a curiously theological approach to Cook's disproval of the theory that a Great Southern Continent was required to balance those in the Northern Hemisphere: 'the same Great Being who created the universe by his FIAT, by the same ordained our earth to keep a just poise, without a corresponding Southern Continent – and it does so'.

In 1788 another empty tomb (this time commissioned by a man with no professional connection with Cook) was erected by Charles Anderson Pelham (1749–1823) on his estate at Manby in Lincolnshire. The maker was Richard Hayward (1728–1800) and the portion of the Portland stone memorial that survives at Brocklesby Park, Lincolnshire, is in the form of a serpentine fluted sarcophagus with a pediment and acroteria. It is carved with shells, hippocampi, dolphins and a relief of the Three Graces.[10]

Cook's international reputation is reflected in a similar commemoration in France. Jean-Joseph, Marquis de Laborde (1724–94), decorated his garden at Méréville with memorials to two sons who perished on the expedition of Jean-François de Galaup, Comte de la Pérouse, which disappeared without trace in 1788. To these he added a monument to Cook designed by Hubert Robert and François-Joseph Bélanger. A relief bust of Cook by Augustin Pajou (1730–1809) was placed in a niche in the plinth, which was surmounted by an urn and stood within a small pavilion. The design was based on Roman funerary altars. Moved in 1895, the memorial stands today in Le Parc du Château de Jeurre near Morigny-Champigny.[11]

Back in England in 1827, Robert Campion, a local landowner, erected a sandstone obelisk on Easby Moor, Great Ayton, near Cook's birthplace. The inscription states that 'while it shall be deemed the honour of a Christian Nation to spread civilisation and the blessings of the Christian faith among pagan and savage tribes, so long will the name of Captain Cook stand out amongst the most celebrated and most admired benefactors of the human race'. This is beginning to associate Cook with the missionary enterprises of the early nineteenth century whose objectives were quite unlike those of his voyages. At the time the memorial was repaired in 1895, it was reputed to be the only one to Cook in his native land. A writer for *The Builder* was of the opinion that 'being Cook's monument, we entirely sympathize with the effort that has been made to put it in better repair'.[12]

---

10 John Lord, 'Richard Hayward: An Early and Some Later Commissions', *Church Monuments*, vol. 12 (1997), pp. 74–75.
11 James Stevens Curl, *Kensal Green Cemetery: The Origins and Development of the Cemetery of All Souls, Kensal Green, London 1824–2001* (Chichester, 2001), pp. 11–12.
12 *The Builder*, 3 August 1895, p. 80.

Imperial heroes

A book reviewer, writing in *The Art Journal* in 1861, said 'the voyages of Cook will always afford so interesting and valuable a narrative, that there is little fear of the old circumnavigator being laid up in ordinary, as unfit for service'.[13] The height of the Empire and the establishment of dominions in Australia, New Zealand and Canada saw a revival of interest in commemorating historical navigators such as Cook, Matthew Flinders (1774–1814) and George Vancouver (1757–98).

One manifestation was the commissioning of public sculpture. Usually a few enthusiasts, inspired by reading accounts of their heroes, would call a public meeting with a view to raising subscriptions: for the erection of a statue, potential earnings from visitors to the town might be stressed as an additional motivation. If the meeting agreed that the proposal was a good idea, it elected a committee. The chairman would then discover that the task was less easy than it first appeared as he went on to encounter problems raising the necessary funds and finding a site (the latter particularly difficult in London). Worries about vandalism were also likely to surface at some stage. Successful enterprises tended to be those bailed out by one wealthy donor. In the provinces and the dominions where the process was easier, commemoration tended to take on a distinctly local flavour.

Australian, American and Canadian money paid for the erection and refurbishment of memorials in Great Britain at the birthplaces and burial sites of their national heroes. One example among many is the gravestone of George Vancouver (1757–98) at St Peter's church, Petersham, which was restored by the Native Sons of British Columbia and subsequently maintained by the City of Vancouver. The Hudson Bay Company put up the plaque within the church.

The most 'imperialist' of the Cook statues was commissioned by the Empire League for a site in the Mall in London, where it was unveiled in 1914. The League, founded in 1894, was one of a number of associations formed to promote the idea of Empire to an enlarged and rather apathetic electorate, at a time when other European nations were competing with Britain for the acquisition of colonies. The inscription reads: '... he laid the foundations of the British Empire in Australia and New Zealand, Charted the shore of Newfoundland and Traversed the Gates of Canada both East and West'; the mention of Canada was added as something of an afterthought in 1928. The proposal to erect the statue was put forward by Herbert Samuel (1870–1963), Member of Parliament for Cleveland, where Cook was still a local worthy.

---

[13] *Art Journal*, 1 February 1861, vol. 7, p. 64; review of John Barrow, ed., *Captain Cook's Voyages of Discovery* (Edinburgh, 1860).

Samuel was a radical liberal of Anglo-Jewish parentage. Another MP, Sir William Gervase Beckett (1866–1937), also became involved in the project. He represented the Whitby division of the North Riding of Yorkshire, and was initially anxious to present a copy of the statue to the town but objected strongly to the committee's choice of sculptor, Thomas Brock. The justification for Brock was that he had produced the sculpture for the adjacent Admiralty Arch. Beckett, after some acrimonious correspondence in *The Times*, commissioned his own statue from John Tweed (1869–1933). This was duly unveiled at Whitby in 1912 on a site that he had presented to the town.[14]

Adoptive antipodean

Copies of the John Tweed statue of Cook were set up in Hawaii, Victoria (British Columbia), Anchorage in Alaska and St Kilda, Victoria, Australia. These gave a somewhat standardized image to the explorer, standing on the deck of an imaginary ship, in his (by now) quaint uniform with his rolled charts under his arm. The earlier statue by Thomas Woolner (1825–92) in Hyde Park, Sydney, was cast in Britain and erected in 1879. The figure holds a chart and a telescope, and has its right arm upraised. The sculptor intended to show 'an animated figure filled with wonder and delight at the moment of discovering a new country',[15] which sounds like a somewhat untypical response from the stolid Cook. When Australia achieved Dominion status in 1901, Cook was seen as the founder of two nations of the Anglo-Saxon race, a popular figure without the unfortunate associations of Arthur Phillip, who had conducted the First Fleet of convicts to New South Wales in 1788 and been first British governor there. The idea of Cook as visionary was taken up by the Reverend W.H.H. Yarrington, whose poem 'Captain Cook Meditating on Australia's Future' was published in Sydney in 1907. Cook's ghost stands on the deck of his ship and watches Australia's transformation from a wilderness to a rose-tinted vision of the English home-counties. These attitudes seem to have been entirely in tune with those of the Cook enthusiast, Sir Joseph Hector McNeil Carruthers (1857–1932), the premier of New South Wales from 1904 to 1908: Carruthers had made the original suggestion for a statue in London.[16] Cook's accounts of the islands of the South Pacific and their inhabitants, which so fascinated his contemporaries, were less emphasized – Hawaii and Tahiti by this time being under, respectively,

---

14 TNA WORK 20/79 and WORK 20/184.
15 Quoted in Juliet Peers, 'Beyond Captain Cook: Thomas Woolner and Australia', in Benedict Read and Joanna Barnes, eds, *Pre-Raphaelite Sculpture: Nature and Imagination in British Sculpture 1848–1914* (1991), p. 37.
16 *The Times*, 3 November 1908.

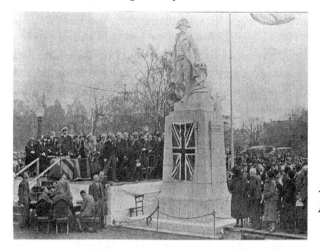

80. *Unveiling the statue of James Cook at Christchurch, New Zealand, in 1932. By kind permission of Christchurch City Libraries, CCL PhotoCD 8, IMG0009.*

American and French rule. The site of Cook's death in Hawaii became a small part of the Empire: an oak cross was planted on the spot by the crew of HMS *Blonde* in 1825 and in 1874 replaced by an obelisk in a small surrounding plot, forty foot square, bought by Great Britain in 1877. After a visit in 1924, Sir Joseph suggested that the surrounding land be taken into public control by the American authorities: it is now a historic park. He had published a lengthy defence of Cook against the criticisms of the American mission-aries who had found his detached approach to native cultures irreligious and over-tolerant. Sir Joseph also took a major part in the ceremonies on Hawaii in 1928 to mark the 150th anniversary of Cook's discovery of the island.

New Zealand had its own Cook statues. One of the most notable was erected at Christchurch, in 1932. During the late 1920s it was a quiet town, with a racecourse, much preoccupied with sport. The Cook memorial statue committee's tardy fundraising campaign was rescued in August 1929 by an offer from a local bookmaker, Mr M.F. Barnett, to fund the entire project. New Zealand had recently suffered an earthquake so there were other demands on charitable giving at this time. Barnett explained his motivation in the *Christchurch Times*: 'He discovered this country, and this country has been particularly good to me.' This was not quite the official version, which also recognized the Dutch navigator, Abel Tasman, and the Maori hero, Kupe, as founding fathers. In his unveiling speech, the Governor-General, Lord Bledisloe, described Cook as the *effective* discoverer of New Zealand and hailed him as a moral exemplar and national hero (fig. 80). The country was now in the grip of the Depression and Barnett also made a 100-guinea donation to the Mayor's Relief of Distress Fund to silence criticisms over the expense of the memorial. The committee and sponsor had wanted a statue similar to the one in the Mall, and gave the commission to a talented local sculptor – William Thomas Trethewey (1892–1956). Trethewey made his

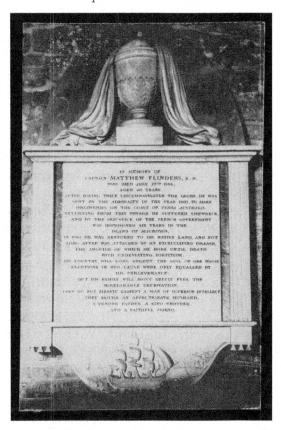

81. *The memorial to Captain Matthew Flinders RN, at St Mary, Donington, Lincolnshire (on a vintage postcard). © On loan to the National Maritime Museum, Greenwich, London, from a Private Collection, FLI/109.*

living as a monumental mason but produced a number of heroic memorials, mostly in stone. This material was cheaper than bronze, which could not be cast locally.[17] Cook is shown, once again, standing on the deck of his ship, but the suggestion of a strong breeze catching his coat tails gives the figure an unusual animation. Fortunately, the statue survived the 2011 Christchurch earthquake.

Flinders

Matthew Flinders (1774–1814), the first circumnavigator of Australia and the man who named the continent, was adopted as another twentieth-century Australian national hero. In the years following his premature death, his family had sought to mark his achievements and his bad luck. Flinders's widow, Mary Ann, erected a marble tablet at his birthplace of Donington, Lincolnshire, as requested in her husband's will, at a cost of £101. It has a draped urn above the inscription and a ship on the apron (fig. 81). It reads:

---

17 *Christchurch Times*, 10 August 1929, 2 August 1932.

IN MEMORY OF
CAPTAIN MATTHEW FLINDERS, R.N.
WHO DIED JULY 19TH 1814
AGED 40 YEARS
AFTER HAVING TWICE CIRCUMNAVIGATED THE GLOBE, HE WAS
SENT BY THE ADMIRALTY IN THE YEAR 1801, TO MAKE
DISCOVERIES ON THE COAST OF TERRA AUSTRALIS
RETURNING FROM THIS VOYAGE HE SUFFERED SHIPWRECK
AND BY THE INJUSTICE OF THE FRENCH GOVERNMENT
WAS IMPRISONED SIX YEARS IN THE
ISLAND OF MAURITIUS
IN 1810, HE WAS RESTORED TO HIS NATIVE LAND, AND NOT
LONG AFTER WAS ATTACKED BY AN EXCRUCIATING DISEASE
THE ANGUISH HE BORE UNTIL DEATH
WITH UNDEVIATING FORTITUDE
HIS COUNTRY WILL LONG REGRET THE LOSS OF ONE WHOSE
EXERTIONS IN HER CAUSE WERE ONLY EQUALLED BY
HIS PERSEVERANCE:
BUT HIS FAMILY WILL MOST DEEPLY FEEL THE
IRREPARABLE DEPRIVATION.
THEY DO NOT HEREIN LAMENT A MAN OF SUPERIOR INTELLECT
THEY MOURN AN AFFECTIONATE HUSBAND
A TENDER FATHER. A KIND BROTHER,
AND A FAITHFUL FRIEND

Flinders was also commemorated by a memorial on Stamford Hill, Port Lincoln (Victoria, Australia), put up by Jane, Lady Franklin, in 1839 on behalf of her husband, Sir John, at that time governor of Van Diemen's Land (Tasmania). The two men came from related Lincolnshire families and Franklin had served on board Flinders's ship *Investigator* in 1802. Mary Ann Flinders wrote to thank Franklin: 'The column you have so generously erected will not only exhibit what he did in the furtherance of navigation but will show that however his services were forgotten by the government at home, there were some who knew & honored his worth.'[18] Flinders's captivity had put back the date of his promotion and there had been disputes with the Admiralty over the expenses of writing the official account of the voyage. The Australian colonies of New South Wales and Victoria were to vote Mrs Flinders a pension of £100 per year in 1853. As she was found to have died the year before, this reverted to her daughter.

---

[18] NMM FLI/109.

The idea of erecting a statue to the explorer at Melbourne was suggested at a meeting of the Victorian Branch of the Royal Geographical Society in 1911 and the task was put in the charge of a local committee.[19] The First World War brought matters to a virtual halt but, after a renewed fundraising drive promoted by the *Melbourne Argus*, they had sufficient money to approach a local sculptor, Charles Webster Gilbert (1867–1925). The work was cast in Paris by F. Barbedienne and unveiled in 9 November 1925. The educational value of the project was stressed throughout. Flinders is shown standing in the prow of a boat in full uniform and sword, with his hat under his arm. Below him, the bending figures of two seamen beach the boat – an image that appears to suggest Flinders's triumphs were achieved on the backs of the workers. The number of memorials to Flinders eventually came to rival those of Cook. Other statues were erected in Adelaide and Sydney, the latter with an associated memorial to Flinders's much-loved black-and-white cat, Trim, the subject of a mock funeral eulogy penned by his owner.

Statues of Flinders have also begun to appear in his home country. A full-length bronze statue by Judith Holmes Drewry was erected at Donington in 2006. Another bronze by Mark Richards, showing the explorer in shirt-sleeves, kneeling by his map, dividers in hand, was placed inside the entrance of Euston Station, London, in July 2014 after being officially unveiled by Prince William at Australia House. This marks his approximate burial place, now reputedly somewhere underneath the site, in what was the St James's Burial Ground. This overcrowded London churchyard was closed in 1854 and after 1883 was partly cleared to accommodate the expansion of the railway terminus. Flinders's remains had, in fact, been removed to make room for more burials even before closure of the cemetery, a common fate for those buried in London.

The family-friendly explorer

By the time of the bicentenaries of Cook's voyages, the attitudes of ethnic triumphalism voiced by Sir Joseph Carruthers seemed very questionable. Nevertheless, enthusiasm for commemorating Cook, Flinders and even the less popular Vancouver is at present undiminished. Efforts to encourage tourism and business are among the motivations behind these projects. Apart from the Donington statue to Flinders (2006), a new bronze one of Vancouver by Penelope Reeve was erected at King's Lynn in 2000, and a bronze Cook by Anthony Stones was presented to the National Maritime Museum at Greenwich in 1994. This was modelled as one of a group of seven

---

19 The Australian Natives Association gave half the proceeds of a fête held in February 1914.

New Zealand explorers, cast in resin, for that nation's pavilion at the Seville Expo 1992, a bronze version afterwards being erected at Gisborne (where Cook first landed, on North Island): the Greenwich one is a second cast.[20] A trend can be seen towards commissions aimed at school parties and families, as for example in the statue of Nicholas Young, the ship's boy who was the first of Cook's crew to sight New Zealand at Gisborne – which Cook named Poverty Bay. A very informal version of Flinders, by Carl Merton, kneels without stockings and in his shirt on a nature trail in the Rumbala Reserve in New South Wales, inviting interaction with the public. A statue of Cook as a boy at his birthplace at Great Ayton, by Nicholas Dimblebee, is intended to appeal to a similar family audience (fig. 82). This is a very different approach from the Victorian statue on its tall plinth protected from contact from 'rough fellows' and small boys.

The North-West Passage

Commemoration of polar explorers, who investigated regions unsuited to colonization or cities, focused on disaster: the casualties became martyrs to new discovery. From 1818, a series of expeditions were sent into Arctic waters to seek a sea route from Baffin Bay to the Pacific and record scientific data in the region. The expedition vessels were inevitably trapped in a frozen sea for many months of the year and gradually their crews began to develop techniques for exploring the surrounding area on foot. They could only *supplement* their food stocks by hunting and, after three winters largely without fresh food, scurvy would set in. There was always a potential threat that a series of poor summers would trap their ships for a fatally long period.

Initially the project of charting the Arctic Archipelago proceeded overland and by sea, involving a couple of narrow escapes but no catastrophic loss of life. Finally, in 1845, the *Erebus* and *Terror* were sent under overall command of Sir John Franklin (1786–1847), to update the surveys of terrestrial magnetism in the Arctic and, if possible, to fill the gap in the route to the Pacific. His ships entered the maze of islands and failed to reappear. Search expeditions found traces of a winter encampment on Beechey Island, with the grave markers of three early casualties – two seamen and a marine. The climate of the Arctic has preserved these ephemeral memorials with the coffins, clothes and bodies of the three men (the subject of investigation in recent years). None of the usual ceremony had been omitted from the burial, although the three were dressed in their working clothes, not the specially-made grave clothes commonly used in civilian funerals. Sherard Osborn

---

[20] In store at time of writing: the others were of the Maori Kupe, Magellan, Pedro Fernandez de Quiros, Alvaro de Mendaña, Tasman and Bougainville.

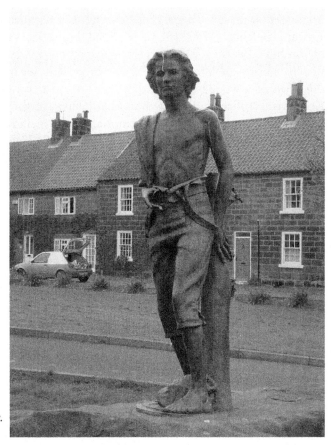

*82. James Cook as
a boy, by Nicholas
Dimblebee, at Great
Ayton, North Yorkshire.
© Author.*

noted, after witnessing discovery of the site in 1850, that 'The good taste of the officers had prevented the general simplicity of an oaken head and foot-board to each of the three graves being marred by any long and childish epitaphs or the doggerel of a lower-deck poet.'[21] The verse on tombstones, as with many other aspects of Georgian commemoration, was under attack in contemporary tracts and Osborn saw in the biblical quotations of the head boards evidence of the evangelical faith of Franklin and his officers.[22]

There were over forty expeditions sent in search of Franklin and these produced their own casualties. William Sharp, of the supply ship HMS *North Star*, died in 1849 while the ship was wintering in Greenland and was buried on shore at North Star Bay. His comrades made a determined effort to replicate the style of stone headstone that would have been produced by a

---

[21] Sherard Osborn, *Stray Leaves from an Arctic Journal* (New York, 1852), p. 91.
[22] 'Choose ye this day whom ye shall serve' (Joshua 24:15) and 'Thus saith the Lord of Hosts consider your ways' (Haggai 1:7). The choice of text suggests that the seaman and marine commemorated may have been troublesome characters.

monumental mason. The last major naval search-expedition, led by Captain Edward Belcher (1799–1877), returned home in 1854, abandoning two of its ships. Beechey Island had now become a rendezvous point for naval vessels, and it was here that Belcher's carpenters set up a cenotaph. It took the form of a wooden post with a ball on top that doubled as a post box. Epitaphs to officers and crew buried elsewhere in the Arctic were stamped on lead plaques affixed to the memorial. These included men from *Investigator*, under Commander Robert McClure (1807–73), whose rescue was the major achievement of Belcher's squadron. This vessel entered the North-West Passage via the Bering Strait and became trapped off Banks Island. When her crew left the Arctic via Baffin Bay they had become the first Europeans to travel through the Passage and survive.

The international nature of the search for Franklin is demonstrated by the nationality of its dead hero, Joseph René Bellot (1826–53), a French naval officer who fell between ice floes and drowned while serving on his second British search expedition. John Barrow junior commissioned a marble plaque to the memory of this officer that was affixed to Belcher's wooden cenotaph on Beechey Island. A granite obelisk designed by Philip Hardwick (1792–1870), then Surveyor to Greenwich Hospital, was set up on the river walk there in 1855 at a cost of £500, the remainder of the subscription fund going to Bellot's five unmarried sisters. A cenotaph was also placed in the cemetery of Bellot's home town of Rochefort, showing the explorer in polar clothing recumbent on an ice floe beneath a canopy in the form of a draped upturned boat, supported by four polar bears (fig. 83). A third bronze memorial, by the sculptor Nicolas Guillemin, was set up in the Naval Museum at the Louvre: its design showed clasped hands, draped flags and the royal arms of England and France.[23] While these two former enemies were fighting as allies against Russia during the Crimean War, the British Government's search for Franklin drew to a close. Dr John Rae (1813–93) of the Hudson Bay Company had brought news that the expedition had perished in the southern part of the Arctic. These second-hand Inuit reports included disturbing suggestions of cannibalism but also that Franklin's men had found a route through the archipelago, pre-empting McClure as discoverer of the North-West Passage. A final government-funded overland search failed to confirm this.

Jane, Lady Franklin

Sir John's formidable widow, Jane, now sent her own expedition in 1857, her funds augmented with contributions from the public. One of the first tasks

[23] The museum moved to the Palais de Chaillot in 1943 and the current whereabouts of the memorial are unknown.

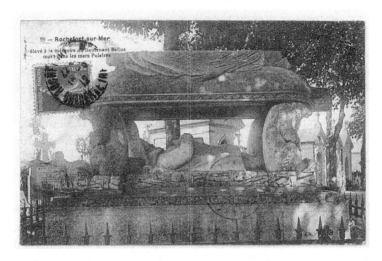

83. *The tomb of Joseph René Bellot, at Rochefort, France (on a vintage postcard).*
© *Author's Collection.*

of its commander, Francis Leopold McClintock (1819–1907), was to set up a marble tablet to Franklin's memory in front of Belcher's memorial on Beechey Island. McClintock's sledge parties found the missing expedition's possessions and equipment scattered along the west coast of King William Island with the remains (many unburied) of its members. They had abandoned their ships after three winters beset by ice, an event noted in a brief document (deposited deliberately in a cairn) that reported Franklin's date of death before this final disaster. His men had indeed found a route to the Pacific in advance of McClure. A party that established their position and the shore line of the island may even have reported their findings to Franklin before he died on 11 June 1847.

Lady Franklin (1791–1875) devoted the rest of her life to the commemoration of her husband and his men, and promoting his claim as the discoverer of the Passage – although McClure had already received the financial reward offered by the government for this discovery. In January 1860 she decided that what she really wanted was 'a public memorial to the memory of my husband and his companions'.[24] She pursued this aim through a group of male allies such as Sir Roderick Murchison of the Royal Geographical Society, Ashurst Majendie of the Royal Society and the former First Lord of the Admiralty, Sir Francis Thornhill Baring. Parliament voted £2000 for a statue of Franklin by sculptor Matthew Noble (1817–76), unveiled in Waterloo Place, London, in 1861. Noble also produced the statue of Franklin set up by the citizens of

[24] Scott Polar Research Institute (SPRI) MS248/119, Lady Franklin's journal, 2 January 1860.

Hobart to commemorate their former governor, and the memorial that Lady Jane commissioned for Westminster Abbey in 1874. Lady Franklin also set up a wall tablet to her husband's memory in St James's, Spilsby, Lincolnshire, which was his birthplace. In St Andrew's mission church, Gravesend, erected in memory of Sir Francis Beaufort (1774–1857), Hydrographer of the Navy and one of the founders of the Royal Geographical Society, Lady Franklin installed three stained-glass windows by Clayton & Bell, depicting Christ, St Andrew and St Peter, with the names of the crews of *Erebus* and *Terror* inscribed on brass dedication plates beneath them. She even erected a wall tablet at Haslar Hospital to Lieutenant William Hulme Hooper of HMS *Plover*, sent to wait and subsequently to search for the missing expedition at the Bering Strait end of the Passage. He died in 1854, three years after his return to Britain 'in impaired health but with undiminished zeal in the cause'.

Lady Franklin's vigorous campaign, waged on behalf of her husband's reputation behind the discreet veil of Victorian widowhood, is revealed in the journal she kept through most of her adult life. Her role should not obscure the motivations of her supporters. The Royal Navy had essentially completed the task of charting the northern boundaries of America at some financial and human cost and, as ever, it was happy to proclaim that the casualties had fallen in the hour of victory. The major loser was McClure. When his death notice in *The Times* said that he 'discovered and completed the North-west Passage',[25] this claim was promptly refuted by both Lady Franklin and Franklin's grandson, Willingham Gell. McClure's plain granite coped stone in Kensal Green Cemetery repeats the claim.

Ice, ships and polar bears

The records of Sir John Franklin's final expedition were almost totally lost. The protagonists were silent and it was left to speculation to give an account of their story. Sherard Osborn, a veteran of the search parties, published a fictionalized account of the expedition's demise. His accounts of the scenery of the region mix the sublime with the gothic and he gives an entirely imaginary account of Franklin's death and funeral: 'The shout of victory, which cheered the last hour of Nelson and of Wolfe, rang not less heartily round the bed of the gallant Franklin.'[26] The relief on the plinth of Noble's London statue follows his account: 'a group of affectionate followers stand round a huge chasm in the ice-stream and Fitzjames ... reads the service for the dead over the grave of Franklin'.[27] Franklin's grave was certainly never found on

25 *The Times*, 20, 22, 28 October 1873.
26 *Once a Week*, 29 October 1859, p. 366.
27 Ibid.

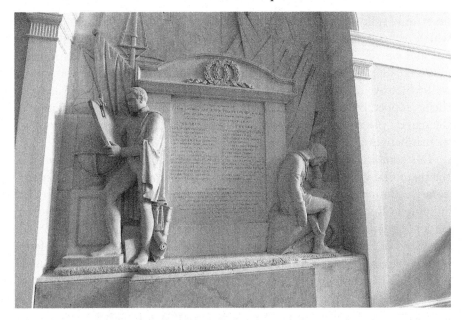

84. *Memorial to the officers of* Erebus *and* Terror, *by Richard Westmacott the younger, at the chapel of the Old Naval College, Greenwich.* © *National Maritime Museum, Greenwich, London, E9021-31.*

the shore where his crews abandoned ship. The statue represents him telling his men that the Passage has been discovered. He wears the uniform of a naval commander draped in a loose fur coat, a rather fanciful way of signifying a polar explorer also employed in contemporary portraits of William Parry, James Clark Ross and John Ross. The formal national monument at Greenwich to the officers of the expedition also makes a half-hearted attempt at depicting polar dress (fig. 84). The sculptor – Richard Westmacott, the younger (1799–1872) – shows the figure of a despondent seaman 'habited in the dress worn in the inclement northern regions'[28] including boots, mitts and an early version of the balaclava helmet. The officer in charge of him is shown in simplified naval uniform. Reports of Westmacott's lectures to the Royal Academy in 1863 note his unfavourable remarks about monuments in which 'the taste for peculiar and minute accidents has often led the sculptor into the most egregious disregard of true art-principals': Westmacott, a classicist, was not a man for pedantically accurate detail.[29] The two ships are shown in relief,

28 *Illustrated London News*, 8 January 1859, p. 35. Originally erected in the vestibule of the Naval Gallery in the Painted Hall at Greenwich Hospital, the monument vanished from public sight to the chapel vestry in the late 1930s when the Hall was restored to pre-Naval Gallery condition, but since 2009 has been easily visible again in the chapel vestibule.
29 *The Builder*, 21 February 1863, p. 130.

beset amid spiky ice pinnacles in the background of this monument, a feature which recurs below the bust of Franklin on his Westminster Abbey memorial and on the two to his second-in-command, Francis Rawden Crozier (1796–1848?), in Banbridge, Northern Ireland. Crozier's siblings erected a wall tablet by Joseph Robinson Kirk in the new church there, and a gothic shrine, topped by a statue of the explorer, was set up by public subscription in the market place. The spur-buttresses are topped by polar bears that both act as guardians and offer a nod toward polar zoology.

This combination of ships beset by ice floes and Arctic wildlife is used in the memorial window in St Mary's, Banbury, to Franklin's younger contemporary, Admiral Sir George Back (1796–1878), a veteran explorer who died at home in London. One of a set commissioned from manufacturers Heaton, Butler & Bayne by the incumbent, Back's nephew, Henry, the window includes two views of HMS *Terror* by Lieutenants Owen Stanley and William Henry Smyth, based on sketches they made during her Arctic voyage of 1836–37 with Back in command (fig. 85).

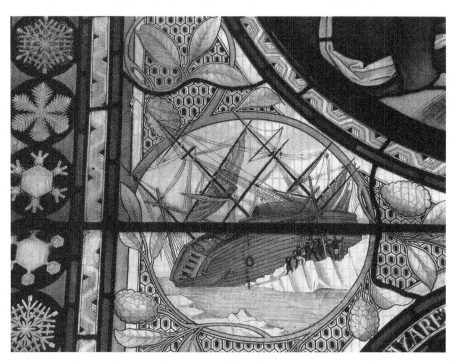

85. *Window commemorating Admiral Sir George Back, by manufacturers Heaton, Butler & Bayne, at St Mary, Banbury (detail).* © *Author.*

A heroic age in Antarctica

The public memory of Sir John Franklin was still relatively fresh during 1912 when Robert Falcon Scott (1868–1912) and his four companions died on their return from the South Pole. They had not perished in the hour of victory but the fortunate recovery of the expedition journals revealed exemplary deaths. Scott's memorials could present the event as a moral triumph and quote his own words. Apsley Cherry-Garrard (1886–1959), assistant zoologist on the expedition and one of its most eloquent chroniclers, chose a quotation from Tennyson's *Ulysses* for the wooden cross set up at Observation Point – 'To strive, to seek and not to yield'. There is an echo of Franklin in his selection, as the poem describes the last, fatal voyage of an ageing explorer. Commemoration was undertaken by local committees and the national Mansion House Scott Memorial Fund. Its objectives of distributing funds to the dependants of the five men, paying off the expedition's debts, publishing its scientific results and setting up a bronze tablet in St Paul's Cathedral, proved relatively straightforward. However, the committee had a difficult time completing the main outdoor monument to the dead explorers. The project was delayed by the outbreak of the First World War, the price of bronze rose and their chosen sculptor – Albert Hemstock Hodge (1875–1917) – died after completing the design and the initial models; finally it proved impossible to find a site in central London. To the chairman's intense relief, a suitable position was provided by the War Office at Mount Wise in Plymouth. The committee had been considering a site at the Royal Naval College, Greenwich, at the time the design competition was held. With that in view, the monument had to be in harmony with the baroque architecture; a design was chosen that approached its subject through neo-classical allegory and Scott is shown crowned by Immortality (sometimes described as Victory). A correspondent in *The Builder* greatly approved and expressed his dislike of the realistic 'imitation in Portland stone of a heap of snow and ice' offered by another competitor.[30]

Like George Back, Scott had clerical connections. His brother-in-law, the Reverend Lloyd Harvey Bruce, was rector at Binton, where a new west window was installed in the church in 1915 (fig. 86). A late work by the firm of C.E. Kempe & Co., the gothic tracery gives the figures of Scott, Wilson, Bowers, Oates and Evans the appearance of a group of Christian apostles (the polar images in Back's window are less dominant, being inserted between scenes of the childhood of Christ). Scott's photographer, H.G. Ponting, was consulted to ensure the authenticity of the design. Scenes of man-hauled sledging are shown in relief on the memorial at St Paul's and the base of the

---

[30] *The Builder*, 17 July 1914, p. 72.

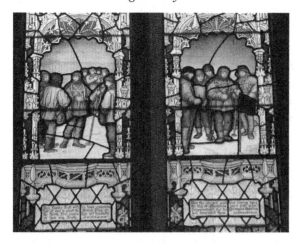

86. *Window commemorating Captain Robert Falcon Scott and his companions, by manufacturers C.E. Kempe and Co., at St Peter, Binton, Warwickshire (detail).*
© *Philip Halling (CC EY-SA 2.0 UK).*

monument at Plymouth – it was a sensible way to show all five men of the polar party and express the hardship of their journey. The memorial at City Hall, Cardiff, by William Wheatley Wagstaff (1880–1962), includes reliefs of seals and penguins and a dog sledge. The officers of the Royal Navy commissioned their own memorial to Scott placed opposite to that of Franklin in Waterloo Place. Their speed in erecting the statue, in 1915, made life even more difficult for the Mansion House Committee who were still looking for a site in London for Hodge's design. The naval officers eventually gave the commission to Scott's widow, a former pupil of Rodin and now recognized as one of the significant British female sculptors of the early twentieth century. Some quite unjustified reservations about her competence were voiced by Lionel Earle, secretary to the Board of Works, who committed to file the opinion that 'for all I hear, she may be an admirable woman, but is absolutely devoid of all artistic sense'.[31] The decision to depict Scott in working clothing provoked further controversy, with a fear among senior officers that the statue of Franklin on the other side of the road would somehow pull rank.[32] Kathleen Scott (1878–1947, later Lady Kennet) produced a copy for Christchurch, New Zealand – in marble due to the bronze shortage[33] – and another informal Scott, dressed in naval overcoat and boots, for Portsmouth Dockyard in bronze. The objections to polar dress were probably a reflection of contemporary class-based political controversies. One of the most successful sculptures of a polar explorer is the memorial to Sir Ernest Henry Shackleton (1874–1922) by Charles Sargeant Jagger (1885–1934) at the Royal Geographical Society. The sartorial realism of this sculptor's military

---

31 TNA WORK20/127. The maquette for the statue was acquired by SPRI in 2013.
32 Max Jones, *The Last Great Quest* (Oxford, 2003), p. 155.
33 The statue broke off at the ankles during the 2011 Christchurch earthquake.

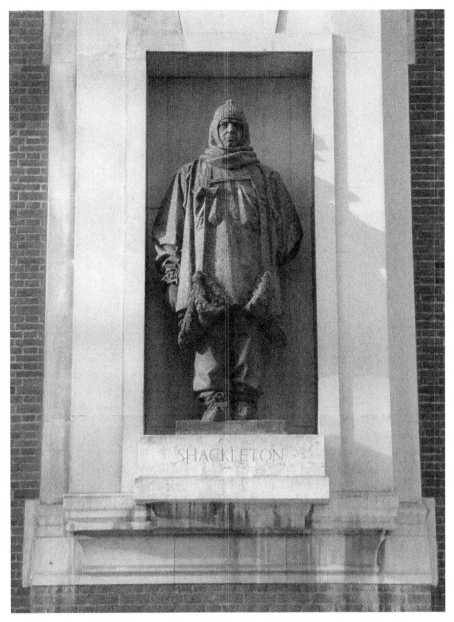

87. *Sir Ernest Shackleton, by Charles Sargeant Jagger, at the Royal Geographical Society, London. © Author.*

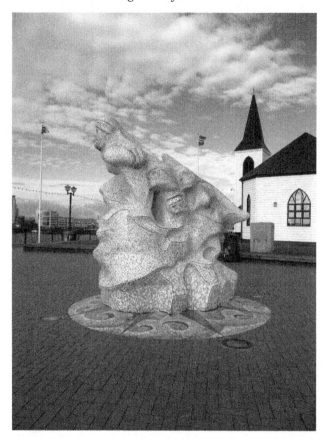

88. *Memorial to Scott
and his companions,
by Jonathan Williams,
at Cardiff Docks.
© Author.*

figures reflected his own pride in his working-class roots. Shackleton's baggy clothing and dangling fur mittens are superbly realized (fig. 87).

In 2003, a new memorial to Scott and his five companions by sculptor Jonathan Williams was commissioned by the Captain Scott Society, and it stands on the dockside at Cardiff, near the Norwegian Church (fig. 88). It takes the form of an iceberg in resin, incorporating the faces of Scott and his four companions and the bows of the expedition vessel *Terra Nova*, which sailed from Cardiff on 15 June 1910. Scott has clearly made the transition to collective memory as a 'historic worthy', justly celebrated for his contribution to the scientific research which continues in Antarctica. Franklin, for long an obscure figure on the British side of the Atlantic, has gained in significance at a time of global warming, the degradation of the icy northern environment that killed him and the increased commercial exploitation of the Canadian Arctic.

In September 2014, Parks Canada discovered the hull of his ship, HMS *Erebus*, on the seabed of Queen Maud Gulf, opening a new chapter in the investigation of this polar mystery.

8

Inshore: fishermen, lifesavers and leisure

Fishing boats, lifeboats and yachts are all small boats, or at least relatively so, from communities in which owners and crews are also subject to the hazards of the sea. This coastal zone, where work and leisure meet, has also been an area of cultural innovation, both artistic and social. Fishing is linked in some way to all of these stories.

Fishermen

Significant memorials to fishermen are harder to find than one might think. Inshore fishing was neither a lucrative occupation nor a full-time one. In eastern England, coastal dwellers took to fishing when other coastal trades declined, and combined it with pilotage, salvage and ship supply, all activities sometimes associated with sharp practice. Other coastal side-lines such as smuggling or plundering wrecks fell completely on the wrong side of the law. 'Fisherman' was not necessarily an occupation to be carved on the family gravestone.[1] At the Old Parish Burial Ground at Wick in Caithness (a port that became a herring boom-town when the Dutch ceased to dominate this industry), there are many inscriptions commemorating men who gained their livelihood from fish processing and trading. Only one surviving stone states that it commemorates a fisherman, John Maskell of Greenwich, whose smack, *Prince of Wales* of London, was wrecked in Sinclairs Bay, in 1802: Greenwich smacks fished for cod in the North Sea.

Fishing villages were often situated some distance from the main parish church in remote coastal locations, inaccessible from the landward side but near to boats pulled up on the shore. Robin Hood's Bay for example was served by Old St Stephen's at Fylingthorpe one mile from the town, until a new church was built between Bay and Thorpe in 1870. Bay town itself had Methodist and Congregationalist chapels, a reflection of the strength

---

1   The gravestones at Barnoon Cemetery, St Ives, mention the occupation of only one of the fishermen buried there, George Quick (1853–1915), a local preacher.

of nonconformist religion in fishing communities. 'Fisherman' could be an occupation with status when individuals were commemorated in an evangelical context: 'I will make you fishers of men' (Matthew 4:19). A good example is the memorial placed in Paul church near Mousehole, Cornwall, to three local fishermen who died in 1851 during Captain Allen Gardiner's ill-fated mission to convert the inhabitants of Tierra del Fuego.[2] At the former offshore fishing ports of Lowestoft and Hull, fishermen's headstones are found in the municipal cemeteries rather than the parish churches, reflecting a new industry moving into an established settlement. Newspaper reports concerning deep-sea fishing talk about 'smacksmen' or 'trawlermen'.

In kirkyards and churchyards

Scotland early developed a tradition of highly carved churchyard memorials, the style related to vernacular woodcarving. In 1588 the General Assembly of the Church of Scotland made burying inside churches illegal, reinforcing an earlier condemnation in John Knox's 1560 *Book of Discipline*.[3] These proscriptions encouraged the Scots to produce not only elite, high-status external monuments, but also more modest gravestones carved with trade symbols, and this was also customary on the Isle of Man. The oars, nets and fish on Scottish tombstones identify the family with fishing, although the iconography may represent the person erecting the gravestone rather than the family members commemorated, and do not indicate precisely what their connection was with the trade. The stones were often carved on both sides and sometimes have later additions. Good examples are found in kirkyards on the Scottish east coast. The church and burial ground of St Vigeans, in Angus, served the nearby fishing village of Auchmithie. The haddock they caught there were salted, dried or smoked. Auchmithie is credited with inventing the Arbroath smoky – a partly split haddock lightly smoked under a barrel.

The sandstone headstones have been protected by their sheltered inland site and display some splendid examples of folk art. The earlier stones were set up in the mid-eighteenth century with numerous additional inscriptions, made more confusing by the frequency of particular surnames in this area. In 1805 John Spink and Jannet Swankie, his wife, who married on 12 November 1773, dedicated a headstone in this location to three children who died young.

---

[2] Supplies to the seven-man mission were delayed and they all starved to death.

[3] John Knox and others, *The First Book of Discipline* (Edinburgh, 1721 edition), p. 598: 'In respect of divers Inconveniences, we think it not seemly that the Kirk appointed for Preaching and Ministration of the Sacraments shall be made a place of Buryall, but that some other secret and convenient Place, lying in the most free Aire be appointed for that Use, which place ought to be walled and fenced about, and kept for that use only.'

It gives Jannet's maiden name, as was customary in Scotland and the Isle of Man, and describes John as a 'Mariner'. The reverse is carved with a winged cherub's head, a boat and anchor, and two fish. A verse below refers to the three dead children:

> We on our bed of rest
> Do take our soft repose
> Nor are we toss'd by boreas blast
> As they that to the ocean go

The nearby headstone set up by John Swankie and Helen Cargill (married 22 November 1757) depicts a fishing boat with drying sails and two crossed fish. A verse in cursive lettering below threatens that

> Tho' man in health at morn arise
> and joyful view the light
> Perhaps a stiffened corse he lies
> At the return of night

A later inscription has been added by Ann Cargill in memory of David Swankie, her husband and a 'Seaman of Arbroath', who died on 21 December 1845. Births to John and Helen were registered into the 1770s: David, born in 1792, may have been their grandson. The stone may initially have been set up to mark a family grave plot, a more modest version of the elite family burying grounds set up in kirkyards such as Greyfriars in Edinburgh.

Later English headstones to fishermen include a sandstone example at Holy Island commemorating John Stevenson, who drowned nearby in a gale in 1875 (fig. 89). Erected by his widow, the headstone has a rope-twist border and a single-masted lugger carved above the inscription. Stevenson's occupation as fisherman is indicated in the 1871 census. The headstone to Benjamin Herrington (d. 1922) at Southwold, Suffolk, is resolutely traditional in style but, here again, his occupation as 'fisherman' is only stated in the census. The stone is carved with a portrait of the 12½ ton longshore boat, *Rapid*: Herrington was one of five joint owners.[4]

Anglican initiatives

In response to the success of nonconformity in fishing communities, some Anglican clergy took an active role in setting up memorials to fishermen in

---

4 Information from Lowestoft Record Office.

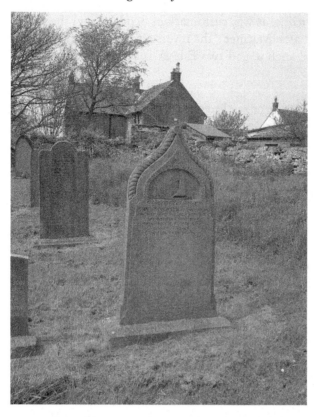

*89. Gravestone
of fisherman John
Stevenson, at Holy
Island, Northumberland.
© Author.*

English churches from the mid-nineteenth century onwards – one aspect of philanthropic and missionary work directed towards seamen in their parish. Many of the series of memorial tiles set up at Brightlingsea, Essex, to local men lost at sea commemorate fishermen. Brightlingsea's fishermen caught sprats and dredged for oysters and scallops in deep-sea smacks with a crew of six men, which was particularly hard and dangerous work. Essex smacks from the Colne and Blackwater ventured as far as the Terschelling bank off northern Holland. Following a particularly heavy death toll during the gales of 1883, when five smacks were lost, the Reverend Arthur Pertwee, vicar of Brightlingsea, put forward a proposal for such a memorial, commencing from the start of his incumbency in 1872.[5] The original idea was to inscribe the names on wooden panels. The scheme eventually took the less conventional form of a series of tiles of uniform design running round the church. Originally intended to consist of encaustic tiles, they eventually took the form of white tiles with the inscription painted over the glaze in enamels, a

5   Alfred L. Wakeling and Peter Moon, *Tiles of Tragedy: Brightlingsea's Unique Maritime Memorial* (Stockton-on-Tees, 2001), p. 25.

cheaper way of producing many different designs. Encaustic tiles, with the pattern produced in two layers of different-coloured clay, were used as floor tiles during the late Middle Ages. The technique was re-invented by Herbert Minton in the 1840s and the tiles were installed in gothic-revival churches and villas. Their use in a collective memorial context was unusual but not unique.[6] The Brightlingsea tiles were supplied by church furnishers Cox & Buckley, who would have ordered them from a ceramics producer, perhaps Minton. In 1858 the Right Reverend Edward Trollope had suggested single rows of Minton's wall tiles as a more architecturally sensitive substitute for conventional wall tablets.[7]

The inshore fishing at Filey in Yorkshire was not dissimilar to that in Angus. The local boats were the famous Yorkshire coble, with its full, high bow to face the surf in beach launchings and landings. The sea has eroded back the softer layers exposing a shelf of hard rock along this shoreline, on which the fishwives found limpets to bait the long lines. St Oswald's church has a commemorative window by the firm H. Bryans depicting the calling of Simon, Andrew and Peter: finding an appropriate biblical subject was very easy in this case. The dedication lists Filey fishermen lost between 1879 and 1896, with a further plaque noting more seamen whose bodies had not been recovered between 1901 and 1948. The 1883 casualties were eight men from Filey, compared to thirty-four at Brightlingsea. St Margaret's, Lowestoft, has a memorial with the names of local fishermen drowned at sea listed on wooden panels. A window above shows St Andrew, their patron saint. This comparatively modern work was designed by Mrs Laurel Cooper in 1965 and shows the saint holding his saltire and a net filled with fish. The window is dedicated to Charles William Dance (d. 1963) and his wife Ida: at the beginning of a successful commercial career, Dance had worked as a fish salesman. Truro Cathedral, a gothic-revival building begun in 1880, has a window scheme devised by the architect John Loughborough Pearson (1817–97) and produced by the London firm Clayton & Bell. Two windows at the west end are concerned with local industry and depict tin miners at Dolcoath and fishermen at Newlyn, both with their respective guardian angels. These particular windows do not, however, directly commemorate, individually or collectively, the labour force in these industries.

6   Note the Memorial to Heroic Self Sacrifice in St Botolph's churchyard, City of London, tiles by William de Morgan and Doulton & Co.
7   The Reverend Edward Trollope, *Manual of Sepulchral Memorials* (1858), introduction, p. 4.

The Russian outrage

During the second half of the nineteenth century, Hull and Grimsby emerged as deep-sea trawling ports, their fishing communities moving into the town from other parts of the country. The fish were distributed to industrial centres by rail and from 1880 the trawlers began to be powered by steam. The work remained extremely risky, with the dangers of death and injury from machinery added to the hazards of weather. The memorial to the fishing community settled in Hull's Hessle Road, however, came about as a result of an entirely different sort of accident.

The Hull trawlers were by then operating in company fleets, with an 'admiral' responsible for the transfer of the fish from trawlers to fish carriers and the general direction of the fleet by means of flags and rockets. On the night of 21–22 October 1904, the Russian Baltic fleet was *en route* to the Pacific to reinforce the naval forces responding to the Japanese blockade of Port Arthur. Nervous about rumours of Japanese torpedo boats in the area, they mistakenly opened fire on a fleet of Hull trawlers. George Henry Smith, skipper of *Crane*, and William Richard Leggate, his third hand, were killed and six more men on the same vessel injured. She subsequently sank. William Whelpton of the trawler *Mino*, also damaged by gunfire, died of shock on 13 May the following year. British public outrage was then appeased when the Japanese Imperial fleet of Admiral Togo destroyed the offending Russians at the Battle of Tsushima on 27 May 1905.

Smith had been a member of the Blyth Boys' branch of the Royal Antediluvian Order of Buffaloes (RAOB), and this fraternal body provided the band and the coffin bearers at his funeral. The Blythe Boys' Lodge of the RAOB also elected the memorial committee. As funds were a comparatively modest £245, the sculpture was provided by the monumental mason associated with Spring Bank Cemetery, Albert Leake. A statue of Sicilian marble is placed on a plinth of red Balmoral granite. It shows skipper Smith, clad in sea boots sou'wester and sweater, holding a pair of binoculars in his left hand, his right raised in supplication (fig. 90). Rather than carving the figure himself, Leake is said to have contracted it out to Italian workmen, for whom he provided a photograph of the required pose, modelled by himself. It was not unveiled by Charles Henry Wilson, Lord Nunburnholme, as stated on the inscription, apparently owing to a genuine indisposition on his part. A local MP with Baltic commercial interests, Nunburnholme had been anxious to dampen down the feud with Russia aroused by the incident.

Hull's fishing industry declined after 1976 when it lost access to its Icelandic fishing grounds, but its longstanding Baltic trade continued. The statue was moved to a nearby location in the Hessle Road and unveiled for a second time on the centenary of the incident in 2004. The naval attaché to the Russian

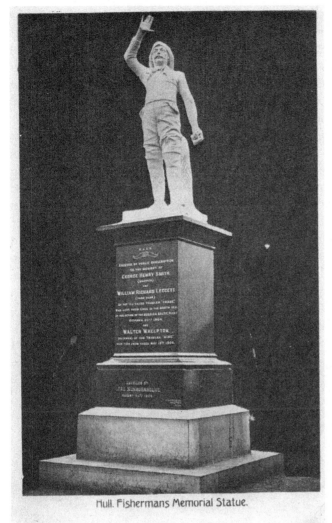

Hull. Fishermans Memorial Statue.

embassy did the honours on this occasion. An additional plaque rededicates it as: 'a tribute to the bravery of the city's trawlermen past and present'.

Lost trawlers

Fishing in Hull's neighbour, Grimsby, also died out although the town retains an involvement with fish processing. A fisherman's chapel in the Methodist Central Hall remains as a memorial to the industry. A painted board records the 102 trawlers and 102 men lost from the port between 1914 and 1975. Three stained-glass windows transferred from the Bethel Mission, Cleethorpes, commemorate particular accidents. The trawler *Sheldon* lost radio contact in

January 1953 and was presumed sunk with all hands. The memorial window was erected by her owners, Sir Thomas Robinson & Son, at a cost of £150 (fig. 91). The window, designed by Gerald Edward Roberts Smith (1883–1959) and made by A.K. Nicholson (1871–1937), depicts St Peter clad in a short tunic and holding a net, with seagulls behind him. Below is a ship portrait of the trawler within a border of shells and fish. The names of her fourteen-man crew are listed on panes bordered by fishing net. The second window shows the steam trawler *Epine*, wrecked with only five survivors on the rugged west coast of Iceland on 13 March 1948. The window was paid for by the relatives of the men lost in the wreck. A third window, showing deck hands pulling in the trawl, commemorates three men killed on board the *St Oswald* when she struck a mine left over from the Second World War off the Norwegian coast in May 1948. These windows form a snapshot of the fishing industry in its heyday. More recently Grimsby has been seeking to attract visitors and develop a sense of place by a more public commemoration of its fishing past. It houses the National Fishing Heritage Centre, and in 2005 a bronze statue of a fisherman hauling in a net was commissioned from artist Trevor Harries. The monument cost £60,000, paid for by the Fisherman's Memorial Trust, with contributions from local residents and businesses.

In contrast to the somewhat run-down aspect of Grimsby, more up-market

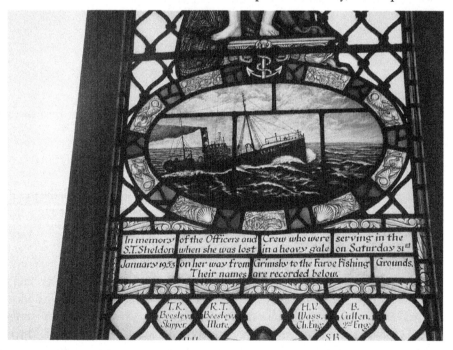

91. *Commemorative window for the crew of the steam trawler* Sheldon, *at Methodist Central Hall, Grimsby.* © *Author.*

seaside towns continue to maintain some inshore fishing to supply local restaurants and farmers' markets. The industry also survives (though much reduced) in Cornwall, based on Newlyn, and in Scottish ports, particularly on the north-east coast. The surviving memorials in churches and local cemeteries are a reminder of the human cost of fish in this most hazardous of occupations.

Salvage

Lifesaving among coastal communities was initially a somewhat mercenary activity. When vessels were lost on the rocky British western shores, local people were reputedly more interested in 'wrecking', meaning salvaging or pilfering cargoes, than assisting survivors: 'wrecking' in the sense of deliberately luring vessels to their doom for such profit is generally a romantic fiction. On the east coast, where vessels were more likely to encounter the hazard of sandbanks, salvage or assistance was pressed on stranded masters, sometimes wanted or not and on onerous terms. Preservation of life from merchant wrecks was first made a distinct ground for a salvage award by the 1854 Merchant Shipping Act:[8] the emphasis of salvage legislation prior to that date was primarily on saving property. Salvage law was thus undoubtedly influenced by the voluntary lifesaving movement and, when lives were lost during nineteenth-century salvage ventures, the lifesaving element was emphasized by subscription funds and on the memorials they raised to the casualties. Lifesaving would eventually transform the public image of coastal communities.

Saving life

The monument to the American loyalist, William Wragg of South Carolina, in Westminster Abbey, shows the shipwreck in which he lost his life in 1777. Wragg himself is seen in the stern of the ship while, in the foreground, Tom Skene, Wragg's slave, is shown rescuing his master's son. Saving the lives of people to whom one owed a personal loyalty was always regarded as an obligation. However, by the end of the eighteenth century it had come to be regarded as a meritorious act to save total strangers from premature accidental death, regardless of their rank, and devising technological innovations to achieve that end became an emerging trend.

This high-minded attitude to lifesaving began among the professional

---

[8]   Prior to 1854, if salvors saved both life and property they received a larger award. After 1854, claims for saving life were paid for from property recovered from the wreck. The Mercantile Marine Fund was introduced to meet lifesaving claims where no property was recovered.

middle classes, initially but not surprisingly among medical men – it was after all their job. Mouth-to-mouth resuscitation was attracting interest throughout the eighteenth century, boosted by an account of a successful case by William Tossach in 1744. The first humane society for recovering the apparently drowned was founded in Amsterdam in 1767 and had to give considerable attention to methods of extracting them from the city's canals. The British society was founded in 1774 by two doctors, William Hawes and Thomas Cogan, and from 1787 was known as the Royal Humane Society after receiving the patronage of George III. Its remit gradually expanded from resuscitation to include lifesaving. It made a charitable appeal to subscribers to empathize with the victims and their family, and a more utilitarian one with a view to preserving breadwinners in dangerous occupations and keeping their families off parish poor-support. As time went on, miracle recoveries from apparent death lost their novelty value and the agenda of the Society became dominated by the need to inculcate a lifesaving ethos, so as to effect speedy rescues. As incentive, the Society offered pecuniary awards and from 1775 presented medals depicting a nude boy trying to rekindle the flame of his torch, the symbol of life. The Society spawned many imitators.

Apparatus

The story of early lifesaving innovation dwells on the trauma of gentlemen who, witnessing wrecks from the shore, had to watch the drawn-out deaths of crews and passengers within sight of safety, as they were washed from rigging or as hulls disintegrated. The Enlightenment belief that technology could change society for the better also played a part, as well as the expansion of print culture and its taste for disaster stories. The memorials to the key innovators in lifesaving boat design or mortar and rocket apparatus play down the patronage of middle-class societies and give an impression of the inventor struggling alone to gain acceptance for his ideas, fitting a general pattern of Victorian narratives of the engineer as hero. The success of the invention might take some while to become apparent. In 1785 Lionel Lukin (1742–1834), who made his living as a fashionable London coach builder, patented a boat with built-in watertight compartments and intended to be unsinkable. Five were purchased for lifesaving purposes but Lukin lacked credibility with the seafaring community. The inscription on his gravestone at Hythe, Kent, has a coat of arms, describes his activities as a coachbuilder and records his hope that 'divine Providence … his guide and Protector during a long and chequered life … would remove him to a better and Eternal inheritance'. The invention of the lifeboat is mentioned in a second inscription on the back, probably added at a later date: Hythe likes to claim him as a local worthy.

After a particularly unpleasant wreck off Tynemouth in 1789, a public competition for a lifeboat design was launched by the 'Gentlemen of the Lawe House'. The winner, Henry Greathead (1757–1818), incorporated some of runner-up William Wouldhave's ideas in his subsequent boats. Being a boatbuilder, Greathead was able to get the lifeboat into production and achieved public recognition for his designs. Rival claims are again staked by their memorials. Wouldhave's stone at St Hilda's, South Shields, has the following inscription:

SACRED TO THE MEMORY OF
WILLIAM WOULDHAVE,
WHO DIED SEPTEMBER 28TH; 1821, AGED 70 YEARS
Clerk of this Church and Inventor of the Invaluable Blessing to Mankind
THE LIFEBOAT.
Heaven genius scientific gave
Surpassing vulgar boast, yet he from soil
So rich, no golden harvest reap'd – no wreath
Of laurel glean'd. None but the sailor's heart:
Nor that ingrate of palm unfading this,
Til shipwrecks cease, or life-boats cease to save[9]

Greathead and Wouldhave are both commemorated by a clock tower by a local architect, J.S. Morton, in the Marine Park at South Shields, opened in 1890. The project was initiated to commemorate Victoria's jubilee but after much debate in the local press took its present form, with a portrait of the rival inventors on opposing sides and with reliefs of lifesaving scenes on the front and back (fig. 92). Wouldhave was by this point embedded in local memory as a neglected genius denied due credit by his contemporaries.

The alternative approach to rescuing men from wrecked ships relied on getting a line on board by which men could be transferred to the shore by breeches-buoy. George William Manby (1765–1854), a Norfolk militia officer who became Barrack Master at Great Yarmouth, and who invented a system for throwing a line on board ship from a mortar on shore, has a family wall tablet at All Saints church, Hilgay, Norfolk: this exhorts that his name be remembered 'As long as there is a stranded ship'. His name there, however, is mingled with those of four brothers and sisters who died in childhood or infancy, with a note that 'The public should have paid this tribute'. Manby's mortar was superseded by the rocket apparatus of Henry Trengrouse, whose anchor-and-rock memorial outside the door of Helston church, Cornwall, notes that he:

9   F.M. Homes, *The Lifeboat: its history and heroes* (London, 1900), p. 21. The original sandstone headstone, carved with a lifeboat, is now inside the church. The granite replacement in the churchyard dates from 1921.

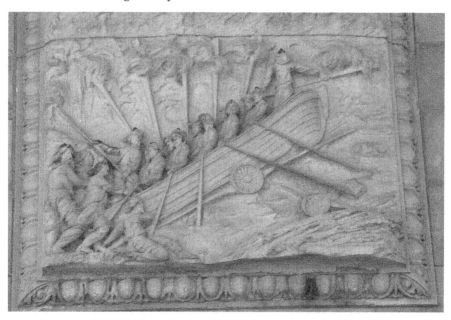

92. Jubilee clock tower, architect J.S. Morton, at South Shields, Tyne and Wear. Panel commemorating the invention of the lifeboat by William Wouldhave and Henry Greathead. © Author.

RENDERED MOST SIGNAL SERVICE TO
HUMANITY BY DEVOTING THE GREATER
PORTION OF HIS LIFE AND MEANS TO
THE INVENTION AND ADOPTION OF THE
"ROCKET APPARATUS"
FOR COMMUNICATING BETWEEN
STRANDED SHIPS AND THE SHORE,
WHEREBY MANY THOUSANDS OF
LIVES HAVE BEEN SAVED

The twentieth-century family gravestone to Augustus William Schermuly (1857–1929) at Morden in Surrey, carved with a ship in full sail, notes him as the inventor of the pistol-rocket lifesaving apparatus. This communicated more conveniently from ship to shore. At the time of his death, lifesaving equipment was being carried in compliance with Board of Trade regulations rather than being bestowed by private philanthropy and Schermuly's rockets and distress flares formed the basis of a profitable family business supplying this equipment. It continued independently until 1973 when taken over by Bryant & May: its Dorking factory only closed in 1981.

Founding father

Although the first Greathead lifeboat was stationed at South Shields in 1789, there was no national organization to maintain or coordinate local initiatives. In 1823 Sir William Hillary (1771–1847) issued *An appeal to the British nation on the humanity and policy of forming a national institution for the preservation of lives and property from shipwreck.* The Admiralty was unwilling to finance such a scheme and Hillary was persuaded to launch another philanthropic organization in 1824, the National Institution for Preserving Life from Shipwreck. This was in difficulties by the time of Hillary's death in 1847 but, following a change of name to Royal National Lifeboat Institution (RNLI) in 1854 – its new royal patrons being Queen Victoria and Prince Albert – and the development of its fundraising techniques, the charity went from strength to strength.

The institution's founder was in some ways a doubtful character whose considerable wealth was acquired by dubious means and spent on grandiose projects, frequently public ones. The risk-taking personality which had emptied his bank account once again at the time of his death led him to hazard his life, in person, in attempts to rescue men from ships wrecked off the port of Douglas. Hillary had only become a resident of the Isle of Man to avoid claims for debts contracted elsewhere. During the twentieth century the reputation of the RNLI reflected more positively on Hillary. In 1924, its centenary year, the Hillary vault in St George's churchyard, Douglas, was restored and an additional inscription added. A bronze plaque had been put up in 1908 on a large rain shelter on the Harris Promenade, commemorating Hillary's role in founding the RNLI and the Tower of Refuge in the bay. It bore his profile, with a victor's wreath above. During the centenary it was re-erected on a wall below Hillary's former residence. The Tower of Refuge, designed by John Welch and erected on St Mary's Isle in Douglas Bay, in 1832, was intended to accommodate sailors wrecked on what is less an island than a semi-submerged reef: in the picturesque form of a miniature thirteenth-century castle, it is still a local feature.[10] Hillary had crusading interests and one of his publications proposed: … *the Christian Occupation of the Holy Land as a Sovereign State by the Order of St. John of Jerusalem.*

Hillary's role as Manx hero is reflected in the two latest memorials to him. A statue of him erected in 1999 on Douglas Head, by local artist Amanda Barton, shows Hillary fastening his cloak and hurrying to the shore. A relief on the Loch Promenade at Douglas is an outstanding work by the distinguished sculptor Michael Sandle, whose monument at Valletta to the Second

---

10 Hillary's scheme may also owe something to the Lord Crewe Trust which provided accommodation, stores and provisions for shipwrecked seamen at Bamburgh Castle.

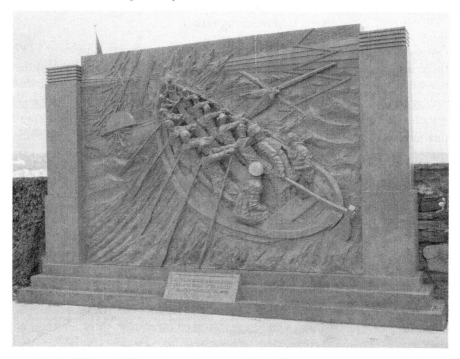

93. *Sir William Hillary rescues the crew of the* St George, *by Michael Sandle, at Douglas, Isle of Man.* © *Author.*

World War siege of Malta has already been covered here. Sandle trained at Douglas School of Art and Technology between 1951 and 1954 and his relief, installed in 2001, shows Hillary's lifeboat rowing to rescue the crew of the paddle steamer *St George*, wrecked on St Mary's Isle early on 20 November 1830 (before construction of the tower). The wreck was hard to reach: the lifeboat had to be backed inside the rocks, some of the boat's oars were smashed and Hillary, who could not swim, was thrown overboard and suffered broken ribs. The *St George's* crew were taken off with difficulty. Finally, all forty men, by now clinging to the upturned lifeboat, were rescued by two other boats from Douglas, one in charge of a naval officer. By a miracle nobody drowned. Sandle's relief appropriately represents the wrecked steamer and the lifeboat from a precariously tilted perspective (fig. 93).

The Navy jumps in

The officers of the Royal Navy were also influenced by the lifesaving ethos. Marine artists recording the major battles of the French wars of 1793–1815 often embellished the foreground of their compositions with British tars humanely hauling not only their shipmates but also their soaking enemies out of the water. Similar scenes appear on monuments, for example in St Leonard's church at Butleigh, Somerset, which holds a memorial to Vice-Admiral Sir Samuel Hood (1752–1814) and his two brothers, Arthur and Alexander. This has a relief at the base by Lucius Gahagan of Bath (d. 1866) showing Samuel, as captain of the frigate *Juno*, rescuing three sailors from a wreck in St Anne's harbour, Jamaica, on 3 February 1791. By the time of Sir Samuel's death, the lifesaving ethos was well established. The memorial to Captain Augustus James de Crespigny (1791–1825) of HMS *Scylla*, in St Peter's church, Port Royal, Jamaica, claims he saved sixteen lives during his short naval career, and quotes in detail a recommendation from Commander George Wood Sarmon that he receive a Royal Humane Society Medal for rescues in 1810.[11] Given the Navy's manning problems during the Napoleonic Wars, its lifesaving motivations at this time were not entirely those of disinterested benevolence.

Between 1835 and 1870, the Royal Humane Society awarded 583 medals to officers and men of the Royal Navy. A surprising number of these recipients seem to have been able to swim. This was less common among seamen than might now be supposed and men who fell into the water, often from high in rigging, could easily drown for that reason, due to injury in the fall or from cold before a boat could reach them. The novel *Pride of the Mess* by William Johnson Pride Neale (set during the Crimean War and leaving no celebrity name unmentioned) begins with a stirring rescue by the hero: '... he pulled the handle which detached the lifebuoy from the stern, and then hurriedly throwing off his jacket, plunged overboard to assist the drowning

---

11 'Sacred to the memory of Augustus James DE CRESPIGNY, 3d son of Sir W. Ch[ampio] n & Lady Sarah De Crespigny, who died on board H.M. Ship 'Scylla', Oct. 24th, 1825. Capt De Crespigny went first to sea under the patronage of Ld. St Vincent, & served under the flag of Nelson, at Trafalgar, from thence, he was taken under the patronage of Ld. Collingwood, who made him study the duties of a seaman, under his particular care. The above gallant officer saved no less than sixteen lives of his fellow creatures during his naval career for which he was presented with a service of plate from his ship's crew, as well as a medal from the R.H.S., in the annual report of which society an account is given, the last paragraph is as follows: These are to certify to the principal officers of the Royal Humane Society that Lieutenant Augustus C[hampion]. De Crespigny served with me as a volunteer midshipman from His Majesty's Ship "Tonnant" in the gunboat service in Cadiz in 1810, during which time I had opportunities of seeing his noble conduct on three very particular occasions. First, in jumping from a boat in a very strong tide way and saving a Marine, second, a boy in the same way, and thirdly, in taking to a small boat & pulling into the very muzzles of the enemy's guns, and evidently saving five men that were near drowning, by the 'Achilles' barge being sunk: his conduct on the last occasion was so truly noble that he not only gained the admiration of the whole flotilla but the envy of the French Commanding Officer, who at last ordered his men to cease firing on him. Given under my hand, this 12th Day of July 1815, West Cowes, G.W. Sarmon. This tribute to a father's memory was erected by his eldest son, Sir Claude Chn. De Crespigny, Bt. 1841.' Quoted in Captain J.H. Lawrence-Archer, *Monumental Inscriptions of the British West Indies* (1875), p. 291.

lad, whom he saw passing under the lee counter evidently unable to swim. "Bravo, youngster!" cried the captain.'[12] An account appears in *The Times* headed 'Feat of Gallantry' and the hero is recommended for a Royal Humane Society Medal.

It was against this background that at least five memorials were erected to the now scarcely known Captain John McNeill Boyd RN (1812–61). Boyd commanded the Dublin district of the Irish Coastguard. A Northern Irishman of Scottish descent, he had, in the course of his naval career, dived in to save men on three previous occasions. During severe gales on 8 February 1861, Boyd and men from HMS *Ajax* were at Dun Laoghaire (then Kingstown), busy saving personal property from the wrecked brigantine *Clyde of Bideford*. The following day saw even worse weather and fourteen wrecks inside the harbour. Unable to launch a boat, fifty to sixty officers and men were gathered on the breakwater and saw the collier brig, *Neptune*, smashed to pieces on the rocks. In attempts to save those clinging to the wreckage, one of Boyd's men had moved forward with a line and a lifebuoy. He was secured with a rope held by Boyd, who was not secured to anything. At this point Boyd and five other rescuers from the *Ajax* were swept away and drowned by a giant wave. His brother, the Very Reverend Archibald Boyd, published a memoir of his sibling: '… this gallant sailor died, not only in the fulfilment of duty, but in the sacred cause of humanity. He fell not in battle, nor in the selfish attempt to save his own life, but in the grand duty of trying to save the lives of others. As he followed his Lord through life, so has he followed Him in death.'[13]

To commemorate Boyd there was a Dublin subscription fund, which was able to commission a statue from Sir Thomas Farrell (1827–1900), who would become Ireland's leading sculptor. Though Catholic, the Farrell family would prosper through patronage from the Lord Lieutenant of Ireland. The marble full-length figure was erected in the Protestant Cathedral of St Patrick in Dublin, and was completed by 28 July 1864, when the trust wound up its affairs (fig. 94). Farrell's father trained under Thomas Kirk and the figure shows the influence of Kirk's statue of Admiral Sir William Sidney Smith (1764–1840) in its pointing gesture and stance. This was the last major work by Kirk (d. 1845), and was one of the early trio of marble statues originally in the Painted Hall at Greenwich but now in the National Maritime Museum.[14] The tousle-haired and whiskery Boyd is shown wearing boots and holding in his left hand a rope firmly secured to the post which forms a support for

[12] William Johnson Pride Neale, *The Pride of the Mess* (1856), p. 6.
[13] Archibald Boyd, Dean of Exeter, *Life in death, a sermon preached on board H.M.S. Ajax 17 Feb. 1861 by the Lord Bishop of Labuan with a memoir of Captain J. M'Neill Boyd, R.N. from authentic sources, by his brother* (Dublin, 1861), p. 12.
[14] NMM SCU0051; see Chapter 3, p. 87.

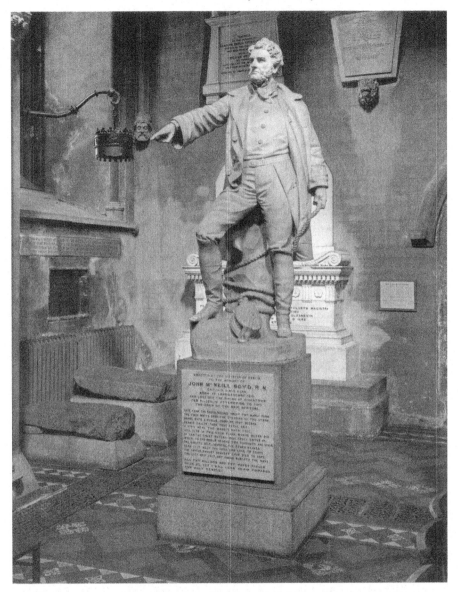

94. *Captain John McNeill Boyd RN, by Thomas Farrell, at St Patrick's Cathedral, Dublin. © Conway Library, The Courtauld Institute of Art, London.*

the figure. The plinth has verses by Dr William Alexander (1824–1911), then Bishop of Derry and, at that time, a poet of some reputation. Like Archibald Boyd, he stresses the Christian nature of Captain Boyd's sacrifice.

> Here it is meet for grief and love to 'grave,
> The Christ-taught bravery that died to save
> The life not lost, but found beneath the wave.

Thomas Farrell also produced the relief surmounted by a figure of Hope on the memorial to Boyd in St Colomb's Cathedral, Londonderry. This shows him pointing seawards again and this time instructing a seaman to throw a lifeline. The Irish Coastguard erected a memorial at Monkstown with a broken mast on a plinth that also commemorates the five crew members of HMS *Ajax*. This takes the same line: 'They glorified God, whose waves went over them, by a death not unmeet for sailors of Christian Britain. "Greater love hath no man than this that he lay down his life for his friends." John IV. 13.'[15] Boyd's fellow naval officers erected a wall tablet in St Ann's church, Portsmouth Dockyard, with the inscription on a carved marble scroll. Finally, thirty members of the congregation of his brother's former church, St Matthew's, Cheltenham, funded another wall tablet. This church had started life as a temporary structure while the parish church was closed, a new building being consecrated in 1879. Even before his death at Kingstown – and given his three earlier instances of lifesaving – Boyd had enjoyed a positive professional reputation and social status, which made middle-class subscribers eager to approve and commemorate his sacrifice.

That sphere of life ...

From 1807, Lloyd's of London made grants for the provision of lifeboats. These were manned and maintained by local organizations. The actual rescuing was carried out not only by the Coastguard but also by fishermen, pilots and salvors. Whitby had such a lifeboat from 1802. Though this had received initial funding from Lloyd's, until 1861 it was run by the Whitby Life-boat Association – an organization with some of the characteristics of an insurance scheme. On 9 February that year, the same storm that had wreaked such havoc on the east coast of Ireland, hit eastern England. In Whitby the lifeboat crew, with some changes in personnel, had taken off the crews of six vessels. The crew of the first, the *John and Ann* of Sunderland, were rescued in a fishing coble, the remainder in the town's new (but not self-righting) West Side lifeboat. On the seventh rescue, with a crew of thirteen men, the lifeboat capsized and all were lost except for one Henry Freeman, who was washed clear and hauled ashore by men on the slipway. Freeman was wearing a lifebelt of newer design, which fitted over the shoulders. The Lifeboat Association

---

15 *Illustrated London News*, 5 October 1861, p. 357.

had no funds to support dependants of men lost in rescues. Two relief funds were set up, one locally based and a second on an appeal to the readers of *The Times* by the rector of Whitby, the Reverend W. Keane. Just over £5000 was raised. In spite of Keane's initially sanguine view of this sum (he considered it would build model cottages for the community), it was only sufficient to provide modest benefits to thirty-four dependent orphans and to the widows throughout their remaining lives. There was no risk of raising anyone above 'That sphere of life in which their parents were'.[16]

Keane went ahead with his second proposal to erect a memorial in St Mary's, Whitby. This cost a modest £53 1s. 1d. and consists of a dome on eight Ionic columns with an inscription on the plinth. It is said to have been based on a model of a 'pagan temple' that Keane found in the Marylebone Road. This story draws a polite veil over its origins as a temple of Venus.[17] The inscription on the plinth, carved by Robert Robinson of Bagdale, refers to the subscription fund and quotes the rector's initial letter to *The Times*.

In 2007 the gravestone of John Storr (the steersman rather than the coxswain of the Whitby lifeboat, as his headstone claims) could be seen standing propped against the side of St Mary's church. Although Storr's body had been recovered and buried on 28 April 1861, the advancing erosion of the geologically unstable east coast later destroyed his grave. The headstones at this site, like the ones further north on the Scottish coast, are of sandstone, and the weather in this exposed spot is wearing away the inscriptions, just as it is the fabric of the surrounding religious buildings. The stone bears the same quotation from St John as the *Ajax* memorial at Monkstown.

The atmosphere of parsimony that hangs over the response to the Whitby appeal has to be seen against many other claims on the middle-class purse from industrial accidents and financial depression. Although the Whitby crew were older and had more dependants than the men of HMS *Ajax*, one cannot but feel a disparity in recognition between the sacrifice of John McNeil Boyd and the rather more effective performance of the Whitby men.

---

16 William Clayton QC, quoted in A.F. Humble, *The Rowing Life-boats of Whitby* (Whitby, 1974), p. 89. Clayton's advice was sought on how *The Times*'s fund could be spent. He was anxious to avoid welfare dependence in recipients but approved the erection of a memorial 'without any ornament'.

17 The temple may be based on the Rotunda at Stowe, Buckinghamshire, a garden building designed by Sir John Vanbrugh and dating from 1721. It contained a gilded copy of the Venus de Medici and corresponds to Pliny's description of the shrine to the goddess on the island of Cnidus. Similar Venus temples featured in other landscape schemes; see David R. Coffin, 'Venus in the Eighteenth-Century Garden', *Garden History*, vol. 28, no. 2 (winter 2000), pp. 173–93.

Heroine

Socially speaking, William Darling and his family fell somewhere between the officers of the Coastguard and the fishermen who manned the lifeboats. Lighthouse keeper in the employ of Trinity House was a responsible position, with lifesaving included in its remit, and William was keeper of the Long-stone Lighthouse in the Farne Islands, off the coast of Northumbria. On 7 September 1838, when his three sons Robert, William and George were away, William Darling took survivors from the wrecked steamer *Forfarshire* off nearby rocks in a sixteen-foot coble. His daughter, Grace (1815–42), was the other rower on the outward leg, and she managed the boat single-handed in heavy seas while her father landed on the rocks and prioritized the passengers to be carried on the first return trip.

Grace, a slight girl, was like Victoria Cross winners in being an ordinary person who performed one extraordinary deed. During the four remaining years of her life, under a glare of press publicity, she avoided conduct which might tarnish her reputation in the eyes of a censorious middle class, and then died, from tuberculosis, a month short of her twenty-seventh birthday. Her heroism identified lifesaving with the feminine virtues of kindness and compassion, although she would also have required strength and daring to participate in this rescue (qualities not unknown to Victorian working women). Contemporaries identified in her the gritty Protestant integrity of Sir Walter Scott's Edinburgh heroine, Jeanie Deans. There is also an echo of her in boatwoman Lizzie Hexham, a character in Dickens's novel *Our Mutual Friend*, who progresses from corpse retrieval for money to lifesaving for love. Local coastal communities, facing the challenges of survival in this social class and environment, were less impressed by her achievements. A commemorative cenotaph, designed by Anthony Salvin in 1842, was rapidly set up in the churchyard of St Aidan's, Bamburgh, intended to serve as a sea-mark. In the fashionable gothic style, it consisted of the canopied effigy of the girl holding an oar (fig. 95). The architects were Hicks and Charles Wood, and the sculptor of the figure Charles Raymond Smith (1799–1888). It was difficult to maintain in its outdoor situation although its current condition is good. In 1885 the figure was replaced, from Smith's design model: the original, now in the church, seems appropriately medieval in its battered state. The sandstone canopy, with its pitched roof, blew down in a storm in 1893 and was restored in 1895 with a flat roof line by Alnwick architect, F.R. Wilson.

The nearby three-light window, dedicated to Grace and manufactured by Clayton & Bell, was installed in 1885 when the statue was replaced. It mixes personifications of the cardinal and theological virtues including Faith, Charity, and Fortitude, with Fortitude holding an oar as her attribute.

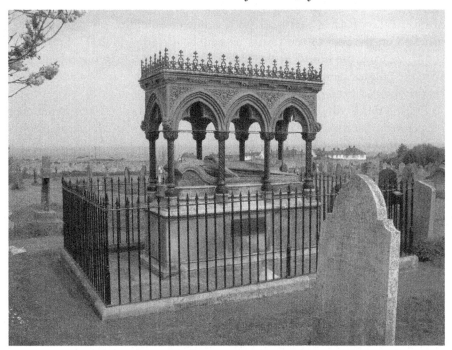

95. *The tomb of Grace Darling, at St Aidan's, Bamburgh, Northumberland. © Author.*

Fortitude or Courage – a traditional male virtue – is here associated with a specific woman. With all this elaborate surrounding commemoration (and an inscribed memorial pillar in St Cuthbert's chapel, Great Farne Island), the Darling grave plot remains separate in St Aidan's churchyard. There, under a simple and also now-replaced headstone, Grace is remembered in family context with her mother, father, brother and sister.

Storm warriors

After the disaster of 1861, the RNLI took over the Whitby lifeboat. Fisherman Henry Freeman (1834–1904) served as coxswain from 1878 to 1899. In the second part of the century the institution, aided by canny fundraising and publicity, went from strength to strength. It provided financial security and status for men like Freeman. Lifeboat Saturdays, when the crews paraded their boats through the streets to the accompaniment of shaking collecting tins, together with the publication of stirring tales of dangerous rescues, further enhanced the status of these men. In the photographs of Frank Meadow Sutcliffe (1853–1941), the burly, bearded and sou'westered Freeman came to represent the archetype of the lifeboatman. A sculpture of Freeman by Richard Sefton, based on one of Sutcliffe's photographs, was installed on the wall of the town's new lifeboat station in 2007. Freeman is shown wearing the lifejacket that saved his life, with a lifebuoy behind him. Like the famous Henry Blogg of Cromer, by the latter years of the twentieth century, he had become a local hero.

During the 1890s, the Margate surfboats remained run as a crew-member cooperative, much like those run by the Norfolk beach-men. Members received a share of any salvage money and provided free lifesaving. Nine men of the crew of thirteen were drowned when the *Friend to All Nations* capsized while racing her rival, the RNLI boat *Quiver*, to the rescue of a vessel in distress on 2 December 1897. Lifeboats and fishermen were now seen as a reassuring part of the seaside experience. *The Daily Telegraph* opened a fund for the dependants of the crew, appealing to its readers' positive holiday experiences of Margate and, as usual in these circumstances, playing down the salvage element. Enough was raised to provide the necessary welfare payments and

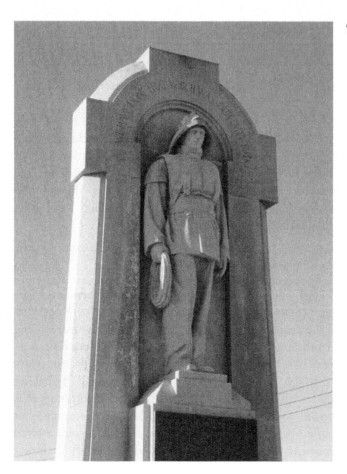

96. *Memorial to the crew of the lifeboat* Mary Stanford, *at Rye Harbour, East Sussex.* © *Author.*

commission two substantial, good-quality memorials. A full-length bronze statue by Frederick Thomas Callcott (1854–79) stands on the seafront. It shows a lifeboatman in oilskins and cork lifejacket striding towards the sea: the inquest had in fact revealed that none of the crew were wearing their lifejackets as they found them cumbersome. Lifeboatmen were something of a Callcott speciality as another figure by this artist was placed at the RNLI headquarters in the Charing Cross Road in London. The second monument marked the men's graves in Margate Cemetery and took the form of a rock, beside which is carved a kneeling woman in contemporary dress, holding a wreath. At the top of the rock are an anchor, lifebuoy and tangled ropes.

When the Rye Harbour lifeboat *Mary Stanford* turned over on the harbour bar in 1928, seventeen men were drowned. The funeral was attended by people from all parts of the country, many of whom would not have known the deceased. A thousand floral tributes were on view: the Princess Diana effect is nothing new. The grave at the church of the Holy Spirit, Rye Harbour, is marked by a statue of a lifeboatman in sou'wester, oilskins and lifejacket holding a coiled rope (fig. 96). Though clean-shaven, the figure has something Christ-like about him. The disaster is also commemorated by a three-light window in Winchelsea church by Douglas Strachan (1875–1950), which depicts St Nicholas, St Augustine and Christ calming the waves, while below a family wait anxiously beside a stormy sea: 'They stayed not to weigh doubt or danger but freely offering their portion in this life for the ransom of men whom they had never known they went boldly into the last of all their storms.'

Yachtsmen

Before it became a mass pastime, inshore fishermen found another source of income serving as yacht crew. Some of these men are commemorated on the Brightlingsea tiles. Only those lost in the course of employment were included in this collective memorial and the yachts they worked on included the famous J-class vessels. Men such as George Henry Lewes were lost overboard taking in sail in rough weather. Lewes lost his footing, struggling with an out-of-control spinnaker on board *Astra*, during a race off Southend in 1935. The design of yachts was initially influenced by local small craft, and redundant fishing vessels might end their careers as yachts. Eventually rescuing yachtsmen became a substantial part of the work of the lifesaving services. As a leisure activity, yachting tended to be less than central to personal identity, so memorials specifically commemorating yachtsmen are somewhat unusual. However, they do include some outstanding memorials: if the family could afford the yacht, they were likely to have deep pockets and artistic interests.

The drowned body was (not surprisingly) an unusual part of memorial iconography, with the exception of two major memorials to the poet Percy

Bysshe Shelley (1792–1822). Both stress the manner of his death in a yachting accident rather than primarily emphasizing the immortality of his poetic works. They were erected by his daughter-in-law, Jane, Lady Shelley – part of her drive to enhance his posthumous reputation. When Lord Byron acquired a yacht, Shelley and his friend Edward Williams wanted one too and had a two-masted, gaff-rigged vessel built, which he named *Ariel*. It was not the most stable of craft. Williams was inexperienced and Shelley inattentive. He was also unable to swim. His friend Edward John Trelawney told Williams: 'You will do no good with Shelley, until you heave his books and papers overboard; shear the wisps of hair that hang over his eyes; and plunge his hands up to the elbow in a tar-bucket.'[18] The yacht and its three crew members foundered in the Gulf of Spezzia, the bodies being washed up three days later and buried nearby. A Homeric cremation on the beach was arranged so Shelley's ashes could be buried next to his son, William, in the Protestant cemetery in Rome, and the remains of Williams could be returned to England.

Shelley's wife Mary was buried, not with her husband, but with her parents in Bournemouth. The poet's heart (or perhaps his liver), which had been snatched from the ashes of the pyre, was buried with her. A memorial to the poet and his wife by Henry Weekes, originally intended for St Peter's, Bournemouth, was erected in nearby Christchurch in 1854. Carved in marble, it includes full-length figures of both writers, Shelley in Pietà pose in his wife's arms (fig. 97). He appears more nautical than poetic, being clad in trousers and bare feet like the seamen on Nelson's Guildhall memorial. There are shells on the beach, seaweed on his trousers and the sculptor has included the prow of the boat. The monument is neither an allegorical treatment of the event, nor is it literally illustrative.

The later memorial by Edward Onslow Ford (1852–1901) was originally intended to replace the slab on Shelley's grave with its Shakespearian quotation, 'Nothing of him that doth fade', in the Protestant cemetery in Rome.[19] It was eventually installed in University College, Oxford. Ironically, Shelley had been expelled from this institution in 1811 for publishing a pamphlet entitled *The Necessity of Atheism*. Influenced by the then controversial, realist tendencies of contemporary French sculpture, the artist used his son Wolfram as a model. The naked body of the poet lies on its side on a beach. The base and plinth are in coloured marble, with the effigy supported by two lions, a mourning muse and a fruit tree (fig. 98). The whole evokes a considerable

---

[18] Edward John Trelawney, *Trelawney's recollections of the last days of Shelley and Byron* (1906), p. 69.

[19] It would have overlapped the Trelawney plot beside Shelley, and Trelawney's daughter objected.

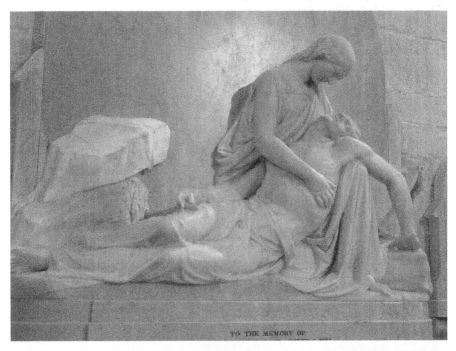

97. *Memorial to Percy Bysshe Shelley, by Henry Weekes, at Christchurch, Dorset.*
© *Author/the Vicar and Churchwardens of Christchurch Priory.*

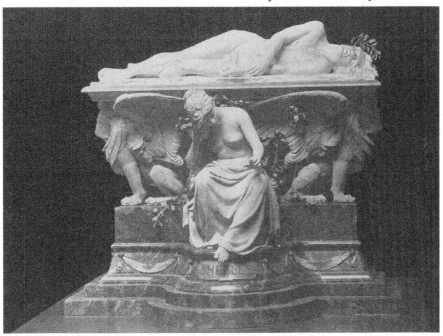

98. *Shelley memorial, by Edward Onslow Ford, at University College, Oxford.*
© *The Courtauld Institute of Art, London*

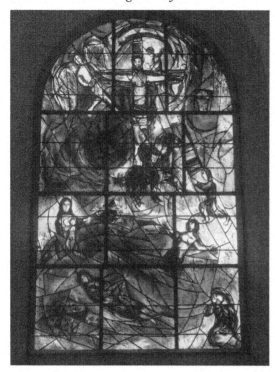

99. *Window in memory of Sarah D'Avigdor-Goldsmith, by Marc Chagall, at All Saints, Tudeley, Kent.* © *Robert Ive.*

emotional response in the viewer, partly due to the realism of the figure and the youth and beauty of the teenage model (Shelley was 29 at the time of his death but looked younger). The body is vulnerable and unconscious but not unambiguously dead. It resembles not only Henry Wallis's painting of the death of the poet Chatterton, Jacques-Louis David's picture of the revolutionary boy martyr, Joseph Bara, and Stephano Moderno's sculpture of the body of St Celia in Rome, but also the less prestigious illustrations of resuscitation techniques distributed to Coastguard stations in 1864.[20] The viewer feels a strong urge to help but knows the unfortunate youth is beyond assistance.

… and women

Another notable memorial to a young yachtswoman is the set of windows at Tudely in Kent to Sarah D'Avigdor-Goldsmith, daughter of Rosemary and Sir Henry, a merchant banker and bullion broker from a distinguished Jewish family. Her mother collected contemporary art. Sarah died of hypothermia while waiting to be picked up following a dinghy capsize in 1963. Sarah and

---

[20] *Illustrated London News*, 28 May 1864, p. 530; 'Restorative treatment of the apparently drowned'.

her mother had seen and liked a Marc Chagall window in Jerusalem and so the artist was commissioned to design new stained glass for this small church (fig. 99). The large east window was installed first and the others added to form a harmonious scheme. The artist had been using the figure of the crucified Christ, which is the principal subject, as a symbol of Jewish martyrdom even before the Second World War. The lower part of the window shows the girl and her yacht in a blue pool, surrounded by figures of her mourning family and the Virgin and Child.

Fisherman as artist

Fishing, art and leisure are combined in the port of St Ives. The Mediterranean light, yellow beaches and vivid blue sea attracted an artists' colony to this small Cornish port after 1912 when fishing began to decline. During the 1920s the paintings of the local rag-and-bone-man, jack-of-all-trades and one-time fisherman, Alfred Wallis (1855–1942), attracted the interest of professional artists such as Ben Nicholson. Wallis took up the hobby late in life, with a preference for ships and local townscapes. His naïve but talented view of 'what use to bee' appealed to modernists and increasingly to the general public. In a cemetery overlooking the sea, filled with headstones in imported marble and slate, Wallis's slab by potter Bernard Leach (1887–1979) is a picture constructed of stoneware tiles, the brown colours reflecting Wallis's own restricted palette (fig. 100). It shows a small figure entering a lighthouse and carries an inscription describing Wallis as 'artist and mariner', with an acknowledgement of his Salvationist faith. This spot truly represents the symbiosis of fishing, art and leisure.

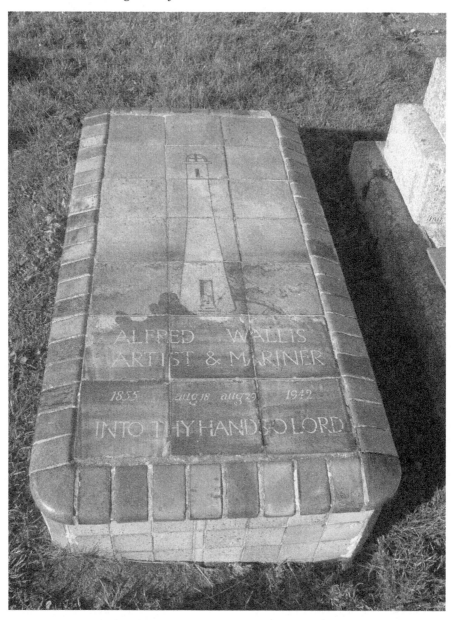

100. *Alfred Wallis, by Bernard Leach, at Barnoon Cemetery, St Ives, Cornwall.*
© *Author.*

Conclusion

The author worked for thirty-five years at the National Maritime Museum, from which a preoccupation with specifically maritime material culture is inevitable. It can blind one to the bigger picture, in this case relationships between memorials to seafarers and to their shore-based contemporaries. I believe that I have managed to argue the case for specifically maritime examples as a rewarding subject for study. As with memorials in general, they have a good deal to say about collective values and their evolution reveals much about the democratization of personal identity. During my lifetime, the relationship between the nation and the sea has greatly changed. Since the Falklands Conflict, the sea as field of war has slipped out of British consciousness and containerization has moved ports away from city centres. A resulting lack of public awareness regarding matters maritime has become known as 'sea blindness'. Interest in the coast and the sea itself as places to pursue adventure and spend leisure time continues.

There is also a growing interest in the sea as an environment. It has provided energy in the shape of North Sea oil, which has spawned its own disasters, notably the Piper Alpha fire. Now it is a site for offshore wind farms. All these activities are a source of employment and danger, although romance has yet to attach itself to wind farms. Love of hobbies has certainly been reflected in individual commemorative projects. Joshua Compston (d. 1996), an art dealer who liked messing about in boats, has a stone recumbent effigy in a dinghy at Kensal Green Cemetery, carved by Zebedee Helm: the quirky cemetery memorial continues to be commissioned. Charles Henry Rew (d. 1972), 'angler and oarsman ...', has a commemorative window depicting the calling of fellow fisherman, St Peter, at the church of St Michel du Vale, Guernsey. The apostle is shown wearing a Guernsey sweater, trousers rolled-up.

There have also been general changes in funerary commemoration, mainly the separation of memorials and memorialization from the remains of the deceased. There is still a need for a special place for the bereaved to mourn and to communicate with the dead. Recent ways of providing this space have included plaques on seats in public places and unofficial, improvised shrines.

Sometimes sponsored park benches can themselves become shrines to the person in whose memory the seat was provided. The illustration of Wallace Hartley's grave at Colne (see fig. 75) shows items recently left there by visiting *Titanic* enthusiasts.

From ancient times, there has been continuous destruction and creation of funerary monuments and this study is just a snapshot taken at a particular moment. Religious change and economic development can both be destructive forces. Church attendance is declining and conversion of churches into private dwellings does not guarantee the survival of their memorials. Cemeteries face clearance for development or road building. However, many churchyards have continued in active use long after the church has become redundant or fallen into ruin. Memorials have been both an outcome and a source of family pride but benign neglect, antiquarian interest and the enthusiasm of the wider public also play a role in preserving them. The influential role played by the press in stimulating memorialization has been demonstrated in previous chapters. Public history is now tremendously popular, thriving online and on specialist television channels. This encourages the erection of memorials and public sculpture, sometimes commemorating new or forgotten heroes. The recent wall tablet erected to Olaudah Equiano at St Margaret's, Westminster, is a good example of this, a product of a drive to include black history in the national narrative. Memorials and the ceremonies which accompany them cement living communities, interest groups and constituencies outside the family.

Recording memorials has been an antiquarian activity since the sixteenth century. Compendia of epitaphs are a longstanding publishing tradition. The internet is in many ways an excellent vehicle for sharing memorial records, potentially making possible the sort of comparative analysis that can open up new insights and avenues of academic study. The need to transfer data between constantly changing commercial systems is a problem in retaining it, and recording has been carried out to different standards by different groups with divergent interests: occasionally I curse the blessed Nikolaus Pevsner's lack of interest in naval officers when he describes church monuments in his *Buildings of England* series. Genealogists, who like graveyards, may also leave out details relating to the visual or literary aspects of memorials. NADFAS (the National Association of Decorative and Fine Art Societies) is proceeding slowly and thoroughly to record the interiors of churches. The Imperial War Museum's National War Memorials Archive has aimed to record all war memorials in the UK with a very wide remit. Public sculpture, with its art historical importance, visual appeal and easy access, has been much more thoroughly covered (particularly by Liverpool University) than church, churchyard and cemetery memorials.

At present there is a widespread popular interest in family history, perhaps through need to establish a personal identity at a time of rapid change. Its academic partner, subaltern history, has been only too happy to use historical resources made available for the mass market through commercial companies. These firms also have an interest in memorial records. Historical interests have been widening and the history of the naval monument has demonstrated the spread of individual commemoration to all ranks. With the actual carvings or inscriptions under threat, the record itself becomes the memorial. That said, the virtual record is unlikely to replace entirely the three-dimensional, sculptural artefact.

Cross-cultural memorialization may be the challenge of the future. The loss at sea of British passengers and yachtsmen attracts more media attention than that of the crew of merchant and fishing vessels. Cargo vessels, in particular, may be crewed internationally. Maritime accidents on the coast involving illegal immigrants could revive the sort of challenges which faced the Reverend Robert Hawker. The twenty-three Chinese cockle-pickers who drowned in Morecambe Bay in 2004 were commemorated by a memorial garden near the lifeboat station in 2007. The local Chinese community had erected a temporary shrine near the scene of the disaster at Red Bank Farm and the tragedy evoked generally sympathetic artistic responses from the British. However, in spite of a disaster fund, the victims' families were left with debts incurred to the people smugglers. A sculpture entitled 'Praying shell' by Anthony Padgett stands at Red Bank Farm today. The kneeling figure faces the sea, and was conceived before the disaster as a spiritual response to the local environment, and a point of interest for walkers.

The sea and that wonderful creation, the ship, continue to inspire artistic responses. A symbol and a cause of death, a source of livelihood and pleasure, and a rich part of the environment, it remains linked to British identity and to the commemoration of the nation's dead.

Bibliography

Archer, Geoff, *The Glorious Dead: Figurative Sculpture of British First World War Memorials* (Norwich, 2009)

Avery, Charles, 'Hubert le Sueur', *Walpole Society Publication 48* (1980–82), pp. 135–209

Ayres, Philip, *Classical Culture and the Idea of Rome in Eighteenth-Century England* (Cambridge, 1997)

Baker, Janis, 'The Representation of Worthy Women' (unpublished Ph.D., De Montfort University, 1998)

Baker, Malcolm, 'Rococo Styles in Eighteenth Century English Sculpture', in *Rococo: Art and Design in Hogarth's England*, edited by Michael Snodin and Elspeth Moncrieff (London, 1984)

Barker, Ralph, *Children of the Benares: A War Crime and Its Victims* (London, 1987)

Barker, Thomas Burgess, *Abney Park cemetery* (London, 1869)

Bathurst, Bella, *The Wreckers: A Story of Killing Seas, False Lights and Plundered Ships* (London, 2005)

Beattie, Susan, *The New Sculpture* (London and New Haven, 1983)

Bergfelder, Tim and Sarah Street, *Titanic in Myth and Memory: Representations in Visual and Literary Culture* (London, 2004)

Biel, Steven, *Down with the Old Canoe: A Cultural History of the Titanic Disaster* (New York and London, c.1996)

Bindman, David, 'Roubiliac in Westminster Abbey', *Oxford Art Journal*, vol. 4, no. 2, 1981

Bindman, David and Malcolm Baker, *Roubiliac and the Eighteenth-Century Monument: Sculpture as Theatre* (London and New Haven, 1995)

Bonehill, John and Geoff Quilley, *Conflicting Visions: War and Visual Culture in Britain and France c.1700–1830* (Leicester, 2000)

Borg, Alan, *War Memorials: From Antiquity to the Present* (London, 1991)

Boston, Ceridwen, Annsofie Witkin, Angela Boyle and David R.P. Wilkinson, *'Safe Moor'd in Greenwich Tier': A Study of the Skeletons of Royal Navy Sailors and Marines Excavated at the Royal Hospital Greenwich* (Oxford, 2008)

Brockliss, Laurence, John Cardwell and Michael Moss, *Nelson's Surgeon, William Beatty: Naval Medicine and the Battle of Trafalgar* (Oxford, 2008)

Brooks, Richard, *The Long Arm of Empire; Naval Brigades from the Crimea to the Boxer Rebellion* (London, 1999)

Bruce, Edith Agnes Kathleen, *Homage, a book of Sculptures by K. Scott*, with commentary by Stephen Gwynn (London, 1938)

Bulley, Anne, *The Bombay Country Ships: 1790–1833* (Richmond, 2000)

Cansick, Frederick Teague, *A Collection of Curious and Interesting Epitaphs ...* (3 vols) (London, 1869–75)

Carroll, Yvonne, *A Hymn for Eternity: The Story of Wallace Hartley, Titanic Bandmaster* (Stroud, 2002)

Carruthers, Sir Joseph Hector McNeil, *Captain James Cook, RN, One Hundred and Fifty Years After ...* (London, 1930)

Cavanagh, Terry, *Public Sculpture of Liverpool* (Liverpool, 1997)

Cecil, Richard, *Memoirs of John Bacon, Esq. R.A. with Reflections Drawn from a review of his Moral and religious character* (London, 1811)

Childs, David, *Growing Remembrance: The Story of the National Memorial Arboretum* (Barnsley, 2008)

Chun, David, *The River Hamble: A History* (Stroud, 2014)

Clutton-Brock, Arthur, *On War Memorials* (London, 1920)

Coad, Jonathan, *The Portsmouth Block Mills: Bentham, Brunel and the Start of the Royal Navy's Industrial Revolution* (Swindon, 2005)

Coke, Diana, *Saved from a Watery Grave: The Story of the Royal Humane Society's Receiving House in Hyde Park* (London, 2000)

Compton, Ann, *The Sculpture of Charles Sargeant Jagger* (Aldershot, 2004)

Couling, David, *Wrecked on the Channel Islands* (London, 1982)

Coutu, Joan, *Persuasion and Propaganda: Monuments and the Eighteenth-Century British Empire* (Montreal and London, c.2006)

Crainer, Stuart, *Zeebrugge: Learning from Disaster: Lessons in Corporate Responsibility* (Herald Families Association, 1993)

Craske, Matthew, 'Contacts and Contracts, Sir Henry Cheere and the Formation of a New Commercial World of Sculpture in Mid-Eighteenth-Century London', in *The Lustrous Trade: Material Culture and the History of Sculpture in England and Italy c.1700–c.1860*, edited by Cinzia Sicca and Alison Yarrington (Leicester, 2000), pp. 94–113

Craske, Matthew, 'Westminster Abbey 1720–70: A Public Pantheon Built upon Private Interest', in *Pantheons: Transformations of a Monumental Idea*, edited by Richard Wrigley and Matthew Craske (Aldershot, 2004), pp. 57–80

Craske, Matthew, *The Silent Rhetoric of the Body: A History of Monumental Sculpture and Commemorative Art in England 1720–1770* (London and New Haven, c.2007)

Craske, Matthew and John Bonehill, *Patriotism and Pathos: War, British Society and the Visual Arts c.1688–1830* (Farnham, 2008)

Credland, Arthur G., *North Sea Incident 21–22 October 1904: Commonly Called the Russian Outrage* (Hull, 1987)

Crellin, Sarah, *The Sculpture of Charles Wheeler* (Farnham, 2012)

Crow, Hugh, *The Memoirs of Captain Hugh Crow: The Life and Times of a Slave Trade Captain* (Oxford, 2007)

Cunningham, Hugh, *Grace Darling: Victorian Heroine* (London, 2007)

Curl, James Stevens (editor), *Kensal Green Cemetery: The Origins and Development of the General Cemetery of All Souls, Kensal Green, London, 1824–2001* (Chichester, 2001)

Czisnik, Marianne, *Horatio Nelson: A Controversial Hero* (London, 2005)

Dafter, Ray, *Guernsey Wrecks: Shipwrecks around Guernsey, Alderney and Sark* (Tonbridge, 2001)

David, Rob, *In Search of Arctic Wonders: Cumbria and the Arctic in the Eighteenth and Nineteenth Centuries* (Cumberland and Westmorland Antiquarian and Archaeological Society, 2013)

Davidson, Luke Anthony Francis, *Raising up Humanity: A Cultural History of Resuscitation and the Royal Humane Society of London 1774–1808* (York, 2001)

Dickens, Charles, *Household Words* (2 December 1854), pp. 245–362; (9 December 1854), pp. 246–392

Doss, Erika Lee, *Memorial Mania: Public Feeling in America* (Chicago, 2010)

Douch, Robert, *Monuments and Memorials in Southampton* (Southampton, 1968)

Dunlop, Durham (editor), *A Memoir of the professional life of William J. Barre, Esq., member of the Royal Institute of Architects, Ireland: with Photographic Illustrations Selected from his Works* (Belfast, 1868)

Eastwick, Robert William, *A master Mariner: being the Life and Adventures of Captain R. W. Eastwick*, edited by Herbert Compton (London, 1890)

Edmond, Rod, *Representing the South Pacific: Colonial Discourse from Cook to Gauguin* (Cambridge, 1997)

Elder, Melinda, *The Slave Trade and the Economic Development of Eighteenth-Century Lancaster* (Halifax, 1992)

Eltis, David, Stephen D. Behrendt, David Richardson and Herbert S. Klein (editors), *The Trans-Atlantic Slave Trade: A Data Base on CD ROM* (Cambridge, 1999)

Esdaile, Katherine Ada, *English Church Monuments, 1510 to 1840* (London, 1946)

Evans, David, *Building the Steam Navy: Dockyards, Technology and the Creation of the Victorian Battle Fleet* (London, 2004)

Fraser, Flora, 'If You Seek His Monument', in *The Nelson Companion*, edited by Colin White (Stroud, 1995)

Fremantle, Sir E.R. *The Navy as I have Known it* (London, 1904)

Gatty, Margaret and Alfred, *Recollections of the life of the Rev. A.J. Scott etc.* (London, 1842)

Gray, Patricia, *The Haunt of Grave Robbers and Murderers: The History of Stoke Damerel Church, Devonport* (Plymouth, c.1979)

Groseclose, Barbara, 'Death, Glory, Empire: Art', in *Orientalism Transposed: The Impact of the Colonies on British Culture*, edited by J.F. Codell and D.S. MacLeod (Aldershot, 1998), pp. 189–201

Halbwachs, Maurice, *On Collective Memory* (Chicago, 1992)

Hamilton, Sir Louis Keppel, *[The Navy League] Diamond Jubilee* (London, 1955)

Harrison, James, *Life of the Right Honourable Horatio Viscount Nelson* (London, 1806)

Harry, R.G., *Tavistock's Sir Francis Drake's Statue and Medal* (Bidworth, 1984)

Hawkey, Arthur, *A Black Night off Finisterre: The Tragic Tale of an Early British Iron-clad* (Shrewsbury, 1999)

Hedger, Michael, *Public Sculpture in Australia* (Roseville East, 1995)

Higgins, Alfred, 'On the Work of Florentine Sculptors in England, in the early part of the sixteenth century; with special reference to the tombs of Cardinal Wolsey and King Henry VIII', *Archaeological Journal*, vol. 51, 1894, pp. 129–220, 367–70.

Higgins, David, *The Beachmen: The Story of the Salvagers of the East Anglian Coast* (Lavenham, 1987)

Hoock, Holger, *The King's Artists: The Royal Academy of Arts and the Politics of British Culture, 1760–1840* (Oxford, 2003)

Hoock, Holger (editor), *History, Commemoration and National Preoccupation, Trafalgar 1805–2005* (Oxford, 2007)

Hoock, Holger, *Empires of the Imagination: Politics, War and the Arts in the British World 1750–1850* (London, 2010)

Hood, Jean, *Trafalgar Square, a Visual History of London's Landmark through Time* (London, 2006)

Hooke, Norman, *Modern Shipping Disasters 1963–1987* (London, 1989)

Howarth, David (editor), *Art and Patronage in the Caroline Courts: Essays in Honour of Sir Oliver Millar* (Cambridge, 1993)

Humble, Arthur Frederick, *The Rowing Lifeboats of Whitby* (Whitby, 1974)

Hutchinson, Geoff, *The Mary Stanford Disaster: The Story of a Lifeboat November 15th 1928* (Brede, 1984)

Irwin, David, *John Flaxman 1755–1826: Sculptor, Illustrator, Designer* (London, 1979)

Irwin, David, *Neoclassicism 1750–1830* (London, 1997)

Janson, H.W., *Nineteenth-Century Sculpture* (London, 1985)

Jones, Dr Max, *The Last Great Quest: Captain Scott's Antarctic Sacrifice* (Oxford, 2003)

Jordan, Wilbur Kitchener, *Philanthropy in England 1480–1660* (London, 1959)

Jupp, Peter C. and Clare Gittings (editors), *Death in England: An Illustrated History* (Manchester, 1999)

Keay, John, *The Honourable Company: A History of the Honourable East India Company* (London, 1991)

Keene, Derek, Arthur Burns and Andrew Saint (editors), *St Paul's, the Cathedral Church of London 604–2004* (London and New Haven, 2004)

Kelly, Robert, *For Those in Peril: The Life and Times of Sir William Hillary the Founder of the R.N.L.I.* (Douglas, 1979)

Kenworthy-Browne, John, 'A Monument to Three Captains', *Country Life*, vol. 161, 27 January 1977, pp. 180–82

King, Alex, *The Memorials of the Great War in Britain: The Symbolism and Politics of Remembrance* (Oxford, 1998)

Lees, Hilary, *English Churchyard Memorials* (Stroud, 2000)

Leslie, Lieut. Colonel J.H., 'Monuments and Memorials of Soldiers in the London City Churches', *Journal for the Society for Army Historical Research*, vol. 6, 1927, pp. 178–80

Lewis, David, *The Churches of Liverpool* (Liverpool, 2001)

Lewis, Michael, *The Navy in Transition 1814–1864: A Social History* (London, 1965)

Litten, Julian, *The English Way of Death: The Common Funeral since 1450* (London, 1991)

Llewellyn, Nigel, 'Honour in Life, Death and Memory: Funeral Monuments in Early Modern England', *Transactions of the Royal Historical Society*, vol. 6, 1966, pp. 179–200

Llewellyn, Nigel, *Funeral Monuments in Post-Reformation England* (Cambridge, 2000)

Lloyd, Christopher, *The Navy and the Slave Trade* (London, 1968)

Lockyer, R., *Buckingham: The Life and Political Career of George Villiers First Duke of Buckingham 1592–1628* (London, 1981)

Luff, P.A., 'Mathews v. Lestock: Parliament, Politics and the Navy in Mid-Eighteenth-Century England', *Parliamentary History*, vol. 10, no. 1 (1991), pp. 42–62

Lynn, Martin, 'Liverpool and Africa in the Nineteenth Century: The Continuing Connection', *Transactions of the Historic Society of Lancashire and Cheshire for the year 1997*, vol. 147, pp. 27–54

MacDougall, Francis Thomas and Archibald Boyd, *Life in death, a sermon preached on board HMS Ajax 17 Feb. 1865 by the Lord Bishop of Labuan with a memoir of Captain J. McNeill Boyd, from authentic sources, by his brother* (Dublin, 1861)

Mace, Rodney, *Trafalgar Square, Emblem of Empire* (London, 1976)

McEwen, John, *The Sculpture of Michael Sandle* (Much Hadham, 2002)

McGoogan, Kenneth, *Lady Franklin's Revenge: A True Story of Ambition, Obsession and the Remaking of Arctic History* (London, 2006)

McGowan, A.P., 'The Royal Navy under the First Duke of Buckingham' (Ph.D., University of London, 1967)

Mackenzie, John M. (editor), *Popular Imperialism and the Military 1850–1950* (Manchester, 1991)

Mackenzie-Grieve, Averil, *The Last Years of the English Slave Trade, Liverpool, 1750–1807* (London, 1968)

McLoughlin, Roy, *The Sea Was Their Fortune: A Maritime History of the Channel Islands* (Bradford on Avon, 1997)

Massie, Robert Kinloch, *Castles of Steel: Britain, Germany and the Winning of the Great War at Sea* (London, 2004)

Maudslay Society, *Henry Maudslay 1771–1831: and Maudslay, Sons & Field Ltd* (London, 1949)

Meara, David, *A. W.N. Pugin and the Revival of Memorial Brasses* (London, 1991)

Minter, Ian and Ray Shill, *Storm Warrior: The Turbulent Life of Henry Freeman* (Birmingham, 1991)

Mitchell, Julian, *The Wye Tour and Its Artists* (Logaston, 2010)

Neale, William Johnson, *The Pride of the Mess. A Naval Novel of the Crimean War* (London and New York, 1856)

Ovenden, John and David Shayer, *The Wreck of the Stella: Titanic of the Channel Islands* (Guernsey, 1999)

Owen, David Edward, *English Philanthropy 1660–1960* (Cambridge, Mass., 1964)

Penny, Nicholas, '"Amor Publicus Posuit": Monuments for the People and of the People', *Burlington Magazine*, vol. 129, no. 1017 (1987), pp. 793–800

Physick, John, *Designs for English Sculpture 1680–1860* (London, 1969)

Porter, Bernard, *The Absent Minded Imperialists: Empire, Society, and Culture in Britain* (Oxford, 2004)

Potterton, Homan, *Irish Church Monuments 1570–1880* (Belfast, 1975)

Powell, John William Damer, *Bristol Privateers and Ships of War* (Bristol, 1930)

Price, John E., 'South African War Memorials in Devonport Park Plymouth', *Journal of the Orders and Medals Research Society*, vol. 23, spring (1984), pp. 16–18

Pugin, Augustus Welby Northmore, *An Apology for the Revival of Christian Architecture in England* (London, 1843)

Quinlan, Mark, *British War Memorials* (Hereford, 2005)

Raban, Peter, 'Nicholas le Messurier (1731–1759) a Guernsey Privateer Captain in The Seven Years War', *Report and Transactions of La Société Guernesiaise*, vol. 22, no. 4 (1990), pp. 878–907

Raban, Peter, *The Channel Islands: Privateers and Prizes 1756–1763* (Market Harborough, 1993)

Raguin, Virginia Chieffo, *The History of Stained Glass: The Art of Light Medieval to Contemporary* (London, 2003)

Read, Benedict, *Victorian Sculpture* (London and New Haven, 1982)

Rees, Siân, *Sweet Water and Bitter; the Ships that Stopped the Slave Trade* (London, 2009)

Robertson, Terence, *Walker RN: The Story of Captain Frederick John Walker C.B., D.S.O. and Three Bars, RN* (London, 1956)

Robinson, J., *Descriptive Catalogue of the Lough and Noble models of Statues, Bas-reliefs and Busts at Elswick Hall, Newcastle on Tyne ...* (Newcastle upon Tyne, 1904)

Roper, I.M., 'Effigies of Bristol', *Transactions: Bristol and Gloucester Archaeological Society*, vol. 27 (1904), pp. 51–116

Roscoe, Ingrid, 'James "Athenian" Stuart and the Scheemakers Family', *Apollo*, vol. 126, September (1987), pp. 178–84

Roscoe, Ingrid, Emma Hardy and M.G.Sullivan, *A Biographical Dictionary of Sculptors in Britain, 1660–1851* (London and New Haven, 2009)

Royal Commission on Historical Monuments (England), *An Inventory of the Historical Monuments in London: Westminster Abbey*, vol. 1 (London, 1924)

Saunders, David, *Britain's Maritime Memorials and Mementoes* (Yeovil, 1996)

Scholten, Frits, *Sumptuous Memories: Studies in Seventeenth-Century Dutch Tomb Sculpture* (Zwolle, 2003)

Searight, Sarah, *Steaming East: The Forging of Steamship and Rail Links between Europe and Asia* (London, 1991)

Seymour, Sir Edward H., *My Naval Career and Travels* (London, 1911)

Smedley, Anne Constance, *Grace Darling and her Times* (London, 1932)

Smith, John Thomas, *Nollekens and his Times* (London, 1828)

Southey, Robert, *Letters from England by Don Manuel Alvarez Espriella* (London, 1807)

Spielmann, M.H., *British Sculpture and Sculptors of Today* (London, 1901)

Spufford, Francis, *I May Be Some Time: Ice and the English Imagination* (London, 1996)

Stanley, Arthur Penrhyn, *Historical Memorials of Westminster Abbey* (London, 1868)

Stark, Francis R., *The Abolition of Privateering and the Declaration of Paris* (New York, 1897)

Starkey, David H., *British Privateering Enterprise in the Eighteenth Century* (Exeter, 1990)

Steer, K.A. and J.W.M. Bannerman, with a contribution from G.H. Collins, *Late Medieval Monumental Sculpture in the West Highlands* (Edinburgh, 1977)

Stewart, David J., *The Sea Their Graves: An Archaeology of Death and Remembrance in Maritime Culture* (Gainesville, Fl., 2011)

Stocker, Mark, '"Loving Hands and an Eye that Knew": The Scott Memorials in Christchurch and London', *Bulletin of New Zealand Art History*, vol. 19, 1998, pp. 55–65

Summerson, J., 'The Monuments in the Church of St. Nicholas, Deptford', *Mariner's Mirror*, vol. 27, no. 4 (1941), pp. 277–89

Toynbee, Jocelyn Mary Catherine, *Death and Burial in the Roman World* (London, 1971)

Trollope, Edward, *Manual of Sepulchral Memorials* (London, 1858)

Usherwood, Paul, Jeremy Beach and Catherine Morris, *Public Sculpture of North-East England* (Liverpool, 2000)

Vale, Brian, *Cochrane in the Pacific: Fortune and Freedom in Spanish America* (London, 2008)

Vandenbussche, Fred, *Raise the Herald: The Battle after the Disaster* (Folkestone, 1988)

Verney, Edmund Hope, *The Shannon's Brigade in India: being Some Account of Sir William Peel's Naval Brigade in the Indian Campaign of 1857–1858* (London, 1862)

Ward-Jackson, Philip, *Public Sculpture of the City of London* (Liverpool, 2003)

Warner, Marina, *Monuments and Maidens: The Allegory of the Female Form* (London, 1985)

Wathen, Bruce, 'Making Drake: The Cultural Construction of Sir Francis Drake from the Late Sixteenth Century to the Present' (unpublished Ph.D., University of Exeter, 2001)

Watt, Quintin, *The Bromsgrove Guild: An Illustrated History* (Bromsgrove, 1999)

Wheatley, Canon S.W., *Historical Notes* (Rochester, 1996)

White, Andrew, *Life in Georgian Lancaster* (Lancaster, 2004)

White, Colin and the 1805 Club, *The Trafalgar Captains: Their Lives and Memorials* (London, 2005)

Whiting, Frederick A., 'The Committee of Taste', *Apollo*, vol. 82, 1965, pp. 326–30

Wilkins, Frances, *Manx Slave Traders: A Social History of the Isle of Man's Role in the Atlantic Slave Trade* (Kidderminster, 1999)

Williams, Glyn, *The Prize of All the Oceans: The Triumph and Tragedy of Anson's Voyage Round the World* (London, 1999)

Williams, Gomer, *History of the Liverpool Privateers and Letters of Marque with an account of the Liverpool Slave Trade* (London, 1897)

Willsher, Betty and Doreen Hunter, *Stones: A Guide to Some Remarkable Eighteenth Century Gravestones* (Edinburgh, 1978)

Wilson, Jean, 'Elite Commemoration in Early Modern England: Reading Funerary Monuments', *Antiquity*, vol. 74, no. 284 (June 2000), pp. 413–23

Winstone, Reece, *Bristol Blitzed* (Bristol, 1976)

Woodman, Richard, *Fiddler's Green: The Great Squandering, 1921–2010* (Stroud, 2010)

Woodman, Richard, *More Days More Dollars: The Universal Bucket Chain, 1885–1920* (Stroud, 2010)

Wright, Thomas, *A History and Topography of the County of Essex* (London, 1836)

Yarrington, William Henry Hazell, *The Landing of Captain James Cook R.N., Botany Bay, 1770. As produced in connection with the Commonwealth Celebrations at Kurnell, Botany Bay ... 7th January, 1901* (Sydney, 1908)

Index

CPSIA information can be obtained at www.ICGtesting.com
Printed in the USA
BVOW06*2147231115

428286BV00001B/1/P

9 781843 839705